A Godsend to His People

A Godsend to His People

*The Essential
Writings and Speeches
of Marshall Keeble*

Edited by
Edward J. Robinson

The University of Tennessee Press
Knoxville

Copyright © 2008 by The University of Tennessee Press / Knoxville.
All Rights Reserved.
Cloth: 1st printing, 2008.
Paper: 1st printing, 2016.

Library of Congress Cataloging-in-Publication Data

Keeble, Marshall, 1878–1968.
  A godsend to his people : the essential writings and speeches of Marshall Keeble / edited by Edward J. Robinson. — 1st ed.
    p. cm.
  Includes bibliographical references and index.
  ISBN 978-1-62190-978-156-3
  1. Churches of Christ—Sermons.
  2. Churches of Christ.
  3. African Americans—Religion.
  4. Keeble, Marshall, 1878–1968.
  I. Robinson, Edward J., 1967–
  II. Title.
  BX7077.Z6K44 2008
  286.6092—dc22   2007043793

For my brothers:
    John
    Wesley
    Lee
    Patrick
    Berry Jr.

And my sisters:
    Velma
    Dorothy
    Cynthia
    Doretha

Contents

Acknowledgments	ix
Introduction: "The Magic Negro" in Churches of Christ, 1914–1968	xi
Chapter 1. The Sufficiency of the Church: Keeble in the 1910s	1
Chapter 2. If It Were Not for the White Christians: Keeble in the 1920s	13
Chapter 3. Disseminating the Bread of Life: Keeble in the 1930s	25
Chapter 4. I Mean to Wear Out on the Battlefield: Keeble in the 1940s	33
Chapter 5. This Is Bible Religion: Keeble in the 1950s	39
Chapter 6. The Global Evangelist: Keeble in the 1960s	87
Chapter 7. The Importance of Trained Ministers	103
Notes	117
Selected Bibliography	139
Index	143

Illustrations

Following Page 80

Marshall Keeble
Andrew M. Burton
Richard N. Hogan
David Lipscomb
James L. Lovell
Preston Taylor

Acknowledgments

This book would have been impossible without assistance and encouragement from the following people: Fred Bailey, Carisse Berryhill, Michael W. Casey, Craig Churchill, Doug Foster, Sara Harwell, Don Haymes, Karissa Herchenroeder, Gary Holloway, Mac Ice, Stan Ivester, Laura Brittney McKinney, Tom Olbricht, Glenn Pemberton, Jack Reese, John L. Robinson, Karin Kaufman, Tobin Shearer, Jennifer Siler, Mark Dwayne Tucker, D. Newell Williams, David Wray, and many other colleagues at Abilene Christian University in Abilene, Texas. I want to thank Neil Anderson, chairman and publisher of the *Gospel Advocate,* for allowing me to reproduce Marshall Keeble's articles. I also express my sincere gratitude to H. A. "Buster" Dobbs, editor of the Firm Foundation, and Jack Evans Sr., publisher of the *Christian Echo,* for allowing me to reproduce some of Keeble's writings.

I dedicate this book to my biological brothers and sisters, spiritual descendants of Marshall Keeble.

Introduction

"The Magic Negro" in Churches of Christ, 1914–1968

In Hollywood's imagination, "Bagger" Vance, a black caddie in Savannah, Georgia, rescues a white golfer from anonymity and failure through his wit, wisdom, and charm, salvaging both the golfer's career and love life. Actor Will Smith portrays Vance as the "Magic Negro," a recurring figure in American popular culture, endowed with saintlike goodness, childlike behavior, and trickster traits—characteristics of what also has been dubbed the "Magical African American Friend" (MAAF). The movie *The Legend of Bagger Vance* plays out in the 1920s South but mentions nothing of the lynching, segregation, and discrimination then common in Jim Crow Georgia. Popular culture critic Christopher John Farley comments that "MAAFs exist because most Hollywood screenwriters don't know much about black people other than what they hear on records by white hip-hop star Eminem. So instead of getting life histories or love interests, black characters get magical powers." In motion pictures as varied as *The Defiant Ones, Ghost, The Green Mile, Remember the Titans,* and *Bagger Vance,* the MAAF, at once clever and naïve, wise and openhearted, serves as foil and friend to white protagonists in order "to soften the punch of racially charged movies, to embody the notion that not all racists are bad people."[1]

Apart from popular culture manifestations, the Magic Negro surfaces in the spiritual sphere as well. When Marshall Keeble (1878–1968), the premier black evangelist in Churches of Christ, traversed Jim Crow America, white listeners often outnumbered black hearers and attributed to him almost magical abilities. White admirers, astonished by the black preacher's wit, charisma, forthrightness, and extraordinary success, lavished him with praise and gifts, but few white Christians, if any, knew the heart and soul of the black man from Middle Tennessee. In 1931 a white minister, J. W. Brents (1884–1963), invited Keeble to preach to African Americans in Muskogee, Oklahoma. Keeble's meeting closed with a remarkable 204 baptisms. "Never in the history of the colored race in Muskogee has there been such rejoicing," Brents declared. Brents's own congregation reaped benefits from Keeble's powerful preaching as four white people and one Native American received baptism "as a result of his [Keeble's] work," and Brents predicted that "there will be many more white people come into the church as a result of the meeting." Attributing to the black evangelist almost supernatural qualities, he then stated that "Brother Keeble is a Godsend to his people."[2] Yet while Brents highlighted and celebrated Keeble's evangelistic success, he never commented on the brutal societal environment that oppressed Keeble and other African Americans.

Two years later, during the throes of the Great Depression, Keeble conducted a gospel meeting in Los Angeles, California. E. N. Glenn, a white preacher in Churches of Christ in southern California, concluded that "California has always been considered a very difficult field in building up the Church as well as with the evangelist in getting the 'one faith' before very many hearers." But Keeble, flying in the face of Glenn's assessment, repeatedly attracted large numbers of eager and responsive listeners in southern California. Amazed, intrigued, and impressed by the black minister's appeal, Glenn, F. L. Young, and other white preachers in the Los Angeles area arranged a conference with Keeble and another black evangelist, Amos Lincoln Cassius, to "talk over a few things." The white clergymen pled with Keeble to "'show us how you do it,' like the magician is called on to do sometimes by a few on the 'inside' of the ring."[3] To Glenn and the other white preachers, Keeble seemed a Magic Negro who could, in some arcane fashion, transform their ineffective preaching efforts into energetic, captivating, and exciting campaigns for Christ.

On the surface, Keeble did indeed appear to be a magician. He virtually spoke black congregations into existence across the South. After preaching, teaching, and toiling in a community for three weeks or more, Keeble often left behind scores of black converts (and many whites as well) who identified with Churches of Christ. His homespun wit, his practical and pointed illustrations, and his insistence that "the Bible is right" mesmerized and captivated white and black listeners who viewed the black preacher as "a great entertainer"[4] bearing a salvation message. He wrangled verbally with black denominational preachers who arose to attack the doctrine and practices of Churches of Christ, but by warding off those whom he deemed false prophets and by defending the doctrinal and liturgical practices of Churches of Christ, Keeble stood as more than an exceptional black preacher to white believers; he was also their Magical African American Friend who, from their perspective, seemed almost infallible and certainly invincible.

Like Booker T. Washington, the Wizard of Tuskegee, who often appeared compliant in public but defiant in private,[5] Marshall Keeble displayed a dual personality, but of another sort. More than one observer noted that Keeble could be as gentle as a lamb when dealing with his religious friends but as ferocious as a lion when encountering his spiritual foes. Floyd H. Horton, a white leader in Birmingham, Alabama, captured the essence of Keeble's duality after the latter established a congregation there in 1938. "I have never heard better preaching than Brother Keeble did during this meeting," Horton reported. "He is so humble that it is an inspiration to be associated with him. To be around Brother Keeble you learn that you do not have to go around with your fist doubled up and a frown on your face in order to preach like Paul, nor do you have to wear a horse face and be a 'sissy' in order to have the spirit of Christ. He is like a lamb in his dealings with his fellow men, but like a lion when it comes to preaching the gospel and defending the cause, and this is the spirit of Christ."[6] Just as Keeble exemplified two personalities when dealing with religious supporters and adversaries, he also revealed dual personas when interacting with whites and blacks. In this regard the black evangelist behaved no different from other black southerners who wore "the mask," camouflaging before whites their deep aversion to racial injustice. One scholar examining race relations in Mississippi observed that the black man "has a kind of dual personality, two roles, one that he is forced to play with white people and one the 'real Negro' as he appears in his dealings with his own people."[7] What was true for black Mississippians stood equally true for other black southerners. Keeble and his fellow African Americans survived the brutal lynch-law system of segregation by suppressing their intense rage and hatred for segregation before white audiences.

As a seeming magician, Keeble also appeared ubiquitous. His evangelistic tours took him virtually to every state in the Union and beyond, from Bradenton, Florida, to Long Beach, California, from Houston, Texas, to Boston, Massachusetts. He also preached in Africa, Asia, and Europe to listeners who never seemed to tire of hearing his sermons. One white leader testified, "It was my pleasure to be there [Atlanta, Georgia] for three nights and hear Brother Keeble. . . . I had to stand, but I could stand flat-footed and listen to Keeble preach three hours and not grow tired."[8] In 1935 Keeble ripped across East and West Texas in successive months like a fierce tornado, leaving behind black congregations in Port Arthur, Waco, and Tyler. In May 1935 he planted the Thomas Boulevard Church of Christ in Port Arthur with forty-one baptisms;[9] two months later he preached three weeks in Waco, establishing the Hood Street Church of Christ with twenty-six immersions.[10] On September 8, 1935, Keeble closed a meeting in Tyler with fifty-five baptisms (twelve of whom came from the Christian Church without reimmersion) and founded the North Tenneha Church of Christ.[11] In light of such extraordinary feats, the black preacher from Tennessee appeared all but superhuman.

Despite these apparently magical powers and extraordinary abilities, certainly Marshall Keeble was a man like his fellows, possessed of ordinary human emotions, touched and shaped by other ordinary human beings in Middle Tennessee. Yet armed with unwavering faith in God and enabled by generous support from whites and blacks in his religious community, Keeble excelled as an evangelist, indelibly marking the history of African American Churches of Christ. The documents that comprise this anthology confirm this view of Keeble. That many white

Christians perceived him as an almost supernal emissary suggests a fundamental lack of understanding of the man. Willie Cato, a white Christian who knew Keeble rather well, asserted that "brother Keeble was no superman. He was very human. His faith and confidence in God and in his Word committed Marshall Keeble to always 'see the hand of God' when he preached. He knew the power was in the Word, not in the man."[12]

Marshall Keeble clearly grasped his own humanness when he listed five reasons for his success as a traveling evangelist before E. N. Glenn and the other white preachers gathered in the 1933 southern California conference. First, he credited "a woman," his wife Minnie Womack (1880–1933), with being "at the bottom of his preaching career."[13] A daughter of Samuel and Sally Womack, Minnie graduated from the High School Department of traditionally black Fisk University. By accompanying him on his preaching tours, leading song services, and offering constructive criticism when he used improper grammar, Minnie proved an essential asset to Marshall's preaching ministry before her untimely death in 1932.[14] Engulfed in sorrow, Keeble trudged ahead, preaching across the United States. He paused briefly to thank Christians for their sympathy, stating, "I want to thank my many friends for the comforting messages that were sent me, after my dear wife passed away, leaving me very lonely; but I mean to hold to God's unchanging hand, so I can meet her in the sweet by and by."[15] Sixteen months after Minnie's death, he married another loving and supportive woman, Laura Johnson, a native of Corinth, Mississippi.[16]

Apart from his wife, Marshall Keeble cited Samuel W. Womack (1851–1920), his father-in-law, as a profound influence on his development and success. From Womack, he "learned the gospel plan of salvation."[17] Womack, who came under the influence of David Lipscomb and the *Gospel Advocate*, the most influential journal among Churches of Christ, withdrew from the Christian Church (also known as the Disciples of Christ) in Nashville and drew away Keeble and his wife. Alexander Campbell (1788–1866) and Barton W. Stone (1772–1844) had led one of the nineteenth century's largest and most dynamic reform efforts, the Restoration movement. By the early twentieth century the Stone-Campbell reformers were dividing into two entities, the Disciples of Christ and the Churches of Christ. After leaving the Disciples of Christ, Womack and another fiery black preacher, Alexander C. Campbell (1862–1930), together founded the Jackson Street Church of Christ, "the mother church"[18] for so many African American Churches of Christ. In this congregation and under the tutelage of Womack and Campbell, Keeble came to believe that the "gospel plan of salvation" meant worshiping without instruments of music, evangelizing without missionary societies, baptizing adult believers for the remission of sins, and following the Bible only in spiritual affairs. Womack was without question the most significant black mentor in the young life of Marshall Keeble.[19]

In addition to the teaching of Womack, Keeble's own internal longings steered him toward the full-time preaching ministry. He testified to Glenn and the others in Los Angeles that he harbored "a burning desire to preach the Word, not only over Lord's day, and come back home as Bro. Womack did, but to engage in that work for full time. So he studied hard and burned 'midnight oil' in getting a few lessons well."[20] Driven by this passion to advance the gospel among African Americans, Keeble committed himself to full-time evangelism in 1914. Likely the city-wide campaign launched at the Jackson Street congregation in 1914, which Andrew M. Burton (1879–1966) called "one of the greatest and most beneficial movements ever started by the brotherhood in Nashville,"[21] inspired Keeble and propelled him into the preaching ministry. During this meeting Keeble copied lessons that Joe McPherson (1877–1918), a white mail carrier, delivered.[22] Keeble never forgot those sermons; he stashed them in his mind and in his suitcase.

Keeble noted that white leaders in Churches of Christ also bore substantial responsibility for his preaching accomplishments. Samuel Henry Hall (1877–1961), a white preacher and writer for the *Gospel Advocate,* encouraged Keeble by inviting him to Georgia to preach, while Andrew Burton, Keeble's principal economic benefactor, "recognized his ability and helped along in a financial way."[23] Burton, a devout Christian and wealthy businessman, generously funded Keeble's preaching campaigns, but other white leaders in Churches of Christ, most notably Filo Bunyan Srygley (1859–1940), Elisha G. Sewell (1830–1924), and Nicholas B. Hardeman (1874–1965), gave him continuing verbal and emotional support. Keeble acknowledged that they "did much . . . toward making his preaching a success."[24]

Finally, he told Glenn and company, having secured monetary and emotional support from white believers, Keeble worked diligently to maintain their trust; to this end, he never openly challenged the racial status quo in Churches of Christ and the larger society. "To these brethren," noted Glenn, Keeble "never betrayed their confidence, but kept his place. He tried never to bring reproach upon the Cause by his conduct, but tried always to keep himself good and humble. He also realized the importance of 'staying in place' when in sections where the racial feelings were quite prominent; winning the confidence of both the white and the colored folks."[25] Among Keeble's techniques for staying in place and skirting racial controversy was allowing white leaders in Churches of Christ to baptize white seekers. When preaching in Houston, Texas, in 1934, his sermons yielded twelve responses, six of them white women. "I always have some of the white brethren to take their confession," Keeble noted.[26] This is how Keeble kept his place and maintained the approval and endearment of whites in Churches of Christ. A key aspect of Keeble's "magical" way was that he knew and understood "the mind of the South"[27] and how to navigate the treacherous waters of Jim Crow America.

The dramatic life of Marshall Keeble, the twentieth century's most celebrated black evangelist in Churches of Christ, embodies in microcosm the heart and soul of African American Churches of Christ. These churches became what Keeble was as he shaped in them a profoundly exclusivistic theological mindset, an imprint so deep that an understanding of present-day black Churches of Christ hinges upon a comprehension of Keeble's persona in its historical context. While a number of important works have examined Keeble, this anthology furnishes readers a unique glimpse into Keeble's mind by allowing the black clergyman to speak for himself.[28] The writings that comprise this book divulge the heart and soul of the preeminent African American preacher in the history of Churches of Christ, revealing the struggles of a black man in violent Jim Crow America and attesting to his challenges as a black cleric in a narrowly segregated religious community. "The Negro didn't like my religion," Keeble once lamented, "and the white man didn't like the color of my skin."[29]

Keeble moved in a complex and turbulent world. Born on December 7, 1878, in Rutherford County, Tennessee, to former slaves, Marshall Keeble entered a social environment flickering with mixed glimmers of gloom and hope. Five years before his birth, a cholera epidemic killed seventy people in Middle Tennessee, and the following year the collapse of the National Freedmen's Savings Bank, with its regional bank in Nashville, obliterated the savings and hopes of countless thrifty African Americans. The Panic of 1873, which precipitated a widespread economic downturn, coupled with the withdrawal of federal troops from the Restoration South four years later, deadened the hopes of southern blacks and spurred the "Exoduster" movement out of Tennessee and other neighboring states. Led by Benjamin "Pap" Singleton and Henry Adams, some forty thousand African Americans from Tennessee, Louisiana, Mississippi, and Alabama flocked to western territories in search of heightened social and economic opportunities for their families.[30] These compelling events plunged Keeble's youthful world into turmoil, doubtlessly contributing to his own complexity as a black man and minister in Jim Crow America.

Even though social and economic disorder pervaded his milieu, an adolescent Keeble in Nashville, Tennessee, could have heard and seen many things to fire his optimism. He probably listened to the melodious voices and soul-stirring spirituals of Nashville's Jubilee Singers. Under the leadership of George L. White (1838–1895), a former Union soldier from New York, the young black choristers began touring the United States in 1871 and soon garnered national and eventually international acclaim. Even if Keeble missed hearing their spirituals or "sorrow songs," he frequently saw the elaborate facility, Jubilee Hall, which their arduous fund-raising tours erected.[31] The success of the Jubilee Singers lingered in Keeble's mind, and when he assumed the presidency of the Nashville Christian Institute in 1942, he accompanied young singers from "his school" as they visited southern cities soliciting monetary support chiefly from white Christians.

If the inspirational songs of the Jubilee Singers and the presence of black colleges in Nashville such as Fisk University (established in 1866), Central Tennessee College (founded in 1866 before evolving into Walden University in 1890), and Meharry Medical College (organized in 1876 to train black doctors) uplifted

Keeble, the virulent white racism of the Progressive era cast a dispiriting pall of oppression, repression, and fear over American blacks. Indeed, Keeble married his first wife, Minnie Womack, in 1896, the pivotal year in which *Plessy v. Ferguson* legalized the shadow of segregation that had been lengthening across the nation after the collapse of the Reconstruction era. Segregated libraries, schools, theaters, parks, hotels, water fountains, residential districts, swimming pools, and railways—prominently displaying For Whites Only and Colored signs—constantly reminded Keeble of the supposedly inferior status his homeland had forced upon him. From 1890 to 1920 southern whites systematically enacted disfranchisement measures such as poll taxes, literacy tests, and grandfather clauses, effectively stripping their black counterparts of the guarantees of the Fourteenth and Fifteenth Amendments and reducing them to a second-class citizenship.[32]

Accompanying the legal machinations, proliferating antiblack literature helped poison the minds of whites against blacks. In 1905 Thomas Dixon Jr. (1864–1946), a Baptist minister-turned-lawyer and novelist, published his inflammatory racist novel, *The Clansman,* which portrayed black men as vicious rapists opposed by the glorious Ku Klux Klan. A decade later Dixon's novel inspired the divisive and incendiary movie *The Birth of a Nation,* which in turn gave rise to the second Ku Klux Klan. This terrorist organization, deeply rooted in the white South's violent irruption against newly freed blacks, was founded by Methodist minister William J. Simmons in 1915 in Stone Mountain, Georgia. This blood-bound revival, in addition to being antiblack, also espoused anti-Jewish and anti-Catholic sentiment, and its coeducational vituperation drew at least half a million women into its ranks. The second Klan sparked what writer James Weldon Johnson has labeled the "Red Summer" of 1919, the "greatest period of interracial strife the nation had ever witnessed."[33] This volatile and poisonous brew fed a twentieth century marked by a surging tide of heinous atrocities against America's black citizenry.

Against this fiery backdrop, Marshall Keeble committed himself to full-time evangelism in 1914. Driven by a desire to convert sinners to Christ "without the aid of any human organization," within a four-year period he planted his first congregation, the Oak Grove Church of Christ in Henderson, Tennessee, drawing wisdom, techniques, and aid from a variety of sources. Monetary donations and emotional support from white believers enabled him to accomplish this task, as several white leaders in Churches of Christ contributed to Keeble's development as a preacher who called blacks to religious reform without challenging the extant racial order. From Hardeman, McPherson, Sewell, and David Lipscomb, Keeble learned how to develop sermons constructed within an exclusivistic theology. From black mentors such as Womack and Campbell he discovered the importance of relying on white supporters. From Booker T. Washington, whose autobiography he read "from lid to lid," Keeble learned how to navigate the complex waters of racial strife in the Jim Crow South. Like Washington, Keeble wore a " mask" to survive the deadly thickets of discrimination and segregation. Even though he passionately hated racism and segregation, Keeble suppressed in public his deep aversion for these injustices, taking up the role of "Br'er Rabbit," who triumphed over the stronger "Br'er Wolf," "Br'er Tiger," and "Br'er Fox" through "wit, ingenuity, guile, cunningness, and humor." By moving through his career as a nonthreatening black man in a white-dominated fellowship, Keeble successfully evaded the explosive minefield of racial segregation.[34]

Keeble lost his most significant black mentor in 1920 when Samuel W. Womack died, but in the same year he gained his chief financial benefactor Andrew M. Burton, whose generosity enabled the black evangelist to move across the South, leaving congregations in his wake. Burton provided the financial lift that made of Keeble a rising star in the evangelism field for Churches of Christ, and his consistent support prompted Keeble to applaud the white businessman as the "greatest missionary in the church to-day." Such white helpers donated their time, energy, and resources to build separate black congregations while scrupulously refusing to challenge the "separate but equal" Jim Crow structures that burdened African American Christians even as they salved white consciences.[35]

In 1921 Keeble conducted a successful evangelistic campaign in Birmingham, Alabama. In this rigidly segregated city, white Christians collaborated with the black evangelist to plant a black congregation. A decade later two white women in Scottsboro, Alabama, Victoria Price and Ruby Bates, falsely accused nine young black men of raping them. An all-white jury found the "Scottsboro Boys" guilty and sentenced eight of them to death. This infamous case played on the animalistic stereotype of the black rapist and exacerbated race relations throughout the nation. Keeble, while traversing Alabama and other southern regions, understood the controversy swirling around such affairs, and it made him even more conscientious about complying with segregation's codes.[36] At his career's inception, Keeble chose the path of evangelism over that of social reform, and he never wavered from this decision.

By 1931 Keeble had emerged as the most visible black evangelist in Churches of Christ. While carrying out an evangelistic campaign in Valdosta, Georgia, he baptized 166 people. Shortly thereafter, Benton C. Goodpasture (1894–1977), a white editor, published the black preacher's sermons, spreading Keeble's fame to an ever-widening circle of both black and white believers, making him a household name among adherents of the Restoration movement. Keeble accomplished his most impressive work as an itinerant preacher in the South during the Great Depression era, baptizing 1,071 black people in 1931 alone. The 1930s also marked a significant change in national politics as scores of black Americans bade farewell to Lincoln's Republican party and gathered in the Democrat fold. Even though Keeble assiduously avoided political affiliation, he admired Franklin D. Roosevelt and his New Deal. In a 1948 speech at David Lipscomb College, Keeble, while arguing that present-day Christians had no need for the baptism of the Holy Spirit, referred favorably to President Roosevelt:

> When Mr. Roosevelt lived he used to make fireside chats over the radio. He used to make them and we enjoyed them because no man has ever been born that could speak over the radio as he could. We all admit that, we miss his voice now, regardless of what party he belongs to. I love his voice. Now, then, when he would make those fireside chats he was not a well man, he would go to bed early and about 12:00 you would hear the announcement telling you that this is Mr. Roosevelt by transcription. Mr. Roosevelt speaks in Washington in the White House. . . . We today don't need the baptism of the Holy Spirit for we have God's word by transcription. We have the record.[37]

Like countless black Americans in the 1930s, Keeble appreciated Roosevelt's symbolic gestures in establishing the so-called Black Cabinet[38] and raising economic hope through New Deal programs. Yet Keeble remained careful to distance himself from overt political alliances, retaining his lifelong focus on evangelism.

Yet Marshall Keeble lived through times of momentous change for his people. World War II engendered a number of pivotal social shifts in the United States. America's response to the bombing of Pearl Harbor (which occurred on Keeble's sixty-third birthday) and its entry into the global conflict helped the nation out of the Great Depression. During the war, one million black southerners exited their homeland in search for economic and social betterment in the North and West. In 1944 the U.S. Supreme Court's *Smith v. Allwright* decision declared the white primary unconstitutional, and four years later President Harry Truman desegregated the armed forces.[39] These events illustrate the far-reaching transformations in American policies that would restructure Keeble's world.

The societal redirections of the 1940s presaged a decade of social and racial upheaval in the 1950s South. The *Brown v. Board of Education* decision of 1954, the lynching of Emmett Till, the Montgomery Bus Boycott, and the Little Rock Nine episode of 1957 laid bare the vicious racism still destructively maiming the lives of black southerners. African Americans established nonviolent organizations such as the Southern Christian Leadership Conference (SCLC) and the Congress of Racial Equality (CORE) to work for equal rights, while rabidly racist white southerners formed their own reactionary groups, such as the White Citizens Council and a revived Ku Klux Klan, which were, along with Strom Thurmond's earlier Dixiecrat political initiative and the 1960s revival of the Republican party in the South, designed to oppose federal intervention in civil rights.[40]

Keeble never publicly commented on these matters, although he was certainly cognizant of them. He in fact delivered several speeches on lectureship programs at Church of Christ–related schools in the South, which barred black students, and he had accepted the presidency of Nashville Christian Institute since the doors of extant colleges in his fellowship remained closed to black students. In a 1950 lecture at Abilene Christian College in Texas, he lavished praise on white administrators at the newly formed Southwestern Christian College, who trained "boys and girls of the Negro race . . . to get out and meet anybody that rises up against the church of Christ." Keeble, of course aware that most Church of Christ colleges rejected aspiring blacks, concluded his speech with a diplomatic rebuke: "May the grace of God dwell in your heart and may the grace of God cause you to look upon no race as being inferior, but let's make him what he ought to be and lift him on a higher plane that Jesus can bless you and give you a crown that fadeth not away."[41]

Yet even in the face of the extraordinary changes sweeping across his nation, Marshall Keeble kept carefully to his chosen evangelistic work while working to shape the morality and ethics of black congregations. Many of Keeble's articles in the 1950s focused on "purity in the pulpit," jealousy among church leaders and members, congregational division and disputes, and gambling. Keeble's passionate love for Christ's church prompted him to chide black parishioners: "It seems like the more our brethren learn from the word of God the more we try to show how smart we are. . . . If we keep on fighting on the inside of the church we should remember that we are committing suicide spiritually."[42] Having established so many churches with his preaching, Keeble felt compelled to help bring them to spiritual maturity, thereby adding to his own duties.

Keeble expanded his roles in the 1950s, working as evangelist, educator, church planter, moral counselor, and missionary. The generosity of white Christians that had enabled him to range across the South now allowed him to travel abroad, touring and preaching in Asia, Africa, and Europe. After his travels Keeble recorded and published an account of his recollections in *From Mule Back to Super Jet with the Gospel*. This book and the articles he wrote in the *Gospel Advocate* took no account of the turbulent social and political events of the 1960s; the assassinations of John F. Kennedy, Malcolm X, Martin Luther King Jr., and Robert F. Kennedy found no explications in his essays. If Keeble showed no public interest in these violent deeds, he was obviously moved by the demise of his lifelong comrades and supporters: Nicholas B. Hardeman (in 1965) and Andrew M. Burton (in 1966). Perhaps more devastating to Keeble personally than the lost of those pivotal figures was the closure of "his school," the Nashville Christian Institute, in 1967. Paradoxically, while the death of Jim Crow had opened doors of opportunity for African American students, it precipitated the collapse of NCI as schools once closed to black students across the South now opened to them. The opportunity to attend public schools led to a declining enrollment at NCI and its eventual termination. After the school's closure, white and black leaders in Churches of Christ fought in court over assets worth half a million dollars, and Keeble sided with the white establishment in

Nashville and opposed many of his black former students. The demise of NCI and its subsequent legal skirmishing left Keeble brokenhearted and fractured the fellowship of white and black believers, leaving wounds that still linger.[43]

That Marshall Keeble's favorite song remained "Hold to God's Unchanging Hand," which focuses on "otherworldly"[44] themes, perhaps offers some insight into his pattern of life:

> Time is filled with swift transition,
> Naught of earth unmoved shall stand,
> Build your hopes on things eternal,
> Hold to God's unchanging hand!
>
> Trust in Him who will not leave you,
> Whatsoever years may bring,
> If by earthly friends forsaken,
> Still more closely to Him cling!
>
> Covet not this world's vain riches,
> That so rapidly decay,
> Seek to gain the heav'nly treasures,
> They will never pass away!
>
> When your journey is completed,
> If to God you have been true,
> Fair and bright the home in glory,
> Your enraptured soul shall view. . . .[45]

This 1904 composition emerged during an era of social and racial repression and inspired Keeble to abandon "all that I might preach the gospel to my people." His preoccupation with leading the souls of black folk to "heav'nly treasures" surely accounts for his almost antipolitical views, his lack of public interest in civil rights, and his virtual rejection of culture.[46] Keeble stood on the sociopolitical sidelines while Dr. Martin Luther King Jr., attorney Fred D. Gray, and so many others fought valiantly and fervently for racial and social equality. One of his closest friends remarked that "Marshall Keeble held God's hand all his life while preaching for the One who took care of him."[47] Having built his "hopes on things eternal," Keeble singlemindedly traversed racially segregated communities in the South, planting African American Churches of Christ while ignoring racial insults, shaking off physical assaults, looking beyond black bodies dangling from trees, brushing off discriminatory For Whites Only signs, and forgiving white believers who barred his young black students from their Christian school campuses. His wholehearted dedication to his preaching ministry precluded involvement in the civil rights movement. Keeble's unshakeable determination to reach as many black souls as possible served as a counterweight to any urge to join in the efforts to rid the land of Jim Crow's plague. The finite amount of energy in his being he would invest wholly in the "souls of black folk," bringing them to "the home in glory."

Marshall Keeble's public writing mirrors this devotion to the care of souls. The bulk of his efforts this comprise this anthology appeared in the *Gospel Advocate*. Keeble contributed numerous articles to the *Firm Foundation*, the *Christian Leader*, the *Christian Worker*, and other Church of Christ journals. His articles also appeared in the *Christian Echo*, the paper published and controlled by blacks in Churches of Christ; but George P. Bowser's paper appeared and circulated irregularly because of insufficient finances. More significantly, Keeble understood that his home base must remain in Nashville, Tennessee, the place of his residence and the city where the *Gospel Advocate* was published. As a consequence, the overwhelming majority of Keeble's writings surfaced in that journal; he knew that the emotional and monetary support of Andrew Burton and other white leaders in Churches of Christ held the key to his work as a traveling evangelist. His articles kept white readers informed, inspired, and convinced of his biblical orthodoxy. This anthology, then, deliberately reproduces extant articles mostly from the *Gospel Advocate*, even though some from the *Christian Echo* and other sources appear. Notwithstanding this selectivity, the anthology uniquely allows Marshall Keeble, unquestionably the most influential black preacher in twentieth-century Churches of Christ, to speak for himself. More significantly, it enables Keeble himself to strip away any mythical and magical debris that may clutter the memory of his extraordinary life.

Chapter 1

The Sufficiency of the Church: Keeble in the 1910s

Like many of his white mentors in Middle Tennessee, Marshall Keeble unwaveringly believed that the church was the only God-ordained and only God-sanctioned institution through which evangelism could be carried out. Keeble vehemently opposed Christians who sought evangelism through missionary societies, and this view prompted him to break from Preston Taylor and the black Disciples of Christ in Nashville, Tennessee. Keeble's aversion for missionary societies derived largely from his perusal of the writings of white leaders in Churches of Christ such as Tolbert Fanning. As early as 1857 Fanning had vented his displeasure with missionary societies, affirming, "The Church of God is the only divinely authorized Missionary, Bible, Sunday and Temperance Society; the only institution in which the Heavenly Father will be honored in the salvation of the world, and in and through no other agency can man glorify his Maker.... We see not, and never have seen, how it is possible for any people professing the Christian religion to attempt to do the work of the church through merely human agencies, such as Missionary Societies, Sunday Schools, etc."[1] Keeble imbibed this ideology, and his conviction of the sufficiency of the church inspired him to move through the world preaching, teaching, baptizing, and planting congregations without the aid of any manmade institutions.

The documents in this chapter portray Marshall Keeble as an emerging church planter. Indeed, Keeble in 1918 established his first congregation, the Oak Grove Church of Christ in Henderson, Tennessee, which still exists today. This congregation became the first of many Keeble would organize before his effective evangelistic career ended in 1968. The documents that follow further reveal that Keeble had help from such white leaders as Nicholas B. Hardeman and such black leaders as Samuel W. Womack and Alexander C. Campbell. Black women, including his wife Minnie Womack and his colaborer Annie C. Tuggle, were also invaluable contributions to Keeble's ministry in the 1910s.

More Gospel Preaching Needed [1916][2]

Two years ago I took up the work of an evangelist. When I started, I found that I would have to leave everything to follow Jesus and proclaim his word. The apostle Paul exhorted Timothy not to entangle himself with the affairs of this life; and to be successful in the evangelistic work, I believe a man ought to give himself wholly to the work, and God will bless his labors. He may suffer for the necessary things of life: but the apostle Paul said that he was sometimes hungry, naked, and many other things he suffered for Christ. He says that with food and raiment we should be content.

Since I have been engaged in this noble work I have gone into homes where I was not wanted because I was a ("Campbellite")[3] gospel preacher; but I went in and remained, and would leave peace in such homes. No one knows what a man meets that preaches the gospel, save the man that does it; and he does not know, if he just goes where everything is smooth, where the work is already built up. I find no time to rest in this work. I am busy every day somewhere, preaching the gospel, for my people certainly need it.

This is my second trip this year among the churches in East Tennessee, and I find most of them dying for the want of preaching. A few of them have a little preaching sometimes, but none of them, in my judgment, have enough, and that is the reason sectarianism (or man-made doctrine) is taking the world. There are one hundred sectarian preachers to one Christian preacher. I often get on the train and ride for miles and meet about fifty or more preachers, and not one of them a Christian preacher. We need more preachers in the church of Christ that are willing to suffer and endure hardness in order to spread the wonderful message that Jesus commanded to be preached to all nations.

A few months ago I was at McMinnville, and the white brethren at Salem Church invited me to preach to them at eleven o'clock, and I did so. I was never treated in a more Christianlike way in my life. The elder, Brother J. M. Green, gave me a cordial welcome and an invitation to come back again. The white congregation at Arlington, about three miles from Salem, invited me to address them at three o'clock in the afternoon. Here I was accorded the same treatment that I received at the Salem Church, and they contributed liberally to me in my work for the Master. I wish others could see our needs or knew our needs; then they would gladly aid us in spreading the gospel. If any one doubts my ability as a preacher, let him write to Brother J. M. Green, McMinnville, Tenn., Route 5 Box 109;

W. R. Mingle, Bellbuckle, Tenn.; or James Stubblefield, Viola, Tenn. These are white brethren who have been greatly interested in our work. I am very thankful to God for the fellowship of these brethren; for without the aid and cooperation of my brethren and sisters, both white and black, I could not do the work that I am now trying to do in a humble way and in everything giving God the glory.

For the benefit of some that might want to know what visible results we have had in our work, I now state that since last July there have been ninety-seven added to the church of Christ; and, with the help of God and the brethren, I want to do more this season. I have several meetings to hold in places where there are but two or three colored Christians, and they are not able to support a meeting; but I am going, trusting that God will send some one to my aid.

There are several places where we have no church of Christ among the colored people in Tennessee—Columbia, Mount Pleasant, Chattanooga, Martin, Dresden, and others too numerous to mention; but the striking part about it is, no one seems to care. The only way I see that these places can be reached with the gospel is for those that are financially able to sacrifice some of the means that God has given them and have the gospel preached where it needs to be; and the way I understand the Scriptures, if this is not done, some of us will fail to enjoy eternal life.[4]

Here is one example of how to reach the Negro with the gospel. Brother A. M. Burton (white),[5] of Nashville, is now giving the congregation on Jackson Street, in Nashville, Brother G. Dallas Smith's Bible drill,[6] furnishing books and some one to teach the class, and, in my judgment, it will be the means of a good many seeing the truth. Brother Burton has been a great help to the work at this place. Several years ago he supported a meeting at this place, and the results were wonderful, many being added. May God send us more such Christian men and women as Brother Burton....

[Life-Giving Sisters, 1916][7]

On the second Lord's day in May I began a meeting at Mount Pleasant, Tenn., and remained there twelve days. This is a hard field, because my people are so far back in ignorance that they do not realize that the Bible, God's Word, is our guide to everlasting life. No one knows what a gospel preacher has to undergo in such places as this, save he that has it to do; and I am glad it has fallen to my lot to do this great work of carrying the greatest message that ever was sent to a perishing world. Just as soon as we entered this town the other preachers began working hard to keep their members away; but they came, anyway, and the blessed truth caught three, and they were baptized for what the Bible teaches, and one was restored. On the last day of the meeting a few disciples from the surrounding county met with us and agreed to keep the work alive, and I endeavored to impress them to meet on the first day of each week. Brother Joe Worley,[8] who lives in the town and who cared for my wife and I while there, certainly made it pleasant for us. Brother Worley has all the responsibility of the work here on him, but he does not seem to be tired. While here I had the pleasure of visiting Brother Wrye (White) at his home, and spent about one hour with him; and he gave me some very good advice, for which I am very thankful. Brother Wrye, in my judgment, is doing a great work at this place, for which, if he is not paid here, he will get his reward in the end.

On the fourth Lord's day in May I began a meeting at Bellbuckle, Tenn., which I consider the greatest meeting that I ever conducted. We had to use the schoolhouse, which is very large, and at times it was full. Here we baptized a young lady who came up from Wartrace, [Tennessee] and made the confession, going down there to baptize her. My wife is so much help to me in my work. She leads the song service.[9] The second week of the meeting Sister Annie Tuggle[10] joined us, and it was certainly a treat, for she gave new life to the work. She is a faithful worker. May God bless her in her field of labor. She is a solicitor for the Bible School at Silver Point. I do not believe I ever met as many white brethren and sisters as interested and eager to get the gospel to the Negro as these are here. Brother W. R. Mingle (white) is, in my judgment, is a great example of true Christianity, and I must say he has a good, Christian wife. The white brethren and sisters knew that the three or four colored disciples here were unable to feed us while here, and they would send cabbage, potatoes, milk, canned fruit, butter, meat, chickens, etc., and Sister Mingle sent over baked cakes and homemade light bread. Now, dear reader, does this look like real Christianity or not? I will leave the answer with you. I only pray that others may be inspired to do more to reach this fallen race of mine. The interest the white people showed in us at this place will ever live in my heart and will cause me to grow stronger and more faithful in discharging my duty and carrying the gospel to my people....

[But God Sustained Me, 1917][11]

For the benefit of those who have contributed to me in my work and also that others may be encouraged to aid us, I submit a brief report of my work for the year 1916.[12] I have worked in four States, namely, Tennessee, Alabama, Mississippi, and Arkansas. During the winter I was busy visiting mission points and congregations, endeavoring to keep them alive, and I believe my work was effective along that line. In the spring I began protracted meetings, beginning at Mount Pleasant, Tenn., in May, and closing my last meeting at Nashville with the congregation I am a member of. It was in this congregation that I was trained as a Christian worker, doing anything that I was asked to do by my older brethren. I have sat at the feet of such men as old Brother Womack and G. P. Bowser. From the time my first meeting began at Mount Pleasant, I held twenty-three meetings, covering a period of eight months and a half, and during the time I lost about one week. I worked so hard during these meetings that my physical strength grew very weak, but the God of Heaven held me up. It may be, dear reader, you would like to know what visible good was done; and if you will listen, I shall humbly give you what you desire: Baptisms, 118; restorations, 47; sermons preached, 365; sick visited, 65; marriages, 1; funerals, 4; number of places or congregations visited, 36; number of miles traveled, 7,000; total cash paid me and donated, $795.15, besides a number of presents given me in the way of clothing and boxes of provisions, without which I could not have done what I have done. God only knows how grateful I am to all who have shared with me in this great work of reaching my people. My wife and children were with me a part of the protracted meeting season, and in singing and teaching the Scriptures privately my wife rendered valuable service. Now I do not believe this is all that I could have done last, and by the help of God I will do more this year. I went to many places where, if it had not been for the white brethren and sisters, we would have suffered greatly. No one knows the hardships of an evangelist but one who has engaged in the work. I always keep in memory the teaching of the apostle Paul to Timothy [2:3]: "Endure hardness, as a good soldier." Let any one desiring our services in any destitute field notify me, and I will see what can be done....

Three Good Meetings [1917][13]

On June 11 I began a meeting at Louisville, Ky., of three weeks' duration. Interest was fine all through the meeting. At each service about half of the audience were white people, some of whom never missed a service. In this meeting one confession was made; but when the time came for her to be baptized, she was not ready. I hope she will before it is too late. This meeting was supported by the Highland church of Christ,[14] and they also furnished the tent and chairs. About twice a week a male quartet from the Highland Church would sing for us.

From Louisville I went to a mission point about seven miles below Nashville, Tenn., and held a ten day meeting. This meeting was also greatly supported by the white people. Brother [Samuel W.] Womack was in this meeting most of the time, and his presence seemed to give life to the meeting. We need more such men as Brother Womack, who has spent his life fishing for men, and who has lived so he is a good pattern for both young and old. In this meeting five made the good confession. Four were baptized while the meeting was in progress, and Brother Womack went back and baptized the fifth one last Lord's day. Several of the Jackson Street Church brethren and sisters came down and rendered valuable assistance.

I began a good meeting at Cookeville, Tenn., last Lord's day. The interest is fine, and the white brethren and sisters are attending well, as usual. No additions yet, but prospects are good. I am glad God has put it into the hearts of the white brethren to reach down with the gospel and bring up this fallen and neglected race of mine. Let us labor and pray....

Keeble Plants His First Church [1918][15]

When I made my last report, I was at Cookeville, Tenn., in a very interesting meeting; but there were no additions. I began a meeting at Latham, Tenn., on the second Lord's day in July and continued it one week. Interest was good and five young men were baptized. The white brethren and sisters attended the meeting regularly and assisted me in the work. From there I went to Henderson, Tenn., and began a meeting on the third Lord's day in July. This is a new field. When I went there two years ago, I found just four members; old Brother [Bose] Crooms and his family and baptized seven more. This time the interest was great. Sixty-nine were baptized. Eighty-four made the good confession, which leaves fifteen yet to be baptized. Very nearly all of these people came from the Baptists and Methodists. When we tried to rent the Methodist Church to hold the meeting in, they refused, although they allowed us to use it last year; and we tried the Baptists, and they refused. So Brother N. B. Hardeman[16] arranged for us to hold the meeting about seven miles from town in a little schoolhouse which was located in a thick settlement of colored people. This meeting lasted three weeks. One day we went to the water to baptize twelve persons who had made the night before, and I preached at the edge of the water, and eighteen more came forward and were baptized, making thirty that were baptized that day. The white Christians did all they could to assist us in the meeting. On the last night Brother N. B. Hardeman and others came out and made remarks in the meeting. This was my first time to meet Brother Hardeman, and in my judgment, he is a fine Christian man....

Four Years of Evangelistic Work [1919][17]

I am now closing my fourth year's work and I am happy because Jesus has blessed my labors, and to him be all the praise. For four years I have daily worked trying to win souls for Christ, because winning brings reward. One thing that has served to encourage me in the work is the assistance that I have received from so many of the brethren and sisters who have been so thoughtful of my needs. A good many places where I have gone to preach to my people, if it had not been for the aid given by the white people, I would have suffered, and I am so thankful for such kind and Christian fellowship, and pray that I may ever live so as to be worthy of all blessings bestowed upon me in the future. I shall now give an account of all my work for the last four years, and I hope it will be inspiring to all who may read it. Year 1915—sermons, 240; baptized, 90; restored, 23; miles traveled, 5,260. Year 1916—sermons, 335; baptized, 135; restored, 30; miles traveled, 5,000. Year 1917—sermons, 297; baptized, 104; restored, 16; miles traveled, 6,295. Total for four years: sermons, 1,161; baptized, 457; restored, 86; miles traveled, 23,052.

I give these figures to prove that the work can be done without the aid of any human organization. I have always believed that the work could be done by the church, and now I know can.[18] During these four years I have established two congregations, and both of them are preparing to build meetinghouses this spring. In accomplishing what I have, I have suffered in many ways, but ever trusting Jesus, who suffered for me. Now, as the old year passes out and we are blessed with the privilege of seeing the new year come, let us not make new resolutions, but put in practice those we have already made. May God help me to do more in the future and bring many souls to Him who redeemed us. May God bless all who have had fellowship with me in my work, and I ask of them their continued fellowship and prayers.

["The Two Old Heroes," 1919][19]

The first Lord's day in the year I met with my home congregation, and it was a joyful day indeed. Brethren A. C. Campbell and S. W. Womack, the two old heroes who have struggled and fought hard to establish a pure worship in Nashville, were present. Brother Womack is now failing in health but I believe his is stronger spiritually than he ever was. I thank God that, as a preacher of the blessed gospel, I have been spared to go over almost all of the work that this old, humble, and meek servant has established. Just to see the many places where he has labored against great opposition and prejudice and to see strong congregations there now would make any lover of the cause of Christ rejoice. The white brethren and sisters who have been his coworkers ought to be happy and filled with joy to know that they have had fellowship in such a great work of building up Christ's kingdom on earth. He often states that if the white brethren and sisters had not come to his aid he could not have done the work that he has accomplished.

Brother A. C. Campbell has labored hard and earnestly everywhere he has gone to tell the world of the blessed Christ. I have known Brother Campbell for many years, and I know of no man who has had more difficulties and hindrances than he has had; but it seems that he has set his affections on things above, not on the perishing things of the earth. Though he is nearing the threescore mark, he is just as active as a young man, and we pray that he may live long and continue preaching the grand, old gospel of Jesus Christ. It was these two godly men that caused me to come out from the "digressive" church and take my stand with a people that are contending "earnestly for the faith which was once for all delivered unto the saints [Jude 3]"; and, whatever may come, I am determined to be faithful until death....

From Spring Valley I went to Corinth, Miss., and spent Thursday and Friday night. I found the church in fine condition. Brother J. Hannon,[20] an evangelist, is located there, and he is doing, it seems, all that he can to keep the work alive.

... I went to Tuscumbia, Ala., and while in that town I saw so many people who possibly had never heard the gospel of Jesus Christ; so I went to the Chief of Police and got permission to preach on the street, and for about an hour and thirty minutes I spoke to about four hundred people, white and colored, and they gave the best attention, and many expressed themselves after dismissal, stating that they had never before heard such preaching in all of their lives.

On the second Lord's day in February I was with the Spring Valley Church again. We had a splendid service.

From Spring Valley I came home to be in attendance at a ministers' meeting at the Jackson Street Church, in Nashville. This meeting began on Thursday, February 13, and continued over Lord's day. In speaking of this meeting, I can say it was a feast of good things. There were about thirty preachers present, besides deacons and elders and a host of visitors. There have been great meetings at Jackson Street Church, but never anything like this one, and I was glad the brethren found the old church standing firm on the truth and willing to be governed by God's government. Many good things resulted from this meeting.

On the fourth Lord's day in February I was with my home congregation; and at three o'clock in the afternoon Brother T. Q. Martin[21] preached an able and instructive sermon, and it had it's effect on all who were present. This man is a white man, but I do not believe he has a spark of malice or prejudice in his heart; and may God bless him with long life so he may continue lifting up fallen humanity. We also were glad to have the white brethren with us who came with Brother Martin. Let us all pray that God's Spirit may rule in his church.

An Interesting Report [1919][22]

. . . The next place I visited was Blackton, Ark., where I preached on the fourth Lord's day in April, and enjoyed two splendid services with this faithful congregation. This congregation was established through the faithful efforts of old Brother Nathan Cathey,[23] who moved in her over thirty years ago from Hickman County, Tenn. If all who move into new fields would go to work as this old servant did, great would be the spread of the gospel of Jesus Christ. Brother Cathey died last year, leaving a wide awake, working congregation as the fruits of his labors. Brother D. J. Bynum[24] and I have been engaged to labor with this church a month in mission work.

On April 28, 29, I was with the little band at Cotton Plant, Ark., and the interest was good at both services. We are planning to hold a meeting there this fall.

I began a meeting with the Memphis mission on April 30 and continued it ten days. The interest was good, but there were no additions. The work there has been hindered in many ways. There are some as faithful and earnest brethren and sisters there as I have ever met, but they need encouragement and instruction. Brethren and sisters from Neshoba and Capleville, who live from sixteen to twenty miles away, attended these services, showing an interest in the work. While here I made my home with Brother D. J. Bynum and wife, and I shall never forget their kindness.

Returning to Nashville, I preached at the Jackson Street Church on the second Lord's day in May, with good attendance at both services. I was proud to find them faithfully working and trusting Jesus.

On the third Lord's day in May, assisted by Brother T. H. Busby,[25] I began a meeting at Sparta, Tenn. Brother Busby did the singing and some of the preaching, and he did his part well. There is a splendid meetinghouse in the town which was given to the brethren by the white congregation there, but its doors had been closed for over two years prior to this meeting. We succeeded in getting regular worship started again, and Brother Busby is to visit them once a month. Though the work has been virtually dead, the white brethren are willing to assist in reviving it. Brother Hal Harris, who is highly esteemed by all the white people, promised to look after the work and see that the doors are kept open for services in the future. I am to go back at an early date and hold a meeting.

. . . I went to Henderson, Tenn., on May 27, and remained three days. The services were well attended and two persons made the good confession. One of these was a Baptist preacher. Two years ago I went there and found four members; now there are about one hundred, and they are preparing to build a meetinghouse. I will hold another meeting there in July. I have never met better white people than those at Henderson. Brother J. Hannon, who lives at Corinth, Miss., preaches for the colored brethren there once a month and they all love him.

On May 30 I preached at Corinth, Miss., and found them still faithful in the work. Although Brother Hannon preaches a good deal, he does not forget his home work.

I am now in a meeting at Bellbuckle, Tenn., which began June 1, and the interest is increasing. This is my seventh meeting here. We have raised thirty dollars to assist in building a meetinghouse. They now have a little over one hundred dollars in the building fund. Brethren who love to do real mission work should send a contribution to W. R. Mingle (white), who is managing the business for them until some colored brother develops who can take the work. . . .

I am glad that I had the privilege of being present at David Lipscomb College on May 14, because I saw the need of Christian education as never before. It was worth the trip to hear the speeches made by Brethren A. B. Lipscomb,[26] Elam,[27] McQuiddy,[28] and others. May these Christian men live on, for such men are a blessing to the church and to the world. Brother David Lipscomb[29] put a coal of fire among the brethren before God took him, which will never die.

[Things That We Should Be Thankful For, 1918][30]

While sitting at home on account of such severe weather and studying God's word, I can see so many things to be thankful for. I thank God for that dear old mother[31] that brought me into this great world and instilled that great principle into me to love God, and for that father[32] that labored hard to give to his family the necessities of life and took me by the hand and led me to church every Lord's day. We need more parents like these, for a child reared this way will never depart from its training. At the age of fourteen I obeyed the gospel, and I am so thankful that I began to serve the Lord early in life, so I never learned so many evil habits that most young men learn. When about eighteen years old, I married a daughter of S. W. Womack. I never thought at first what a blessing it was to marry into this Christian man's family, but I am thankful now. If there ever was a Christian anywhere, this old servant is one. While I am young, I am trying to live humble and meek like him, and I thank God for the impression his life has made on me. Some people send flowers and put them on the casket after death, but I believe in giving them while we live. I am a young preacher endeavoring to make a success in life; and if I can just make the man that Brother Womack is, I will be so thankful. His success in life, in a material way, has not been very great, but I have reference to the great treasures he is laying up in heaven. He has established more churches and done more to keep "digressivism"[33] out of this State than any colored man I know of anywhere; and had it not been for the instruction he received from such men as Brother David Lipscomb and Brother E. G. Sewell,[34] he could not have succeeded as he has. I have been in conversation with him thousands of times on scriptural subjects, and he rarely ever finishes without mentioning one or the other of these great men. About nineteen years ago Brother A. C. Campbell[35] decided to pull out from "digressivism." And he had courage enough to begin mission in his own home. As soon as Brother Womack learned of it, he joined hand in hand with him, and they worked for some time this way, and the interest grew so we had to get a larger place to worship; so we purchased a piece of property on the corner of Jackson Street and Fourteenth Avenue, North, known as the "Jackson Street church of Christ," and we are so thankful for this work that these two worthy Christian preachers have done. Brother Campbell is nearly sixty years of age, but is yet active in the ministry, and I know of no man that is doing more to convert the world than he. As I have been closely connected with these two brethren for about twenty years or more, I can truthfully say they have suffered while preaching the gospel, and their wives need to be praised for their great endurance, and for all of this we thank the Lord. It was these two men that encouraged me to preach the gospel, and I shall never be through praising them and thanking God for such blessings. Neither of these men know that I am writing this article. I just thought it proper to say a few words about the good they are doing and have done. Brother Womack and Brother Campbell say that the Gospel Advocate has been second with them, and the Bible first.[36]

    Speaking concerning the Advocate, it has been a great help to me in studying the Bible. I have been reading it ever since I learned to read. My grandfather[37] took it until his death; then, after I married into Brother Womack's family, I found it there. So I am still reading it. May God bless and lead those in whose hands the paper is to remain, and may it go forth, blessing the world as it did when that great and noble servant, David Lipscomb, lived. Some brethren think that the paper will not be what it used to be, but I believe such men as J. C. McQuiddy, A. B. Lipscomb, and T. B. Larimore[38] are fully able in every sense to cause the paper to hold its present position in the world, and, like Joshua, they will lead us across Jordan. For all of these rich blessings we thank our Heavenly Father.

I want to thank the editors of the Gospel Advocate for publishing my articles and reports from time to time.

Keeble in the 1910s

Chapter 2

If It Were Not for the White Christians: Keeble in the 1920s

Marshall Keeble learned early in his evangelistic career that his success as an itinerant preacher depended largely on the financial support of white Christians. Like many of his black mentors and contemporaries in the Stone-Campbell movement, such as Samuel W. Womack, Alexander C. Campbell, and Samuel Robert Cassius (1853–1931), Keeble understood that black Christians lacked the financial resources their white counterparts possessed. "Dear white brethren," expressed Campbell in 1909, "some of the loyal colored brethren have the zeal, the whole truth, and the courage to do the right thing, and you white brethren who are loyal have the zeal, the whole truth, the courage, and the money."[1] Cassius put it more bluntly: "I have not gone to the white churches because I liked to preach to white folks. I went to them to get aid that I might go to my own race. There was nowhere else to go."[2]

While Keeble was not as forthcoming as Cassius, he certainly recognized the importance of relying on financial support from white Christians. In 1920 Keeble lost his most significant mentor, Samuel W. Womack, but in the same year he gained his most important supporter, Andrew M. Burton. In the documents following, one learns that Burton, a wealthy white businessman in Nashville, Tennessee, stood as Keeble's chief benefactor. Burton's consistent and generous donations enabled the black evangelist to travel the country, disseminating what he called the "pure gospel." Keeble's writings also show that other white believers generously supported his evangelistic campaigns. Even though antiblack sentiment may have vitiated their generosity, their efforts were sincere, impressive, and commendable. By the end of the 1920s, Keeble had emerged as a potent and successful evangelist, having planted congregations in Birmingham, Alabama, Jackson, Tennessee, Lakeland, Tampa, and St. Petersburg, Florida, and Fort Smith, Arkansas.

[Keeble in Detroit, Michigan, 1920][3]

I have been in Detroit three months to-day (February 15). Since coming here I have labored with the Atione mission, and we have succeeded in bringing the two factions together; but a few are still unwilling to come together so there will be no division. This is a fine field, because the true laborers are few; and if the brethren and sisters here will labor together, a great work can be accomplished in Christ's name.

The first of the year the brethren decided to start a building fund, and they are progressing nicely. We are now worshiping in a rented storehouse. If we were in a more suitable place, a great work could be done.

Since coming here I have labored with my hands[4] and preached at every opportunity. I came here for the benefit of my son's health, and I am glad to say that he has rapidly improved. I am planning to remain until the first of May, and then I will go home and rest up for my protracted-meeting work. I hope to begin my first meeting for the season at Bellbuckle, Tenn.

Several of the churches have remembered me with boxes and some have sent money to aid me. I am glad they believe me to be worthy, and trust that I may never betray their confidence. Brother W. R. Mingle (white), of Bellbuckle, has fellowship[p]ed me greatly ever since I entered the evangelistic work. For four years he has given me a nice pig to raise and also contributed regularly to me. He has done more to encourage me in the work than any one else.

Spiritually, the Gospel Advocate has given me great strength. No one can read its pages regularly without growing stronger in the faith of the Lord Jesus. My wife sends it to me each week; and when it comes, I never stop reading until I have read it through. Every brother ought to read this paper. I am glad to see the Advocate standing so firm on the truth, and I am praying that the brethren who have it under their management will live long so the world can be benefited and bettered by their strong articles.

I ask the prayers of all while in this wicked city.

[Division in Nashville, Tennessee, 1920][5]

After spending six months in Detroit, Mich., I am now back home to take up protracted-meeting work for this season. Although I went to Detroit for my boy's health,[6] I labored in an automobile factory for our support and preached at the mission on Antoine Street. This was a fine field to labor in. Interest grew in every service, and four were baptized and three restored while I was there. I have been engaged to hold a few weeks' meeting there this fall. Since being home I have met with the Jackson Street Church, and I am glad to say they are doing well. This is the congregation old Brother [Samuel W.] Womack and Brother Alexander Campbell labored so hard and earnestly to establish some years ago. I shall never forget those good [white] brethren—A. B. Lipscomb, Joe McPherson, F. W. Smith, S. P. Pittman, and F. B. Srygley[7]—who came and gave us scriptural instruction on two occasions, but those who went out and now worship on Jefferson Street[8] refused to hear or receive their instruction. Although Brother Joe McPherson has gone from us, his labors and his influence among us still live. I only ask that these good men bear with us and pray for us that a better state of affairs may exist in the future. We cannot build congregations and schools with division, strife, and hatred existing among us; so I long for the day when we will confess our wrongs and forgive each other and not divide God's people over our faults. I pray that I may be instrumental in bringing many precious souls to Christ this season. Let brotherly love continue [Hebrews 13:1].

[A Eulogy of Samuel W. Womack, 1920][9]

On July 13, 1920, Brother S. W. Womack departed this life. He had been sick for nearly two years, and had been confined to his room about ten months. His suffering was great at times, but he never once murmured, but was cheerful all the time. I was absent when he died. I was in a meeting in Latham, Tenn., and they wired me three or four messages, but I failed to get either one until it was too late for me to attend the funeral. It had been my desire to be present at this good man's funeral. Old Brother [Henry] Clay,[10] who had labored with him for years, spoke over the remains; also Brother [Calvin] Dowell,[11] a young brother who is a product of Jackson Street Church, spoke encouraging words. Brother F. W. Smith and Brother A. B. Lipscomb were present and spoke words of comfort and all who heard them were uplifted and edified. Brother A. M. Burton was also present. This Christian man never talks much in a public way, but his life tells what he is. These brethren were all interested in Brother Womack and his work, and during his life of over forty years in the ministry they greatly helped in supporting him in his work.

I have often heard Brother Womack say he had gone to places to preach where there was not a colored member of the church of Christ, and his own race would fail to aid or support him, and the white people would supply his needs; and I believe if there ever was a dollar safely invested, it was when given to this faithful preacher of the gospel of Jesus Christ.

I married in this family about twenty-five years ago, and I have been closely connected with him ever since, and I must say that I never heard him speak rashly or get angry. He seemed to keep a joyful spirit all the time. He has been a great help to me. He first got me to see that I was wrong while working with the "digressives," and I came out from them over twenty years ago, and from that [time] on

I tried to make my life like his; and though he is gone, I shall continue to try and imitate the Christian life he has left behind.

Last September he was with me at Sugar Grove, Ky., where I was holding a meeting. He established this congregation and was highly esteemed by them all. While there he was very feeble, and told them that he would never meet them on earth any more, but to live so they could meet on the other side of Jordan.

His funeral was conducted at the Jackson Street Church, where he worshiped when at home; and when he got so weak he had to walk with a stick, he would often preach to congregation while sitting in a chair. He considered this congregation to be the cream of his labors; and although some time ago some trouble arose and caused division, he remained and endeavored to unite us again and stop the division, and we who remain are yet working and praying that unity may be brought about in the future. The Jackson Street Church never once neglected him in any way. They contributed regularly to him, and the members were always giving him something to comfort him in his sickness. Other churches would send donations to him often. The white brethren and sisters all over the South sent him comforting messages. Some of them would say they had never seen him, but they had read of his life in the Gospel Advocate.

It was Brother Womack's delight when he was in town to visit the Gospel Advocate office, because, he said, he was always made welcome by the whole staff. Whenever he got puzzled over any passage of scripture, he would always have a conference with old Brother David Lipscomb during his life time. After Brother Lipscomb died, he continued to go and talk with Brethren A. B. Lipscomb, J. C. McQuiddy, F. W. Smith, and others, and by this means he was always prepared to instruct his people. He [Womack] always read his Bible daily. . . .

[White Christians with Black Servants, 1920][12]

. . . I wish more of the white brethren and sisters would attend more of the meetings conducted by my people, and then they could see the neglected work right at home. Every white brother or sister that has a servant should often speak to him or her about obeying the gospel, and this would cause them to open their eyes to the truth. Several years ago I held a meeting at Henderson, Tenn. A great number of white brethren and sisters lived in that vicinity, and, of course, had a good many colored people working around, and they would teach them the word of God and tell them to go out and hear me preach, and, as a result, sixty-nine obeyed the gospel. I think we could call this mission work at home. The influence of Freed-Hardeman College[13] in that section is great. There are several merchants in Henderson that are members of the church of Christ, who are never too busy or ashamed to grasp our hand and freely talk about the church and its work. . . .

["A Great Missionary Spirit," 1921][14]

For the last seven years I have been engaged in mission work among my people, and during this time nine hundred and fifty-seven souls have obeyed the gospel under my preaching. My support during these seven years has not been at all times what I would have liked for it to be; but I have pressed on trusting Jesus to supply my needs. Since entering the work I have been encouraged by such Christian men as A. B. Lipscomb, A. M. Burton, S. W. Womack, and a great many others. Several of the white brethren remembered me during the holidays; and a good many colored brethren and sisters among whom I have labored.

I am glad to see such a great missionary spirit among the white churches, trying to reach all nations with the gospel; and I am forced to say right here, brethren, do not forget, in arranging your plans for this year, to include mission work right at your door among my race. To use all the time and money to reach the foreign nations, and neglect your cooks, house girls, farm hands, chauffeurs, and nurses, I think, is a sad and serious mistake; because if we can get the gospel to those who serve your homes and care for your little ones, you can put more trust in them, and save them from ignorance of the blessed gospel of Jesus Christ. The white brethren tell me in a good many places I go to do mission work that they hope all of the negroes in their section will obey the gospel, because when one accepts the gospel it seems to make a different man out of him in every respect. While I was at Tuscumbia, Ala., last fall, several of the leading white brethren there wanted to see a colored Christian preacher; and when they saw me and heard me preach, they seemed to be happy because they had lived to see a colored man preaching the pure gospel. Now, brethren, I do not mention this for any selfish reason or motive, neither am I opposed to mission work across the waters; but please do not forget those who work by your side and in your homes. . . . [15]

[Stirring Up Birmingham, Alabama, 1921][16]

On the fifth Lord's day in May I began a meeting at Birmingham, Ala., under a tent furnished by the West End church of Christ (white). This church, through Brother W. C. Graves,[17] had me to come here and preach the pure gospel to my people. This meeting was a success in many ways. Interest grew in every service until there were more standing outside than there were on the inside. The first week I had to preach and lead the song service. The white brethren saw this was too hard on me; so Brother W. C. Graves led the song service the balance of the meeting; and when he was absent, Brother Mosley led. These white brethren were not ashamed to help us in every way possible. They paid my board with a Baptist family, and told me to just preach and not worry about anything. The Christian fellowship that these brethren and sisters showed me is the only way to manifest to the world that the gospel is to every creature. I preached about two weeks before any visible good could be seen.

One night a Methodist preacher attacked the teaching that I was doing; but when I humbly answered him with God's word, a young woman came forward and made the great confession, and from that time on interest was high. Forty-five made the good confession. Forty were baptized while I was there, and the others are to be baptized later. Among the number baptized was a little band of what are called "sanctified" people. They were worshiping in a nice hall. When they heard the pure gospel and learned how to become really sanctified, they were all baptized for the remission of sins. So the hall where they worshiped was turned over to us, and the brethren and sisters will worship there until they can buy them a house in which to worship God according to his word. . . .

One encouraging thing about this meeting was that we left everybody reading the Scriptures. The brethren and sisters were to meet in the hall on the Lord's day and take the Lord's Supper. Brother W. C. Graves was to meet with them and teach them how to keep house for the Lord. If we had more white brethren like Brother Graves and those whom he worships with at West End, my race would soon be lifted out of darkness. These brethren did not give their money and stand back somewhere; but they came to every service and rendered every assistance possible, and the results were a great ingathering of souls for Christ. . . .

[The Influence of Joe McPherson, 1921][18]

. . . I am glad to see the white churches turning their attention toward my race, trying to lift them with the gospel of Jesus Christ. There are thousands of negroes living right around some of our largest white churches who have never heard the gospel of Jesus Christ, and it is a serious condition when we remember that Jesus said: "Go ye into all the world, and preach the gospel to every creature" [Mark 16:15]. It does my soul good when I read the Gospel Advocate. The first thing I look for is "At Home and Abroad," because I can see where the brethren see hammering away with the truth and thousands are being brought to Christ; and then I think of how few negroes are given the chance to hear the pure gospel, and I tremble. Jesus said: "Go . . . teach all nations" [Matthew 28:19]. We need some more preachers like Joe McPherson, E. G. Sewell, David Lipscomb, and S. W. Womack, who went about preaching "Jesus Christ, and him crucified" [1 Corinthians 2:2] to the rich and the poor, black and white. Brother Joe McPherson did more toward teaching me how to preach than any man I ever heard. A. M. Burton supported a meeting[19] once for the Jackson Street church of Christ (colored), in Nashville, and got Brother McPherson to do the preaching. This meeting continued one month, and many souls were brought to Christ. In this meeting I copied every lesson Brother McPherson preached; and though he is dead, I am still preaching his sermons, and these lessons are still bringing men to Christ. Brethren, wherever you go and find an opportunity to preach to my people, please give them God's word, and it will bring forth fruit to the glory and honor of Jesus Christ.

[Tension in Mississippi, 1921][20]

During the last two weeks in October I was in a meeting at Utica, Miss. The colored people there had never heard the pure gospel. Brother R. L. Sweeny (white) became interested in having the truth taught to my people, but felt that he was not able to support the meeting; so he wrote Brother A. M. Burton and explained the condition to him, and asked him to send some colored preacher into this section. Brother Burton asked me to go, saying he would give me fifty dollars; so I consented to go.

In many respects my faith in Christ was tested as never before, but I am glad to say that all of this made me stronger and more determined to hold up Christ to the world. Brother Sweeney secured the meetinghouse of the people called the "Sanctified Church"[21] for me to teach the word of God in, and also got one of the deacons[22] to care for me while there; and I must say that I have never been better cared for, because this brother and his wife did all they could to make my stay a pleasant one. After the second night these good people began to see that something was wrong; so they sent to Jackson, Miss., for their pastor,[23] and he came. He heard my lesson that night, but never said one word against it, and left the next morning. However, he came back the following Lord's day and suggested that I be stopped, that the doors be shut, and his people obeyed him and advised me to stop. This preacher saw what effect the truth was having on his people. A good many of the people, seeing how they treated me, said openly that they never intended going to hear these people any more. I am glad that the sentiment of the people was in favor of the truth. The man whom I was [staying] with was so anxious for me to continue preaching that he went to the principal of the Utica Institute (colored)[24] and asked him to let me preach in the school chapel; and he gladly consented. I preached each night to several hundred students, and many others who lived in the community came and were well pleased. Although there were no additions, I consider it a victory for the truth. . . .

After arriving home, I went up to Brother Burton's office and talked to him about my trials and hardships at Utica, and he said to me: "I am going to increase my contribution twelve dollars and a half more." Brother Burton suggested that I go back there next year. . . .

[Trials at the Jackson Street Church of Christ, 1922][25]

. . . I left for home to be with my family a few days and on the first Lord's Day in the new year I preached at the Jackson Street Church. This is where my membership is and a place that is dear to me. Although we have passed through some hard trials at this place, the future looks good to me. The attendance was good both day and night. Brother [Calvin] Dowell a young man just beginning to preach, spoke at night. Brother S. W. Womack did some good work at Jackson Street; and though he is dead, it still lives. Brother A. C. Campbell, who was a colaborer with Brother Womack, was present and the church enjoyed having him. Brother Henry Clay, who is growing old and feeble, is a great blessing to the church and we are proud to have him. On the first Tuesday night in 1922 I was with the Jackson Street Church. This is our regular prayer meeting nights; but as there was to be baptizing; Brother Campbell was asked to preach and he gave a splendid talk on baptism. Brother Alonzo Jones was also present. Sometime ago the church and Brother Jones had a little difference and he came to see if we wouldn't adjust the matter scripturally. This was done and we want all to know that the Jackson Street Church and Brother Jones are in full fellowship again. Brother Jones is opposed to division, strife, and envy among God's people. I am sure he will suffer in many respects, but all that will live godly must suffer. I pray that God will give him grace to overcome. I am now ready and willing to indorse [sic] Brother Jones as a sound gospel preacher. Brethren, let us all work hard to bring about perfect unity among the brethren wherever we go....

[Preaching in California, 1924][26]

On January 24 I began my work with the mission at Oakland, Cal., and spent seven weeks there trying to build up the work in every way possible. When I arrived in Oakland, I found Brother D. C. Allen[27] waiting at the depot for me. After I had become rested from my long trip, Brother Allen and I began our work as best we could. This is a hard place to get people to attend religious services; but we hammered away with the truth, and one man from the Methodists became obedient to the truth and was baptized, and one was restored who had been out of fellowship over twenty years. The white people attended the meeting fine and encouraged me much.

The white church at Santa Rosa, Cal., about fifty miles from Oakland, invited me, through Brother Felix Owen to come up there and speak three times on Lord's Day, and I went, and spoke to a packed house at three services. I shall never forget the Christian kindness shown me by these good people. This was the first meeting ever conducted in California by a loyal colored preacher.[28] The meeting house is a nice, neat place to worship. Brother and Sister Larimore[29] are seeing after the meeting of the notes. If more of our white brethren and sisters would take a greater interest in getting the pure gospel to my race, there would be a great change in the religious conditions among us. Brother D. C. Allen's home was my home while in Oakland, and he and his Christian wife did all in their power to make me happy. Brother Allen is a strong preacher and has a good report. This congregation is small, but there is some fine talent in it. They all helped in making my stay a pleasant one....

[A. M. Burton's Generosity, 1925][30]

... The meeting at Muncie, Ind., grew more interesting at each succeeding service. I began there on March 8 and continued nearly three weeks. Nine were baptized and one was restored, making sixteen members there now. They have agreed to meet from house to house for the present, and I am to go back there as soon as I can. Brother A. M. Burton sent me a check covering my railroad fare and some over, and the church that I established at Birmingham sent me a liberal contribution to assist in supporting me in this destitute field. This is the second mission field that has helped to support me this year. To my mind, Brother A. M. Burton is the greatest missionary in the church today. If it were not for him, much of my work would have to go undone. I am now at Lebanon in a fine meeting, with interest increasing at each service.

[Keeble in South Carolina, 1925][31]

I began a meeting at Greenville, S.C., on May 3 and remained nearly three weeks. Brother G. F. Gibbs (white) arranged for this meeting among my race. He is one man that wants all nations to hear the gospel, and he and the congregation, he labors with did all in their power to encourage me while there. Brother Gibbs and several other white brethren led in the song service. The sectarian preachers did all they could to keep the people from coming to the meeting, but the meeting grew in interest and resulted in twelve precious souls obeying the gospel. Also several white people were converted and [they] had Brother Gibbs to baptize them.[32] Brother A. M. Burton's financial support in this meeting was highly appreciated. This makes two destitute fields he has sent me to this year, and at each place a new congregation was started. I have, by the help of God, started three new congregations to work according to the New Testament this year.

[The Keeble Strategy, 1927][33]

During the last year I labored in six States, preached three hundred and sixty sermons, conducted twenty-one meetings, baptized one hundred and sixty-three, and thirty were restored. I am proud to make this report and yet I feel like I ought to have done more. I thank all who had fellowship with me in this work. On the first Lord's Day in this year I began a meeting at the Jackson Street Church, which continued two weeks and resulted in three baptisms, one restoration, and five by membership. All seemed to enjoy the meeting. We had large crowds every night. Brother A. M. Burton's arrangement to broadcast[34] the services at Jackson Street Church on January 9 put new life into the whole congregation. We thank God for such friends. On January, 12 I was invited to speak at the Russell Street church of Christ. While they listened I told of some of my hardships in destitute places among my people. After dismission [sic] they encouraged me to press on. Brother S. H. Hall's[35] remarks after I had finished created in me a greater desire to suffer and work for Christ.

[The Love of A. M. Burton, 1927][36]

... On March 6 I closed a very successful meeting at Birmingham, Ala., with sixteen additions. Next day I went to Bleecher, Ala., where I spent four days, preaching in a Baptist meetinghouse. The people were hungry for the gospel. Five came out for Christ and were baptized. I am to go back as soon as possible. On March 11 I stopped over at Chattanooga and preached to a splendid crowd that had gathered at the mission where Alonzo Jones works. The white church is supporting Brother Jones in this work, and he is as busy as he can be. All seem to love him. On March 13, through the kindness and love of A. M. Burton, we were privileged to broadcast again over station WLAC, at Nashville. So many of my own race who would never come to our services at the meetinghouse have complimented the program. On March 14 I began a seven day meeting at Louisville, Ky. The house was crowded from the beginning. There were three baptisms; all from the sects, and seven came from the "digressives."[37] G. P. Bowser began this work, and it is a credit to him. He is a hard, earnest worker....

[Keeble Plants Church in Jackson, Tennessee][38]

In August I was called to Jackson, Tenn., by the Highland church of Christ (white) to conduct a three week meeting for my people. This meeting was held under a large tent, which was packed at every service. Interest continued to grow as the meeting progressed. The tent was pitched in two blocks of Lane College; a colored school that sends out Methodist preachers. Bishop Lane[39] attended several nights. One of the professors attacked me one night and attempted to show to the crowd that I was teaching false doctrine. When he was through, I followed him with nothing but the truth; and when I extended the invitation seven precious souls came forward and made the good confession. I am more convinced since holding this meeting that sectarianism must be fought with a humble and meek spirit. The Central church of Christ (white) also cooperated with the Highland Church. There was not a colored Christian in the town when the meeting began but thank God, we left fifty-eight to keep house for the Lord. We had baptizing one Sunday afternoon, and the white brethren estimated the number present at around four thousand. Many white people attended the meeting and some said they had been converted and would go to the white churches of Christ. When the meeting closed the white brethren had provided a splendid place for those who had obeyed the gospel to begin at once to worship God like the Bible teaches. The white brethren are meeting with them every Lord's Day and training them in the way of the Lord....

If It Were Not for the White Christians

["I Baptized Twelve Preachers," 1929][40]

On my second Lord's Day in November I began a meeting at Birmingham, Ala., and continued it four weeks. Much interest was manifested throughout the meeting. There were ten baptisms and the church was greatly encouraged and edified. While in Birmingham, Dr. White, a white brother who has always assisted me in my work, had me to come to his office so he could treat my teeth, and he also gave me a fine job of bridge work, for which I am very thankful.

On December 11 I began a meeting at Huntsville, Ala., which continued one week. There were two baptisms. This church is in a fine spiritual condition and it is a real pleasure to labor with them. On December 18 I began a meeting at Decatur, Ala., and continued it one week, with interest fine throughout the meeting. This was my last meeting for 1928.

I am glad to say that many that I have baptized remembered me during the holidays. I am thankful for such friends. In the way of visible results, 1928 was my greatest year, with three hundred and fifty-eight baptisms. I hope to be able to do more this year.

I preached my last sermon for 1928 at Hopkinsville, Ky., and will begin my year's work for 1929 at the Jackson Street Church, in Nashville, Tenn., the first Lord's Day in January. I am greatly encouraged over the interest the white churches of Christ are taking in getting the pure gospel to my race. The gospel is the only thing that will serve to decrease crime and all kinds of disorderly conduct. The harvest is ripe, but the laborers are few. Let us pray the Lord to send forth laborers into his field. There never was a better opportunity for the church among my people than now.

Last year I baptized twelve preachers. Of course, they will have to start all over, because they came from the sects and had never preached a gospel sermon in their lives. If we can capture the preachers, much false teaching will cease. In my work many white people come to hear me and are converted. They are too prejudiced against the church of Christ to go and hear the white brethren, but they come to hear me to get something to laugh at, and they get caught in the gospel net.

[A Church Planted in Lakeland, Florida][41]

On the first Lord's Day in February I began a meeting at Lakeland, Fla. I was called to Lakeland by the white church to labor among my people. When I arrived there, three very kind white brethren met me at the depot and carried me to a very nice place, where I was to make my home. I found the man of the house a Methodist and his wife a Baptist, and their son was not a member of any church; but when the meeting ended they were all in Christ. I baptized them all and left them rejoicing. In arranging for this meeting, I promised to spend two weeks, but interest grew so rapidly I was forced to remain four weeks. Every night some one confessed

Christ and would demand baptism "the same hour." Several of the white brethren used their cars to carry these people to the water to be baptized and then to carry them home with their wet clothes on. To work with such people is uplifting and inspiring. One white brother led the song service every night until we baptized a good song leader, and then he turned the song service over to him. White brethren came from St. Petersburg, Plant City, Tampa, Mango, and other points. The colored brethren and sisters chartered a large bus every Sunday and came to help in the work, and their presence greatly stimulated the meeting. Brother Douthitt, who preaches for the white church, encouraged me much. He made a fine talk to us one night, which all enjoyed. He has offered his services in building up this work while it is young. Almost all of these people came out of sectarian churches, and the sectarian preachers were glad when the meeting closed. One white sister asked permission to teach a class of colored sisters every Monday afternoon, and all of the colored sisters were glad to have her teach them the way of the Lord more perfectly. There were sixty-five baptisms in the meeting.

[A Church Planted in Arkansas, 1929][42]

... On September 1, I closed a four week meeting at Fort Smith, Ark., which resulted in eighty-one members of my race being baptized for the remission of sins. Three white persons also made the good confession in the meeting, and Dr. Billingsley took their confessions. The white brethren had a fine quartet that sang each night before and after prayer. Brother Rodgers (white) led the song service every night. Our attendance increased each night. One Lord's Day while there, I baptized thirty-nine before coming out of the water. Brother Laird and Dr. Billingsley did everything they could to encourage me in my work while there. I have never worked with any greater men in my life. They asked me to return and I gladly consented. It is a pleasure to labor with such Christians as the Park Hill Church. Brother A. M. Burton agreed to pay my railroad fare to Fort Smith; but when his check came, it was twice the amount of my fare. Brother Burton has stood by me in my struggle to proclaim God's word. The white churches that are calling me to labor among my people are doing a great work, because my people are burdened under the yoke of sectarianism. I thank God for the great missionary spirit that is now among the white churches of the Southland to have the pure gospel preached to my race. ...

Chapter 3

Disseminating the Bread of Life: Keeble in the 1930s

The year 1931 was pivotal for African Americans in the Stone-Campbell movement. First, Preston Taylor, a black preacher and affluent businessman in Nashville, Tennessee, died. Samuel Robert Cassius, an itinerant preacher and racial reformer in Churches of Christ, also expired in August of the same year. Indeed, the very night of Cassius's death, Keeble began a protracted meeting in Valdosta, Georgia, which ended with 166 baptisms. During this campaign Benton Cordell Goodpasture (1894–1977), editor of the *Gospel Advocate* from 1939 to 1977, arranged for Keeble's sermons to be transcribed. This consequent book of sermons catapulted Keeble to national prominence in the Stone-Campbell movement. Throughout the 1930s, Keeble enjoyed one of his most successful decades as a traveling evangelist, prompting one white supporter to affirm, "Brother Keeble is a Godsend to his people."[1]

In this determinedly Jim Crow era, Keeble paradoxically led countless black and white southerners into the fellowship of Churches of Christ during the Great Depression. The writings that comprise this chapter portray Keeble as a distributor of both physical and spiritual bread. After immersing twenty people at Dickson, Tennessee, Keeble announced, "This was a place where my people were starving for the Bread of Life."[2] Six years later Keeble and other members of Jackson Street Church of Christ in Nashville distributed food to flood victims in Middle Tennessee.

The impetus behind his preaching efforts, however, still contained anti–missionary society elements. "In 1931," Keeble reported, "I baptized one thousand and seventy-one people of my race and converted a number of white men and women, who went to the white churches and were baptized." "This shows," he continued, "that we do not need the missionary society to do the work of the church."[3] This statement not only demonstrates that Keeble enjoyed one of his greatest years as an evangelist but also attests that after having moved away from Preston Taylor and the Disciples of Christ at the turn of the twentieth century, he remained opposed to doing evangelism through missionary societies.

[Cutting Down False Doctrine in Florida, 1930][4]

On Sunday, May 18, I closed a three week meeting at Lakeland, Fla., with twenty-five baptisms and the church greatly inspired. The white church there assisted me greatly in every way. A "sanctified" woman preacher attacked the doctrine that I taught two nights, and I gave her the best I had in my shop, and I also showed her that she was at the wrong job and that she was dodging the job God gave her. With the truth we won the sentiment of the large crowds that came. The doctrine of the church of Christ will cut down every false doctrine. Brother W. C. Phillips was present at many of the services and encouraged us much. I am now in a fine meeting at Jacksonville, and the outlook is good. I have been here two days. I was called here by the white church. Brother H. N. Rutherford is a fine coworker. I have never met a more Christ like man in my life. It is a blessing to be in his presence. Brother Luke Miller[5] and wife are here to assist in the song service and they are doing their part well. Brother Miller is the young evangelist working in this State. The white brethren are much impressed with his humble, meek, Christ like disposition. Since coming here I have met my old friend, P. G. Millen. Brother Millen is the white brother who kept alive the work that I established at Tampa; and if a congregation is established here, he is waiting to go to work with them and teach them "the way of God more perfectly" [Acts 18:26]. Brethren pray for me.

[A Church Planted in Valdosta, Georgia][6]

In June I spent four weeks at Valdosta, Ga., in a tent meeting. The white church here arranged for this meeting, and they gave me their support in every way possible.

Brother A. B. Lipscomb preaches for this church, but he was away during the time that I was there. I regretted his being away very much.

Brother G. E. Claus, who lives at Valdosta, worked hard to make the meeting a success. In fact, this church has some of the best brethren in it of any church that has called me to labor with my people. This church bought a large number of New Testaments and gave them to those who had no Bible. The Central church of Christ, of Nashville, Tenn., sent a large number of leaflets to be given out; and my friend, Brother B. C. Goodpasture, of Atlanta, Ga., also sent some very fine leaflets. This meeting increased in interest until the close, and I consider it the best meeting of all my work. Brother Luke Miller and his good wife were of so much help in the meeting in every way. He led the song service.

One Lord's Day I baptized fifty-nine precious souls into Christ. During the time of baptizing a hard rainstorm came up, but we went right on; and when the rain ceased everybody was soaking wet, and it was impossible to tell who had been baptized. White and colored stood in the rain throughout the time of baptizing. On the following Sunday Brother Miller and I baptized sixty-three before we came out of the water. One night twenty-nine came forward at the invitation, all grown. There was great rejoicing. Eleven came from the "digressives." Total number of additions, one hundred and sixty-three.

The white church was greatly inspired over this work. I left the white brethren busy arranging for a place for them to worship, and they also want a colored man to come there and locate so he can keep the work going. I promised to return for another meeting.

To God be all the praise, honor, and glory. Pray for me.

[Two Churches Planted in Mississippi, 1931][7]

On November 1 I began a three week meeting at Jackson, Miss. The white church there called me to preach to my people. Interest grew in each service. We began the meeting in the so called "Sanctified" people's meetinghouse. (The white brethren rented it.) Three nights were all the "Sanctified" people could stand of the doctrine taught by the apostles. Four of their preachers attempted to show that I was teaching false doctrine; but in the spirit of love I turned the light on their false teaching, and they ordered us out of their meetinghouse. We left pleasantly, and the white brethren rented a Methodist meetinghouse, and we finished in it. This meeting resulted in twenty-seven baptisms five of them preachers, two Baptists, two Sanctified, and one Methodist. I also baptized the man and his wife with whom I lodged. He was a Baptist preacher. The truth will cut its way when handled in love and with courage.

Brother C. B. Thomas, the white minister, was very nice to me. He assisted in every way possible, and it was an inspiration to be in his company. He also led the song service most of the time. The white church there is wide awake and working hard to spread the kingdom of God. The Central church of Christ, in Nashville, Tenn., sent me a large bundle of literature to be distributed, and it was anxiously received by the people. It did much good, causing the people to read their Bibles. Brother A. M. Burton is highly praised by them all in Jackson, because he assisted them in getting established. Brother Thomas will meet with those I baptized and teach them "the way of the Lord more perfectly."

On December 14, I closed a meeting at Ripley, Miss., in which ten precious souls were baptized. Interest grew as the meeting continued. The white church there called me to teach the pure gospel to my race. Brother Walker, the white minister, encouraged me very much; and Brother J. Roy Vaughan passed through while I was there. He always does all he can to help me in my work. He is deeply interested in getting people to hear the truth. The white church there is anxious to have the colored people taught the pure gospel. The white brethren there treated me with the spirit of Christ.

The past year has been a very successful one in my work. I have preached three hundred and ninety-six sermons, preaching forty-six weeks, baptizing nineteen preachers, conducting fifteen meetings, and baptizing, in all, four hundred and twenty, with forty-one restored. From the "digressives" came twenty-nine; new congregations, six. To God be all the praise, honor, and glory! Many thanks to all who have had a part with me in accomplishing what I have for the Master last year. I hope to be able to make a better report, this year. I pray that this missionary spirit that the white churches manifest, in having the pure gospel preached to my race, will continue until many thousands have heard the word of God. Pray for me.

[A Church Planted in Jonesboro, Arkansas, 1931][8]

... June 4th I closed a three week meeting at Jonesboro, Arkansas. The attendance was great, the white brethren estimated from one to two thousand present each night, over half at each service were white brethren. The white church supported me in every way they could. I will never forget the kindness shown me by Brother H. D. Jeffcoats and all the white brethren and sisters who proved that they wanted the gospel preached to all nations. I have been called back for 1932. This meeting resulted in twenty-two colored additions, and fourteen white, the whites were baptized by Brother H. D. Jeffcoats. If Christ be lifted up he will draw all men unto Him. I also had the privilege of visiting Jonesboro Orphan Home and made a short talk to the little children. It will touch the heart of anyone to see how well these little folks, who have no parents, are cared for. The Lord will certainly bless Brother and Sister Jeffcoats for looking after these dear children. Brother Jeffcoats also has some wonderful helpers in the Home assisting him, and we all know that if it was not for the hearty cooperation that churches are rendering the work would go down. God bless such work.

[A Church Planted in Bradenton, Florida, 1931][9]

... I have just closed a fine meeting at Bradenton, Florida in which there were 287 baptisms.

The white churches in this section sponsored this meeting. Brother D. B. Whittle did all the arranging. They all treated me Christlike. Before coming here I closed at Jackson, Miss., with 69 baptisms. Brother C. B. Thomas managed this meeting, and the white church he preaches for, stood behind him; these are great workers for Jesus.

The colored people are so thankful to the white churches for bringing them the pure Gospel. I am mailing you one of the baptism scenes at Bradenton, Florida in which 115 were baptized the same day. Brother John Vaughner, a young man I baptized, did the baptizing. To God be all the praise.

[A Church Planted in Tyler, Texas, 1935][10]

M. Keeble, Nashville, Tenn. On September 8th we closed a meeting at Tyler, Tx., with 55 baptisms and 12 from the Christian Church. The white church at Tyler called us there to labor among the colored people. Brother Harvey Scott[11] labors here, and I have never in all my life labored with a more Godly man. It was a blessing to be in his company. Many preachers of the church of Christ, white and colored came, and their presence encouraged us much. All seemed highly pleased with Brother Smith[12] leading the singing. To God be all the glory. Pray for us.

[Meetings in Missouri and Kentucky, 1936][13]

On July 26, William Lee and I closed a meeting at Springfield, Mo. We were called there by the three white churches to establish a colored church. Only two colored people were baptized. (Five with people were baptized by the white brethren during the meeting.) Brother Williamson and Brother Harriman, white preachers, did all in their power to encourage us while there. The crowds grew every night until they reached about four thousand the last night. The white churches were so well pleased that they invited us back for 1937. We are now (August 4) in a meeting at Bowling Green, Ky. The Twelfth Street Church (white) called us here, and is doing all it can to make the meeting a success. A loud speaker system was installed yesterday, so the preaching is being heard for some distance. Two old people, man and wife, over ninety years old, were baptized Sunday, and there was much rejoicing. Pray for us.

[Helping Flood Victims in Nashville, Tennessee, 1937][14]

... Upon my arrival home I found that Central Church of Nashville had requested the Jackson Street Church to feed the colored flood sufferers. The Jackson Street members gladly consented to prepare the food and give out the clothes. It was a great work. While these sisters prepared the food I taught them the Bible, and found that they were also hungry for the Bread of Life. Central Church provided the food, and the colored sisters prepared and served it. Although it was a hard task, it was a pleasure to do it, and we thank Central Church for giving us the opportunity of having a part in such a great work.

On January 9 we left home for St. Petersburg, Fla. On the way we stopped at Chattanooga, Tenn. We were greeted by a large crowd, including a number of the white brethren. Brother Jones is doing a good work at Chattanooga.

At Atlanta we also had a fine stopover. The work there is doing fine under the preaching of A. C. Holt.[15] The white churches are just as interested in the colored work now as they were at the beginning.

We also had a stopover with the church at Valdosta, Ga. The brethren are working in peace and love, with D. English[16] laboring with them. . . .

[In Tennessee and Florida, 1938][17]

On the first Sunday in the year, Brother [William] Lee and I began a two weeks' meeting at Jackson Street, my home congregation, in Nashville. Eighteen were baptized, three restored. The interest grew in each service. Every seat was occupied at almost every meeting. Many heard the gospel for the first time. Brother Lee gave a song drill each night before the preaching hour. All were inspired by the wonderful training which he gave in "Christian Hymns," the new songbook. I wish this book was in every congregation.

Since being in Florida we have visited St. Petersburg, Bradenton, Haines City, Lakeland, and we are now in a meeting at Tampa. Interest is high. Two baptized to date. We will close February 6 and begin at West Palm Beach, February 7. The white church here is assisting in supporting the meeting at West Palm Beach. As soon as we are through there the white church at Fort Myers is arranging to support a meeting for the colored people. For over thirty years the white churches have been calling me to establish churches among my people, and God has wonderfully blessed our efforts. He will bless these white churches for their unselfish and unceasing efforts to deliver my race from the bondage of sin and false doctrine.

I thank God for a wonderful coworker like Brother Lee. While at Nashville we had the privilege of attending the lecture course at David Lipscomb College. It was a great privilege to hear the speeches delivered there. The president and faculty spoke on two occasions. We were greatly encouraged.

[Keeble in Alabama, 1938][18]

On May 12 we began a tent meeting at Montgomery, Ala. It was estimated that more than a thousand people were present each night, half of the number being white. M. B. Myers (white) furnished his loud speaking system. By this means the gospel went into the homes in the vicinity where it was hated. There were thirty-five baptisms and one restoration. The Highland Church called Brother Lee and me to labor in teaching our race. Brethren Rex Turner and McBroom encouraged us much. William Whitaker[19] preaches for the colored church and is doing a great work. We are now (June 4) in a fine meeting at Decatur, Ala., and large crowds are attending. Brother Allen, who preaches for the white church that is supporting this meeting, is encouraging us in every way. The white brethren have made arrangements for us to be on the air six days while here, from 5:30 to 6 P.M.

[Keeble in Oklahoma, 1938][20]

On July 24 we began a meeting at Mangum, Okla., and continued for two weeks. Six were baptized. William Lee conducted the singing, and all were pleased with his work. Many white people came for miles to attend. While there we met Don Hockaday, who is doing a great work in Montana. The white church at Mangum is doing all it can for the colored work. They have built them a nice place of worship and are helping support the colored preacher. On August 10 we started at Tupelo, Miss., under a large tent, and continued two weeks. J. W. Dunn assisted us greatly, and all the white brethren attended from Tupelo and near by places. The white brethren are planning to build a place for the colored brethren to worship. There were three baptisms. While there we had the privilege of hearing Roy Vaughan[21] debate with a Primitive Baptist, Mr. Holder. It was one of the greatest treats of my life. Brother Vaughan knows how to take care of sectarian preachers. I am more convinced than ever that debates like this one are a blessing to the church....

[Keeble at Home, 1939][22]

Every year I begin my work at home with a meeting at Jackson Street Church, in Nashville. The meeting usually lasts two weeks, but this time interest was so high that Brother Lee and I continued for thirty days. Interest increased throughout the meeting. And while the meeting was in progress, we worked every day on an addition to the building. This makes the building much larger and more modern and the church seems greatly inspired. During this meeting there were eight baptisms and three restorations. The white brethren came in large numbers to every service and encouraged and inspired us in the work....

[Keeble in Gadsden, Alabama, 1939][23]

On July 9 William Lee and I began a tent meeting at Gadsden, Ala. Interest increased from the beginning until the crowds were estimated to be over two thousand. There were sixteen baptisms. One had been a deacon in the Baptist Church for many years, and one was more than eighty years old. On the last night of the meeting a white man and his wife confessed Christ and were baptized by Brother Smith (white) the same hour of the night. The man was reared a Catholic, and his wife was reared a Methodist, but they are one in Christ now. The white church at

Gadsden supported the meeting, and we are invited back in 1940. It seems that all of the writers of the Gospel Advocate are getting better and better, and I am feasting as I read and reread their wonderful articles. . . .

[Keeble in Denison, Texas][24]

On September 10, [1939,] Bro. William Lee and I began an outdoors meeting in Denison, Texas, and continued for fifteen days. The white people attended in large numbers, but the colored people were afraid because their pastors had told them not to attend and if they did they would turn them out. So, we are more convinced that if the blind lead the blind they both will fall in the ditch.[25] One young man obeyed the gospel and went on his way rejoicing. The Armstrong Street Church of Christ (white) sponsored this meeting and we give God the praise. Pray for us.

Chapter 4

I Mean to Wear Out on the Battlefield: Keeble in the 1940s

During one of his preaching campaigns, Marshall Keeble encountered an African American preacher in a denominational church who asked him, "What is the Greek word on that?" Keeble replied, "Listen Brother, I want everybody in this audience that knows Greek to raise his hand." When no one in the audience raised his hand, Keeble quipped, "Don't waste your time, Nigger."[1] "That slowed him down," Keeble recalled. Later, however, he admitted that a day would come when preachers would have to be better trained. "My friends," he explained, "the day is coming though that the audience is going to know Greek, and that won't work."[2] This experience intensified Keeble's awareness of the need for better equipped ministers, and he wholeheartedly threw his support behind educational movements designed to train young African Americans.

In 1940 A. C. Holt, an African American preacher and educator in Nashville, Tennessee, helped launch the Nashville Christian Institute (NCI) as a night school. Within two years Keeble had become president and expanded the school to include black youth from kindergarten through high school. Key components of the school's curriculum involved daily Bible teaching and a training program for aspiring ministers. From 1945 to 1955 NCI graduated 235 students, 97 of whom became preachers. By 1943 the NCI board had changed from all black members to predominantly white ones.[3] The writings that make up this chapter reveal a Keeble not only preoccupied with leading lost souls to Christ but also concerned about educating the minds of young people, especially those aspiring to be preachers. Keeble's battlefield encompassed both the mission field and the classroom.

[A Tour of the Deep South, 1940][4]

I began my work for the year at my home (Jackson Street Church, colored) in a three weeks' meeting. Interest increased throughout. Many of the white brethren attended every service, and many sectarians attended. For all of this we thank God.

On February 7 I started south for Florida. My first stop was at Chattanooga, where I was met by a packed house. Half of them were white, and there were some sectarians present. Alonzo Jones[5] preaches for the colored church there and is doing a great work. He is loved by white and colored for his work's sake.

Next I stopped at Atlanta, Ga., where I found a large number anxiously waiting to hear the gospel. A. C. Holt[6] preaches for the church and is highly thought of by both white and colored.

At Valdosta, Ga., I found the church doing a great work, under the leadership of that great Bible teacher, D. M. English,[7] who is appreciated by all.

On February 11 I began a tent meeting at Tampa, Fla., continuing for three weeks. Interest increased throughout the meeting. There were two baptisms. John Vaughner[8] preaches for the church, and is loved by all for his great missionary work.

I am now, March 8, in a tent meeting at Bradenton, Fla. The interest is high and the outlook good. F. L. Thompson[9] preaches here. I am glad to say that he is preaching for the largest colored church in the United States. He is doing a great job, and the church is holding up his arms. He is loved by all.

[A Eulogy of F. B. Srygley, 1940][10]

It hurt me and it also shocked me when I read of that great soldier of the cross, F. B. Srygley, passing. But when I think of what a blessing he was to us all for years, my heart rejoices, and I pray the Lord to send us more workers like him who will hold back nothing that is profitable to us. I am glad he lived to see the Gospel Advocate in hands that will keep up the great fight he made for over half a century. It is impossible for those who use the pen to know what a great blessing they are to the brotherhood. The Advocate gets better every day.

[Keeble in Los Angeles, California, 1941][11]

I began a meeting at Los Angeles, Calif., with the congregation at 9512 Compton Avenue. It was an inspiration to labor with these Christian brethren and sisters. Brother A. L. Cassius[12] preaches for this church and he is loved by all because of him living what he preaches. I also preached at the other two congregations and they assisted in every way to make our efforts a success. Brother [Richard Nathaniel] Hogan established these congregations and it is a great work, and he is a great preacher.[13] The cook at George Pepperdine College and his wife were baptized while we were in this meeting. On our way home we visited Phoenix, Ariz., Tucson, Ariz., Las Cruses, N.M., El Paso, Texas, Dallas, Texas and Memphis, Tenn. Brother Cassius brought us through in his car and it was a very pleasant trip for us all. Brother Cassius was going out for his evangelistic work for this year. He has developed into one of our greatest preachers. Let us work while it is day for night will soon come.[14] It was a blessing to meet Brother [George P.] Bowser in Nashville a few days ago, and to hear him preach.

"A Great Opportunity" [1944][15]

For a number of years, brethren, both white and colored, have looked for an opportunity to contribute to the preparation of colored people for better service in the kingdom of God.

The Nashville Christian Institute offers everyone a chance to help build an institution where the colored youth can be taught the word of God, with literary work and trades, as a Christian foundation for citizenship and service in establishing God's kingdom in the hearts of mankind.

We believe that education must be interwoven and connected with the correct knowledge of Christ; otherwise the youth's foundation for resourceful and courageous Christian leadership becomes brittle.

The present enrollment of the institution is one hundred fifty students, fifteen of whom are studying for the ministry. Both we and they are inspired and grateful. A. M. Burton gave the institution $50,000 to make it one of the greatest Christian assets in the world.

The current expenses of the school slightly exceed $1000 a month. We employ seven faithful teachers and board twenty fine young men students. This most useful and serviceable school offers everyone this godly chance to help develop men and women for the great Christian task that will confront them after the war.

Brethren please accept the opportunity to help meet the demands of this great institute and make it one of the best in the world.

"Students Are Baptized" [1944][16]

I want to thank all of the brethren and sisters for their liberal donations to help us prepare our boys and girls of the Nashville Christian Institute for service in the Master's kingdom. Since our school opened on September 24, twenty-three have obeyed the gospel, most of them coming out of sectarian families.

On account of having so much needed improvements made at the school we have been forced to call on our many friends to help us. We have about sixty boarding students and over one hundred seventy-five from the city. The outlook is good. About twenty of our students are preparing for the ministry. On my last three trips out in the interest of the school I have carried three of the boys with me, and they impressed everyone who heard them. If they continue as they are, some day they will make wonderful gospel preachers.

Brethren, please help us make this school a blessing to the world by sending us a liberal donation, and please pray for us. I am so anxious to see this school running in a permanent way before the Lord calls me from this earth.

"Encouragement Letter [to G. P. Bowser]" [1945][17]

Mr. G. P. Bowser; Dear Sir and Bro. in Christ:
I am inspired over the new arrangement of the ECHO. You are now doing your greatest work. I hope you will live to see your plans fully developed; because you have never become discouraged, and your faithful wife[18] has stood by you through these many years of hardships and trials. You have been a blessing to the church ever since I saw you obey the Gospel. You have been a blessing to me; and anytime I can be of any assistance, please call on me. G. E. Steward, H. H. Gray, J. S. Winston, R. N. Hogan, and Levi Kennedy are great workers in the Kingdom of God. With such men standing with you, there is nothing but success. We are now, May 15th, in a great meeting in Atlanta, Ga. Eleven have responded to the Gospel call. I have two of our little boy preachers with me, and all that hear them are greatly impressed. To God be all praise, honor and glory. Pray for us.

BROTHERLY, M. KEEBLE

"Nashville Christian Institute" [1947][19]

In my travels I find that many brethren do not know that we have a school where colored boys and girls can be taught the pure gospel daily at Nashville, Tenn.

This last term many white congregations called us to render programs, so that they could see our work in action. Thousands of dollars were given during these programs, and everywhere we rendered a program we were invited back.

Many of our leading preachers visit the school, white and colored, and state that there is nothing to excel it anywhere. Many of our students are unable to pay their tuition, but there are congregations that give as much as $2,000 a year to help us to develop these fine boys so that God can use them to bless the world. Some of our boys go out every Lord's Day and preach for congregations as far away as Memphis, Birmingham, Louisville, and Cincinnati. Brethren at all of these places write us letters of praise and congratulations.

Brethren, I appeal to you to help us develop these boys for the age that is confronting us. I am now sixty-eight years old, and I am struggling to leave hundreds of strong preachers after I am gone. We closed with three hundred fifty students enrolled and eleven teachers this year. Please help us keep the doors of Nashville Christian Institute open, so that we can fill this land with real gospel preachers, who will hot be ashamed to tell the old story of the cross....

"Nashville Christian Institute Commencement" [1949][20]

Our commencement started in David Lipscomb College chapel May 22. The president of that great school permitted us to use this fine chapel for Sister Lambert Campbell's public speaking class program, and everybody who attended said it was great, because she had them so well trained, and $500 was given. Willard Collins, the vice president, introduced Sister Campbell. This was her ninth program with the Nashville Christian Institute and she says that she enjoys teaching them. Ever since she has been on our faculty she has given her time, because she loves Christian education. She is a blessing to the institution, and we all pray that she lives long.

Our next program was at the Jackson Street Church in its beautiful building. A. Rose[21] of Atlanta, Ga., preached the commencement sermon to the graduating class. There were thirty-one of them, over ten of them gospel preachers. The sermon was an inspiration to not only the graduating class, but the great crowd that packed the building. O. H. Boatright[22] is the principal of the Nashville Christian Institute, and is doing a great job, and he is also the minister of the Jackson Street Church.

Our commencement address was made by A. A. Thomas of Lubbock, Texas, and it was great. Two of the members of our board, S. H. Hall and I. N. Finley, said it was the best that they ever heard. The graduation class was encouraged to continue its education, and prepare to make better workers in the kingdom of our God.

At David Lipscomb College a donation of about $1,500 was given to the school during our lectureship at the Nashville Christian Institute, and they are still working to raise more because this is not enough to put our school where no high school will surpass it. If this appeal touches your heart, just send the donation to B. B. Baxter or Wendell Clipp, at David Lipscomb, to help make the Nashville Christian Institute come up to the standard that the board of education requires.

Our colored boys and girls stand greatly in need of Christian education, and I believe that in my old days the brethren, white and colored, are going to make this school what it should be before the Lord calls me home. I am now seventy years old, been in the church of Christ about fifty-six years, and preaching the pure gospel over fifty-three years, and I am at this writing in a month's meeting in the great city of Atlanta, Ga. I mean to wear out on the battlefield.

Brethren, please help us build this great school so it will never fail. I have thousands of friends, and I am appealing to you to do what you can now while it is day.

For several years S. H. Hall, a member of our board of directors, has worked hard to get the City Bus Company to run a bus line out to our school, and the first of this month (June) the first bus came right by our school, and we are very thankful to Brother Hall and others who helped to bring us this great blessing. We get a bus in the morning hours every ten minutes, in the evening every fifteen minutes until midnight. We thank God. In our board meeting in April I was told to order the bus for the school at once, so we now have a bus ordered, and it will be delivered September 15. This bus will be used to carry our preacher boys and singers wherever we are invited. It will seat fifty-four. Now brethren, please invite us, so you can see what Christian education can do for making the world a better place to live in, and finally give us a home where our Savior is.

I am sure we will be invited by all of our friends. Just send your invitation in at once, and let us book your invitation.

A. M. Burton and I are about the same age, and he is leading us with his great wisdom, and we thank God for all friends who are anxious to help the Negro boy and girl to paths of righteousness.

The Gospel Advocate Company has given us financial help several times when it looked like we could not make it. All I had to do was go down and tell my old friends, B. C. Goodpasture and Leon B. McQuiddy, and we thank God for the Gospel Advocate, Firm Foundation, Christian Chronicle, Apostolic Times, and other papers for giving us space in these great papers.

Many hundreds of dollars have been sent us after articles were read in these papers about the school. . . .

Chapter 5

This Is Bible Religion: Keeble in the 1950s

The articles that comprise this chapter reveal Marshall Keeble's rigid theological and conscientious ethical views. His cardinal tenets included the exclusivism of the Church of Christ, baptism for the remission of sins, the authority of Scripture, the senselessness of emotionalism, and worshiping without musical instruments—all of which remain key doctrines of almost all African American Churches of Christ today. Like his white spiritual forbears, Keeble viewed the Bible as a divine blueprint designed to govern how Christians lived and worshiped. Keeble's literal and scientific approach to Scripture shaped his perspectives of other religious groups. Since he found no mention of Baptists, Methodists, and Pentecostals in the "written record" of the New Testament, Keeble excluded them from the family of God.

When preaching in Valdosta, Georgia, in 1931, Keeble cited as an example the importance of maintaining store receipts and having a recorded deed to verify payment, warning his audience, "Don't you go fooling around without a receipt. You have got to get a receipt." He elaborated: "That is true of a piece of property I might say I owned; and the same thing would be true of the church I am a member of, if it were not mentioned in the written—recorded—word of God. I would suggest that you go to the record and see if you can find your church on record, and if your church is not on record, you did the same thing about the church that I did about that property."[1]

Keeble's rationalistic view of the Bible caused him to look askance at emotional outburst in worship services. "But my friends," he explained, "I am of the opinion and belief that the more of the word of God you get in you, the less emotionalism, and the more of the word of God you get in you, the less excitement. You are compelled to acknowledge that this is the quietest and least emotional service that you have ever attended in your life and this is an intelligent audience, and when you accept the gospel of Jesus Christ, it knocks all the monkey notion out."² Compared to other black religious groups, African American Churches of Christ tend to be more reserved in their emotional expressions in worship.

This chapter of Keeble's writings also witnesses to his conscientiousness about moral rectitude, especially among preachers. He himself carefully lived a morally upright life, knowing that any inappropriate actions would hinder outsiders from obeying the "pure gospel." Indeed, Keeble at times sounded like a Holiness preacher who condemned Christians who played cards, smoked cigarettes, went to theaters, dipped snuff, and drank alcohol. He consistently advised Christian men, especially ministers, to shun wicked women, and he warned preachers against dressing too nicely. Hence, by the 1950s, Keeble had seemingly shifted from a full-time itinerant evangelist to a moral counselor and a concerned bishop of African American Churches of Christ. This apparent shift suggests that black Churches of Christ transitioned from a fledgling to a more stable and substantive status.

Interspersed among Keeble's ethical and theological writings of the 1950s are references to his relations with students of the Nashville Christian Institute, especially as the school's choral groups traveled in fund-raising efforts. As president and fund raiser for NCI, Keeble indoctrinated his spiritual grandsons to carry on the "hardstyle" legacy of excluding those religious groups that did not submit to what he understood to be the tenets of the "pure gospel."³

*"Faith" [1950]*⁴

All churches teach faith, and they all teach that we must have faith; but they differ on the ways to obtain faith. Some say that we must pray for faith. Bible faith comes not through prayer, but by hearing the word of God (Romans 10:17), and we must learn that we cannot please God without faith (Hebrews 11:6). We must learn that faith alone is not acceptable to God, because faith without works is dead. Read James 2:17–20. There are some preachers who teach sinners that they must see some mysterious or excitable thing to prove that they are really converted, but this is contrary to the word of God. We are taught by the word of God that we do not have to see some miraculous thing or have a mysterious feeling to prove that we are saved (Hebrews 11:1). So many people have been lost because this doctrine was taught them. Let us preachers come back to God's word and search it prayerfully.

Jesus taught after he arose from the dead that he had all power in heaven and on earth, and he commissioned his twelve apostles to go into all the world and preach the gospel to every creature. He taught them to preach: "He that believeth and is baptized shall be saved" (Mark 16:16). When Ananias came to Saul and found him down praying, he commanded him to arise and be baptized and wash away his sins (Acts 22:16). This is what must be taught to all men who want to be saved. All men who desire to be saved must lay down their feelings, imaginations, dreams, and take God's word. On the day of Pentecost Peter preached that baptism was for the remission of sins (Acts 2:38). This must be taught as long as men and women live on earth.

Nashville Christian Institute Chorus [1950][5]

The Nashville Christian Institute Chorus[6] visited the following churches in Nashville: Otter Creek, Lindsley Avenue, Reid Avenue, Green Street, Vultee Boulevard, Jackson Park, Central, Rains Avenue, Twelfth Avenue, Donelson, Chapel Avenue. All of these are white churches, and they gave very liberally to help us give our boys and girls a Christian education. Many of our students are fatherless and motherless, and they are among our best students, and many of them are making fine preachers. Many white churches are giving large donations to help us teach the Bible to about three hundred students daily. J. W. Brents (white) teaches the Bible daily in our school. He is a great Bible teacher. Many of our boys go out on week ends and preach for weak congregations near by, and during the summer hold meetings and bring precious souls to our Lord.

Sister A. R. Holton (white) teaches the Bible daily to the girls. Some of our girls can repeat the whole Sermon on the Mount. Sister Holton enjoys teaching them.

If there was ever a time when the Bible needed to be taught, it is now. No one can dispute this. Christian education is the only hope of the world today; and if we neglect to give our children this training while they are young, we will fall short of our duty as Christian parents. Several white churches are sending students to our school annually. This is a fine way to make the world a better place in which to live.

The chorus also visited four colored churches, Jackson Street, Jefferson Street, Green Street, and South Hill. Everyone who heard our chorus enjoyed the programs. O. H. Boatright, our principal, and Mrs. Battle, our music teacher, did a fine job training these young people to sing many of our old time spirituals and other fine hymns. If you want a real treat, invite our chorus to sing for you; they will stimulate and inspire you. We have received many compliments and invitations to return for another visit at the places where we have gone. We were invited to Memphis, Tenn., to sing on Thanksgiving Day in the Booker Washington High School.

The teachers from David Lipscomb College brought the seventh grade students over December 14 to render a Christmas program. The program was wonderful, and was a stimulation to our boys and girls.

We took our chorus to David Lipscomb High School for a program November 9. The students at Lipscomb gave our school $150, and many of them gave our students nice clothing and books for our library. We thank God for a school that is doing the work that David Lipscomb is doing....

"Great Rejoicing among Students of Nashville Christian Institute" [1951][7]

On December 14 a group of students from David Lipscomb High School came and rendered a fine program in our chapel, and at the conclusion of the program they gave the Nashville Christian Institute a fine set of commentaries on the Bible. On December 15 another group of high school students brought food and gifts for Sister Holton's Bible class of girls, consisting of about thirty-five or forty. These girls were very happy because of the Christian spirit these students from David Lipscomb High School brought to the colored students. Sister Holton brought candy to all the small students. At the chapel service on December 15, another group of students from David Lipscomb High School brought shoes, shirts, and other wearing apparel for the ten boys who were not going home for the Christmas holidays, and oh, how happy they were! But it seemed that those who gave these fine gifts were happier than those who received them, and I am made to believe, after seeing this fine spirit of giving, that it is really more blessed to give than to receive.

This is the result of real Christian education. I wish we all understood the need of Christian education. May God bless the teachers who taught these fine students the word of God.

Our principal, O. H. Boatright, and faculty of the Nashville Christian Institute were thrilled and inspired by these students who came and made us all happy. Mr. J. W. Brents, who teaches the Bible daily to our boys, was made very happy over the way our students were remembered.

Prayer [1951][8]

This subject is greatly misunderstood by most all teachers of the word of God. If we read the Bible carefully, we can understand this subject and learn who God will hear. On the day of Pentecost the apostle Peter preached the first gospel sermon after the resurrection of Christ, and the church started off with about three thousand converts, and he never taught any of them to pray for the pardon or to get religion. When they asked the apostle what to do to be saved, or to get their sins remitted, they were told to repent and be baptized in the name of Jesus Christ for the remission of sins. This is what God demands all sinners to do today to be saved from their sins.

God wants all men to pray everywhere, but they must be qualified to pray acceptably to God. They must be able to lift up holy hands without wrath or doubting (1 Tim. 2:8). So we are satisfied that this passage is not to sinners, because many Christians cannot lift up holy hands; certainly an alien sinner cannot.

Why teach sinners to pray for pardon when God has provided everything in writing so we do not have to ask for anything? In water baptism our sins are washed away (Acts 22:16), and we are born again. And in water baptism we are sanctified and cleansed from every sin (Eph. 5:25, 26).

Let us speak where the Bible speaks and rightly divide the word of God (2 Tim. 2:15). In our modern stores today we do not have to ask for anything, because everything is labeled with a name and a price. And God in his word has labeled everything so we will not have to ask or mourn for anything. So let us search the Scriptures.

Are You a Stumbling Block? [1951][9]

I am sure the church of Christ would be more convincing and appreciated more by the world if we who claim to be Christians were more careful about how we live before the world. Jesus taught that we are the salt of the earth and the light of the world, and this proves that there is a great responsibility resting on the church of Christ. It is the only church in which a man can be saved, and I hope we as Christians will be careful not to put our light under a bushel by going into places that will cause people to stumble.

All of us should read Gal. 5:15, 26. All Christians should read this chapter regularly, and it will help us to avoid doing the things that are mentioned in this chapter; "fornication, uncleanness, lasciviousness, idolatry, sorcery, enmities, strife, jealousies, wraths, factions, divisions, parties, envyings drunkenness, revellings, and such like." Paul said they who do such things "shall not inherit the kingdom of God."

Not long ago I held a meeting at a place, and a good many people refused to attend because they saw the members in places that are not popular places for Christians, and also doing things that disgraced the church. We are taught in Heb. 12:1, 2 to lay aside every weight and the sin that so easily besets us, so we can run with patience the Christian race and not cause the church to suffer and be pointed at with a finger of scorn. We must live the life that James 1:27 teaches, and in this way keep ourselves unspotted from the world.

A real Christian would not be caught at a card party, because it is a form of gambling and has caused thousands to stumble. At most parties, beer, whiskey, and wine are served; and if you refuse to play cards and drink these strong drinks at these parties, they will make fun of you; and sometimes the pressure is so heavy we yield, and then we cause someone to stumble, and the church of Christ is hindered in its work of saving souls and lifting Christ up. It is impossible to lift Christ up while drinking beer, whisky, wine, and dancing at these worldly parties. They destroy our souls. Now, if you refuse to partake of these disgraceful things, you will never become popular among men, but you will be saved if you live faithful unto death.

The Church Jesus Bought [1951][10]

There are nearly three hundred or more churches in the world, but only one bought with the blood of Jesus Christ, and I am going into the Bible to identify the one bought by the precious blood of our Lord while he was on the cross. We should be careful to not become a member of a church not in the Bible or not purchased with his blood (Acts 20:28). Be sure to look in God's word for this church and accept no other.

This church was built by Christ (Matt. 16:18) and started in Jerusalem (Acts 2:47), and about three thousand became members of it on the day of Pentecost. The prophets and our Lord told us where this blood bought institution was to begin, and the place they named was Jerusalem (Luke 24:46, 47; Isa. 2:2, 3). Now the next important thing is how to get into the blood bought church. We must do what they did on the day of Pentecost. They were told by the apostle Peter to repent and be baptized in the name of Jesus Christ for remission of sins (Acts 2:38). If they had to do this to enter this blood bought church, everyone would have to do it in order to be saved or to become members of this church. It proves that God has only one church, and his Son paid the price for it, and we know that we who are members of it were bought with a price. If we are members of churches not in the Bible, we have not been paid for by the blood of Christ. In baptism we reach the benefits of the blood of Christ. He shed his blood in his death, and when we are scripturally baptized we reach the death of Christ (John 19:34). We are baptized into his death (Rom. 6:3). We are born again when we are baptized (John 3:5). May the day soon come when the world will be taught according to the Bible that we do not have to pray for pardon. God does not hear and answer a sinner's prayer (John 9:31; 1 Peter 3:12). In baptism we are also put into Christ, and there is no salvation out of Christ (Gal. 3:26, 27). May we all search the Scriptures daily.

The Word of God [1951][11]

The Word was in the beginning when God created the world, and the Word was made flesh and dwelt among men. The Word was crucified, was buried in the grave, and the Word arose from the dead with a message for the world (Mark 16:15, 16). The word of God is the seed of the kingdom of God, and it makes Christians. The seed must be sown in the hearts of men and it will take root and spring up to the glory of God. The word of God, the seed of the kingdom, will not produce anything but Christians (Acts 11:26).

Sometimes people claim or teach that we must go to the altar and pray and roll to bring the Holy Ghost down so they can get the power. But we who read the Bible and rightly divide it know that the power is in the word (Rom. 1:16). When the apostles were told to tarry in Jerusalem, the New Testament had not been written. They needed the Holy Ghost baptism to guide them so they could write the New Testament to guide men into the kingdom of God. Now the Bible teaches that the power is the word of God or the seed of the kingdom of our God (Heb. 4:12).

The word of God will judge us in the last day, so let us obey it. If a man wants to become a Christian or be saved, he must obey God's word. I shall now tell you dear reader, what the word of God tells sinners to do to be saved or sanctified: (1) Hear the gospel (Mark 12:29). (2) Believe the gospel (Heb. 11:6). (3) Repent of your sins (Luke 13:3). (4) Confess Christ (Matt. 10:31). (5) Be baptized (Acts 2:38). When a sinner is baptized, his sins are washed away (Acts 22:16). He is born again (John 3:5). He becomes a new creature (2 Cor. 5:17).

This proves that the power is in the word of God, and it also proves that sinners do not have to pray for pardon or pray for power to come down and sanctify and save them. . . .

Preachers and Elders [1951][12]

What is it that qualifies elders in the sight of many preachers? If the elders agree to every program the preacher suggests and never disagrees with the preacher, he is qualified. If he disagrees with the preacher he is not qualified. What a pity! Some elders agree with every thing the preacher says or plans, so the preacher can praise them. A preacher who takes advantage of elders this way is the one that is not qualified and not the elders the preacher has attacked, and made them cowards by threatening to move them. And when such a preacher gets all of the elders afraid of him, he takes over the whole church and becomes the only one qualified to take the oversight. He then becomes the boss and ruler and he thinks the church cannot dismiss him because he has all of the elders afraid, men who have served as elders for years before he came along. But the preacher crushed them and they resigned or stopped working as elders because they are made to believe that the preacher must lead. It goes on this way for years, sometimes twenty or more years and none can qualify. It seems to me that a preacher who cannot train or prepare elders fit to take the oversight after twenty years of teaching is the one who is not qualified. The fault is in the preacher who is not qualified and who is not able to see himself as he is. This preacher needs to look in God's mirror and see himself as he really is. There are too many like "Diotrephes, who loveth to have the preeminence" in the church today (3 John 9).

Sometimes we read a report from a congregation that says the church is doing its greatest work "under the leadership of our preacher." Whenever you read a report like that you readily know that the preacher is the best overseer and not the elders. I believe most of our preachers are honest, but with love in my heart I hope these articles will cause preachers to stop this unscriptural practice and prepare men to be elders. I am sure by proper teaching and patience elders can be developed and then the preacher can do his duty preaching the pure gospel.

An Opportunity to Do Good [1951][13]

I am sure the brotherhood is proud of the Nashville Christian Institute and the great work being done by this institution. Our young preachers are going out on Sundays to near by places and many have obeyed the gospel. Our boys are also doing some house to house work. In these meetings from house to house several have been baptized and people who are members of sectarian churches are inviting them into their homes for Bible study. For this we thank God. These boys are kind and very nice in these homes and they are always invited back to teach the word. They are causing many people to read the word of God daily. This is a great work, brethren, and if you want an opportunity to do good, please send us liberal donation to help us meet our heavy expenses. Many of our students are not able to pay their tuition. Some are fatherless and some motherless.

Among the white Bible teachers in the Nashville Christian Institute are J. W. Brents and Mrs. A. R. Holton. Mrs. Lambert Campbell teaches public speaking.

Weights and Sin [1951][14]

This subject is an important subject because so many of us don't know the harm weights are. When we are loaded down with weights we are likely to sink into sin and be eternally lost. So let us watch these weights such as smoking, card playing, theatergoing, dipping snuff, petting, drinking wine and strong drinks. Many other things I could mention.

In my first meeting at Birmingham the white church paid my board at a so called sanctified lady's house and she attended the meeting every night.[15] After I convinced her that the doctrine was right, she began to look for signs of smoking and ashes. If she had found ashes or the smell of smoke in my room she would have decided that I wasn't a Christian, but as she could not find signs of smoking she obeyed the gospel. Although this has been about thirty years ago she is a faithful woman in Christ today. Now had I had this weight hanging on me it might have caused her to never obey the gospel.

Here is another weight that might not be a sin, but is causing many to sin. Card playing is found in many Christian homes. I held a meeting about twenty or more years ago where there were ten young married people who played cards every night from house to house. They attended the meeting I was holding at Huntsville, Ala. They wanted me to go home with them one night and I consented. After I got there I found that they wanted to know if they obeyed the gospel could they continue to play cards. I told them to obey the gospel and they wouldn't desire to play cards any more and all of them were baptized. Had I played cards with them they may have refused the gospel. It is best to never let weights cause people to be lost. We are all so careless about causing people to stumble. The apostle Paul teaches us to lay aside every weight and sin (Heb. 12:1). No one who attends theaters ever talk[s] about Christ while in there. Why? Because this is a heavy weight and causes them to sink into sin and they are using their liberty as a stumbling block. Not many preachers teach against card playing and smoking and theatergoing because they are popular weights and considered harmless. May God speed the day when we will cry aloud against weights and sins and let our light shine. Let us shun the appearance of evil.

Purity in the Pulpit [1951][16]

I am worried over the many traps that are being set for our preaching brethren, and I am afraid that some will walk into these traps if caught and not watching. If Satan overthrew Adam, Noah, Lot and Moses, he will overthrow us and cause us to fall and disgrace the church if we are not careful. Satan is going about as a roaring lion seeking whom he may devour (1 Pet. 5:8), and we must buffet our bodies and bring them under subjection lest after we have preached to others we be a castaway (1 Cor. 9:26, 27). WE must remember that Satan caused Peter to fall while he walked with Christ on this earth. Peter repented and was allowed to preach the first sermon on the day of Pentecost (Acts 2).

Here are some of the danger sign of a preacher weakening. When we begin to be successful and people begin to praise us, most of us are not able to stand it. We begin to dress in a way that makes us appeal to some weak sisters and they soon discover that we are trying to entice them. Now my advice to all preachers is to not try to dress so attractively, because in dressing in this way you make the wrong impression on both the brothers and sisters and cause them to lose confidence in you and your sermons will lose their power. When a preacher loses control of himself and begins to let weak sisters entice him, he not only loses power and influence but finally he will have to stop preaching because no none appreciates is sermons. Preachers are allowed in our homes at any time because the brethren have confidence in them. But when a preacher takes advantage of this confidence and betrays this trust and begins to flirt with the women, he begins the most dangerous thing he could allow himself to do, because it will surely destroy him. There are some women who just stay set for weak preachers and they are so perfect they know a weak preacher the first time they lay their eyes on him. I am sorry we have weak preachers among us, and weak sisters who delight in ditching or to overthrowing a weak preacher. Brethren I hope this article will cause our preaching brethren to resist these temptations. Here is my last warning to all weak brothers and sisters.

Please stop visiting certain homes so often and causing people to talk about you. "Keep thyself pure" (1 Tim. 5:22).

I Love the Church [1951][17]

I have been a member of the church of Christ for more than fifty-four years and I have been preaching about fifty-two years. I hope to never do anything to cause the church to suffer in the eyes of the world. Many of our brethren are trying to find fault with everything the church does and this causes hatred and jealousy to come into the church and in this way cause us to bite and devour one another. It seems like some preachers are not happy unless they are tearing the church to pieces and causing the world to say that we are not as good as sectarian churches. So while we fight and attack one another and put Christ to an open shame sectarianism grows. The man who treats the church so ungodly is worse than those who, about two thousand years ago, crucified our Lord. They tore his fleshly body, but when we cause discord and hatred among brethren we destroy the spiritual body of our Lord.

It seems like the more our brethren learn from the word of God the more we try to show how smart we are. Selfishness makes us desire to show everybody what we know and that we are able to tell the churches what they can do and if they don't do as we teach, or as we see things should be done, we cry out that the church is leaving the word of God. If we keep on fighting on the inside of the church we should remember that we are committing suicide spiritually.

I have shed tears over this dreadful and pitiful condition. Brethren let us stop and think and see the damage we are doing to the body of our Lord.

I am closing with the words of our Savior. "Except our righteousness shall exceed the righteousness of the scribes and Pharisees, ye shall in no wise enter into the kingdom of heaven" (Matt. 5:20). So let us stop troubling the church and seek peace and love because love hides a multitude of sins. "Finally, brethren, whatsoever things are honorable, whatsoever things are true, whatsoever things are just, whatsoever things are pure, whatsoever things are lovely, whatsoever things are of good report; if there be any virtue, and if there be any praise, think on these things" (Phil. 4:8).

Pure Religion [1951][18]

Most everybody believes in some kind of religion but few understand it as the Bible teaches. The Bible teaches that religion is a duty. It is something we do and not something we get. When we think of the way we have been taught about religion and how thousands have been misled by false teachers, our hearts are made sad and we pry that the day will soon come when preachers will stop teaching that religion is something a man gets but he can't explain how he got it.

If a watch has been stolen and you are caught with one just like the watch that was stolen, you will by law be forced to tell where you got the watch that you have. And if you can't explain where you got it you are subject to arrest. So it is when one says he or she has religion. If they can't prove by the Scriptures how they got it, or where they got it, they are unlawfully in possession of something that they have no right to have or claim.

When anyone has something that he can't explain or tell where he got it, he usually gets angry when examined or searched. And as a usual thing, when anyone claims that he has religion he at once begins to tell you how he felt when he got it. But the Bible teaches us that we must prove by the Scriptures every step we make in our religious efforts. "Prove all things; hold fast that which is good" (1 Thess. 5:21). This must be done. Now James says, "Pure religion and undefiled before our God and Father is this, to visit the fatherless and widows in their affliction, and to keep oneself unspotted from the world" (James 1:27). From this we understand that religion is a duty, not something we get or feel. No man can even do religion until he understands according to the Bible what religion is and how to get in position to do religion. It takes obedience to God's word to fit one for doing religion. He must hear the gospel (Mark 12:29), believe on the Lord (Heb. 11:6), repent of his sins (Luke 13:3), confess Christ (Matt. 10:32), and be baptized (Acts 22:16). When this is done a man does not have religion but he is prepared and ready to do religion. To visit the fatherless and widows and to keep himself unspotted from the world (James 1:27). This is Bible religion. Let us examine ourselves and see whether we be in the faith. We should live so that we are never afraid to be examined concerning the things we are doing in order to be saved. Our Savior said he would judge us in the last day (John 12:48).

The Works of the Flesh and the Fruit of the Spirit [1951][19]

I wish every member of the church would read the fifth chapter of Galatians, because so many of us are practicing the works of the flesh and causing people to lose respect and confidence in the church. If we would read carefully Gal. 5:19, 21 we would know when we are being led by the flesh or the devil. I am glad the apostle mentions some of the works of the flesh so all children of God who desire to avoid these dangerous things, may know them. So they can shun the appearance of evil.

Many people do not read the word of God, but they read those who claim to be children of God. The apostle Paul teaches in his letter to the Corinthian church that they were living epistles, known and read of all men. Suppose we examine some of the works of the flesh. Adultery is mentioned first and this is causing many children of God to fall. I am sorry to have to say that many preachers are guilty of adultery, and I am offering this suggestion to my preaching brethren. Don't try to look so attractive in the pulpit, because there are a good many weak women in the church and they begin to admire the preacher. Now here is my brotherly advice to all preachers. Dress neatly and clean but never allow yourself to become a fashion plate. If you do you hold yourself up and not our Lord. Another very dangerous thing is trying to use big words. It often causes people to not appreciate our message. And another dangerous thing is preachers allowing an envious spirit to enter their hearts. If your fellow preacher can preach better than you, don't envy him, but learn to praise one another. The Scriptures teach that we should give honor to whom honor is due and praise to whom praise is due. I hope all of us will remove all envy, malice, and jealousy from our hearts, because these are works of the flesh and they cause us to lose our influence and effectiveness as we strive to bring people to Christ.

When we manifest the spirit of envy and jealousy the whole congregation discovers it. It matters not how perfect you are, just remember that nobody appreciates jealousy and envy among preachers. How to treat a visiting preacher is a lesson we should all learn. The churches are close observers of our attitude toward one another. When we show a lovable and kind attitude toward our fellow preacher, men will admire us. I am writing this article because I have discovered that the devil desires to make all of us envious and jealous of each other. So let us fight ourselves and drive out the works of the flesh.

Now the fruit of the Spirit is love, joy, peace, longsuffering, gentleness, goodness, faith, meekness and temperance. Against such there is no law. "They that are Christ's have crucified the flesh with the affections and lusts. If we live in the Spirit, let us also walk in the Spirit. Let us not be desirous of vain glory, provoking one another, envying one another" (Gal. 5:24–26).

Mixing with the World [1951][20]

Many of our brethren say that it is hard to convert people now. They fail to see or know the cause for people not coming to Christ like they use to. For years I never baptized less than one thousand people each year, but not so now. But I think I know the cause of this drop off. The church is mixing with the world and causing the world to stumble and point at us. They say we are no better than they are and all the preaching we can do cannot get them to see the light, because we have our light under a bushel, sitting at card tables, dancing, drinking beer and wine and whiskey and doing many other things I could mention. This is causing people to look at the church as no more than a worldly institution.

The Bible teaches us to come out from among them and touch not, handle not and taste not these things, for all are to perish with the using. We are also taught to shun the appearance of evil. Christ asked his father not to take his disciples out of the world but to keep them from the evil (John 17:15). It is therefore possible to live in the world and not mix with the world. "Love not the world, neither the things that are in the world. If any man love the world, the love of the Father is not in him. For all that is in the world, the lust of the flesh, and the lust of the eyes, and the pride of life is not of the Father, but is of the world" (1 John 2:15, 16). We are also taught to lay aside all worldly weights and run this race with patience. When we begin to keep ourselves from the world and let our light shine, the people will be constrained to come to our Savior. I am sure this article will make all of us think and will cause some to obey the word of God. Think on these things and keep unspotted from the world.

Suffering for Christ [1951][21]

Churches are being disgraced because no one wants to suffer or to endure hardships. All of this comes from too much selfishness among the members. It seems like no one wants to suffer for Christ. The spirit of Christ should be in our hearts and we would not seek revenge when someone speaks evil of us, but rejoice (Matt. 5:12). The Christian is told that vengeance belongs to God. All of this is brought about because everyone wants to boss or rule. I believe if the preachers would manifest the spirit of meekness and kindness they would soon cultivate the spirit of Christ among every member.

The apostle Paul lived so godly and clean until he was able to tell the brethren to follow him as he follow Christ. I believe all of us should study 2 Pet. 1:5–8. Peter tells us to supply to our faith virtue "and in your virtue knowledge; and in your knowledge self control; and in your self control patience; and in your patience godliness; and in your godliness brotherly kindness; and in your brotherly kindness love. For if these things are yours and abound, they make you to be not idle nor unfruitful unto the knowledge of our Lord Jesus Christ." These Christian graces are to be added to our faith if we are saved. The first one to add is virtue. This means courage, moral courage. It takes courage to resist wicked women who have decided to do all in their power to wreck the preacher. And if he doesn't have the courage to resist the temptation he is a wrecked man. He gets where he can't fight sin. Sin has weakened him spiritually and his power to save is gone and his sermons are weak. We have some great teachers among us and these wicked persons want to destroy the preachers. So we better resist the devil so he will flee from us.

Another one of these Christian graces is patience. We must be willing to suffer for the truth and for Christ, and be steadfast and endure and not murmur and complain. This is what it means to be patient. If we want the church of Christ to stand out above every church in the world, we must practice what we preach what we preach. It may cause some of us to suffer for Christ, but we must stand fast in the liberty wherewith Christ hath made us free.

When we decide to preach the gospel we should also decide to suffer for Christ and even if you are not a preacher and decide to be a Christian, you must be willing to suffer for Christ. Paul told Timothy to "suffer hardship, and do the work of and evangelist." "Yea, and all that would live godly in Christ Jesus shall suffer persecution" (2 Tim. 3:12).

At least I would refer you to 1 Pet. 4:1, 2. "Forasmuch then as Christ suffered in the flesh, arm ye yourselves also with the same mind; for he that hath suffered in the flesh hath ceased from sin; that ye no longer should live the rest of your time in the flesh to the lusts of men, but to the will of God."

Which Church Did Jesus Build? [1951][22]

I hate to hear people say that all the churches were built by Christ. When we read the Bible we can find but one that Christ built and I am willing to be a member of the one Christ built and take no chances. Jesus said, "Upon this rock I will build my church" (Matt. 16:18). People have always been mistaken about who Christ is and who owns the church. If Christ says that it is his church why should any man attempt to give the church to John the Baptist? John the Baptist never came to build a church and he always referred to the kingdom as to come something later on. Isn't it a pity to see learned men, highly educated, claim that people have a right to become members of the Baptist Church when this name and such a church cannot be found in the word of God? Christ said, "Search the Scriptures." Some people wear these human names because they believe that there is nothing in a name. But the word of God says, "In none other is there salvation: for neither is there any other name under heaven, that is given among men, wherein we must be saved" (Acts 4:12). "If ye are reproached for the name of Christ, blessed are ye; because the Spirit of glory and the Spirit of God resteth upon you. For let none of you suffer as a murderer, or a thief, or an evil doer, or as a meddler in other men's matters: but if a man suffer as a Christian, let him not be ashamed; but let him glorify God in this name" (1 Pet. 4:14–16).

Some people belong to the Methodist Church, some belong to the dancing Sanctified Church, but when we look for one Scripture where the apostles danced or taught the church to dance we cannot find it. And when we look carefully and prayerfully for the passage of Scripture that teaches us to have our babies sprinkled, can we find it? We must say, no, it cannot be found in the Bible where any of the apostles ever taught that any man should be sprinkled for baptism. But the Bible teaches that we are buried with the Lord in baptism (Rom. 6:3, 5; Col. 2:12). Let us thank God for the plainness and power of the gospel.

An Open Door [1951][23]

Millions of Negroes in America are starving for the bread of life, the pure word of God. The teaching they are getting is false and misleading. The preachers who are teaching the Negroes of America do not know how to rightly divide the word of God. This makes them blind teachers and the Bible teaches if the blind lead the blind both will fall into the ditch.

I see a great opportunity for the churches of Christ in America. The Negroes are anxious to obey God's word, if we can find preachers who will teach them the word of God rightly divided. For over fifty years I have given my life preaching the pure gospel to my race. Today I find them more anxious to hear the pure gospel than ever before, so here is an open door, an opportunity to bring thousand to our Savior. But our problem is, we do not have enough pure, sound gospel preachers. But we have a school at Nashville, Tenn., that teaches the Bible to its students daily, by men and women who are able to prepare the students to preach the pure gospel. These young men can go out and preach the gospel to these millions who are hungering after righteousness.

Now brethren, as you read this article I hope your hearts will be touched and that you will send donations to the Nashville Christian Institute so we can soon have hundreds of gospel preachers on the battlefield, fighting sin and the doctrines of men. I am now (November 16) on a tour in the interest of the school and I am glad to say that donations are being freely made. Many are small but if we get enough of them they go a long way in assisting us to teach the Bible to our boys and girls.

While on this tour with three boys who are preachers, there have been four baptisms. This is worth more than all the money that can be given. The churches where we have stopped have been inspired and greatly edified. Brethren, please help us prepare for this open door and save thousands of my race. For over fifty years the white churches have been having the gospel preached to the Negro. But now we are short of preachers and they must be trained and prepared. If we do not produce the preachers that are so greatly needed, we will lose much ground that we have gained. Again, brethren, let me beg you to hurry up and help us meet this great need and enter this open door that is before us. God will bless us. . . .

The Only Hope of the World [1952][24]

Men and women are called out of the world to be saved in the church that Jesus bought with his blood. There he will keep the faithful until he returns to take them to an everlasting home. But men of the world do not appreciate or like the conditions that they must comply with to be saved from the world. Our Savior prayed that his father should not take his disciples out of the world. Our Savior prayed that his father should not take his disciples out of the world but to keep them from the evil one (John 17:15). He said "they are not of the world even as I am not of the world." It is hard to teach people that they can stay in the world but not of the world. In James 1:27 we are taught to keep ourselves unspotted from the world. So if we hope to be saved we must not mix with the world after obeying the gospel of Christ.

We must remember that the Christian must lay aside every weight and the sin that besets him and run with patience the race set before him (Heb. 12:1). We must also remember that the world needs light. We who have come out of the world must let our light shine before men. But when we partake of the things of the world we are putting our lights under a bushel. When we are found at a card table or dancing on the floor, or drinking strong drinks and going to theaters, our lights are under a bushel and Christ is disgraced and not glorified, by untaught Christians. They crucify Christ afresh.

In his sermon on the mount, Jesus said, "Ye are the salt of the earth." So if the world is saved the church of Christ will have to do it. Therefore we must abstain from the appearance of evil.

The gospel was first preached to the world in Jerusalem on the day of Pentecost (Acts 2), and the people were taught to believe, to repent and to be baptized for the remission of sins. About three thousand came out of the world and were added to the Lord. This is the only way the world can be saved today. So let us preach the word.

The Door [1952][25]

Jesus once said, "I am the door; by me if any man enter in, he shall be saved and shall go in and go out, and shall find pasture" (John 10:9). He also said that the thief and robber "climbeth up some other way." Since Jesus is the door and he says if we climb up any other way we are thieves and robbers and no thief or robber can enter heaven, we had better come in through the door. I would suggest that we find out from God's word who has the "keys of the kingdom." Jesus said to Peter and the apostles, "I will give unto thee the keys of the kingdom of heaven" (Matt. 16:19). Now since the apostles have the keys we will have to hear them in order to get into the kingdom. On the day of Pentecost the apostles used the keys and opened the door of the church, and about three thousand precious souls obeyed the gospel and entered the kingdom. They did not ask God for anything, but they asked the apostles who had the keys, "Brethren, what shall we do?" This proves that we do not have to pray for pardon. The apostles told the people to repent and be baptized for the remission of sins and baptism put them in the kingdom and their sins were blotted out. The Lord added the saved to the church (Acts 2:47). Those who did what the apostles commanded them to do that day were saved and added by the Lord to the church (Acts 2:38; Gal. 3:27; 2 Cor. 5:17).

This is the only way they got into the kingdom then and it is the only way to get in as long as the world stands. In the act of baptism we are also born again (John 3:5), and after being born again we are in position to do religion. James says, "Pure religion and undefiled before our God and Father is this, to visit the fatherless and widows in their affliction, and to keep oneself unspotted from the world" (James 1:27). Religion is not something we get and it cannot be gotten, thank God. It's something we do.

False Doctrine [1952][26]

There is so much false teaching until it is hard to tell what is true. Men have added so much to God's word and unless you read the word of God you will be misled. We are told not to add to God's word (Rev. 22:18, 19). And those who are guilty of adding to or subtracting from God's word must reap what they sow. By studying the Scriptures we can keep false teachers from misleading us.

When we are taught to "get religion" we are taught a false doctrine and this is also adding to God's word. When we are taught sprinkling is baptism, we are taught false doctrine. The word of God teaches that baptism is a burial and if we believe that sprinkling is baptism we are letting people mislead us. I would advise anyone not to believe it, because they that teach such are adding to God's word. The Bible teaches that we are buried with Christ by baptism into death (Rom. 6:4), not sprinkled into Christ. We are also taught by some false teachers that our sins are forgiven before baptism. If this is true why does the word of God teach us that our sins are washed away in baptism? (Acts 22:16). We are also taught that any church will do. But again the Bible teaches that Christ purchased only one church with his blood (Acts 20:28). Such false teaching has confused the world. Jesus taught that he would build his church (Matt. 16:18). He built only one and he gave the apostles the keys to the kingdom, the church. So in order to not be misled by false teachers we must follow the apostles, not the doctrines of men. It is a dangerous thing to be misled. Jesus taught that false teaching is vain (Matt. 15:8, 14). Let me beg all who have been misled by false teachers to search the Scriptures (John 5:39).

Commencement at Nashville Christian Institute [1952][27]

Many considered our eighth commencement our best. Some of the best students we have ever had were in the graduating class this year. Several of them are fine gospel preachers. We are sure they will be an honor to the school wherever they go.

Today we have students from Nashville Christian Institute in seventeen different colleges in America. They are carrying the gospel to their fellow students and teachers in these colleges. Many of them are in the army, converting many of their fellow soldiers to Christ. So the kingdom of God is spreading and Jesus is being lifted up in every walk of life. To God be the praise and the glory.

Vanderbilt Lewis,[28] a former graduate of Nashville Christian Institute and also a graduate of George Pepperdine College in Los Angeles, delivered the commencement address this year. He made a great address and it was an inspiration to all who heard him. Brother Lewis is now preaching for the Compton Avenue Church in Los Angeles.

Keeble's Boy Preachers [1952][29]

The white church at Springfield, Tenn., called me to hold a tent meeting there. The interest was high and one find lady was baptized. Brother [David] Shanks, one of our students at Nashville Christian Institute, is their regular preacher. The white brethren are supporting him. He has baptized several since he has been there. He is also a good student in school. The white church at Spring Hill, Tenn., called Alvin Simmons[30] to hold a meeting there for the colored people. He is also one of our students. He preached some very strong sermons and baptized twenty-one. I was blessed to be with him in the meeting. The great work that these students are ding makes me see more and more the need of trained workers in the kingdom of God. I want to thank the brethren fro the depths of my heart for the donations they are sending to help train these students. These young preachers are a blessing to the church. Many of our best students are not able to pay their tuition and when you give to the Nashville Christian Institute you are helping some worthy students to get Christian education. I am so thankful to Brother McMillan[31] for inviting me to make the first commencement address at Southwestern Christian College. It made my heart rejoice to see those fine students graduate at the only college we have for colored boys and girls. Brother McMillan is doing a great work and may God bless him in this great work.

Nashville Christian Institute Has Many Friends [1952][32]

I feel it my duty to thank all the brother and sisters for their encouragement and endorsement of our great school in Nashville. Our friends are assisting us in making our school a permanent blessing for our boys and girls in the future. We have a good number of young men out this summer, preaching in missionary work and some of our boys are filling pulpits in the place of the regular preachers, while they are engaged in meetings. When the regular preacher returns home these boys will return to Nashville Christian Institute to resume their school work. This gives the young preachers an opportunity to develop in the work they desire to prepare themselves for. Nashville Christian Institute is therefore a blessing to these young men. We are thankful to the many brethren who are sending help regularly so we can pay our teachers and our expenses promptly. We are asking that brethren please help us prepare these fine boys and girls to make better workers in the kingdom of our God. In the future we must prepare preachers to meet the ministers of the denominational churches. If our preachers are not educated and the sectarian preachers are educated, when our brethren are called upon to meet them and to defend the truth, they are handicapped and the cause of Christ is hindered. When brethren help us in the work at Nashville Christian Institute, they are helping us prepare these young men to meet anyone who may oppose them or who may challenge the church of Christ. We are making the greatest growth we have ever made among the colored people. When a preacher can present his message intelligently he has a great effect and power. We thank every brother and sister who has helped us bear this heavy load of trying to honorably operate this great school to the glory of God....

A Scholarship Fund for the Nashville Christian Institute [1952][33]

As I am being forced to turn down worthy students who daily are making application to enter Nashville Christian Institute to prepare themselves to preach the gospel I am therefore making an earnest appeal, as president of the school, to every person who is interested in this good work. This condition worries me greatly and I believe if the brotherhood knew of this opportunity to prepare worthy students they would at one help us start a scholarship fund so we could enroll these young men who are so anxious to preach God's word to over fifteen million Negroes in America and capture them before sectarianism swallows them. Brethren, this is an alarming situation and if we fail to make provision for these worthy students we might have to account for it before God. I appeal to the white and colored brethren all over our great brotherhood to help us keep the doors of Nashville Christian Institute open. If you will help us build up a scholarship fund to be used to train these worthy students who are knocking at the doors of our school, then when I am too old to go the work will continue. I am getting older every day and I would like for the brotherhood to help us provide a fund before I am forced to stop traveling by bus, train and plane, because of being over worked trying to keep the doors of Nashville Christian Institute open. Brethren, where better could you invest your money to do good for years to come? Send a contribution now to the scholarship fund. It may be that long after many of us are gone, this money will be still working for us and the Lord in training young colored preachers to do the work of evangelists. Please carefully and prayerfully consider this scholarship fund....

Hindrances [1952][34]

In this article I mean to mention some things that are hindering the progress of the church. First we need preachers who are careful and clean in their way of living because everybody is watching the preacher. And they have a right to. He should teach and practice clean living. Paul said, "I buffet my body, and bring it into bondage: lest by any means, after that I have preached to others I myself should be rejected" (1 Cor. 9:27). Preachers, I fear, are attempting to look too attractive in the pulpit. Don't you think there is a possibility of drawing the people away from Christ, in all of our efforts to lift our Lord up, by acting and dressing in such a way as to call attention to ourselves? Preachers should hide behind the cross and preach Christ and not themselves. When people go away after hearing you, they should go away talking about Christ and the gospel and not your sermon and you. We need to be careful lest we lead people away from Christ instead of to Christ. We look too much in the mirror at our physical man and not enough in the mirror of God's word at our spiritual man. Brethren, I write this in love for you and the Lord and his church, to call attention to the danger of selfishness, pride, and vanity. Remember the people read while you tell them to read the Bible. So be thoughtful and practice what you preach. Remember Jesus said, "If the blind guide the blind, both shall fall into a pit" (Matt. 15:14). And Paul said, "Take heed to thyself, and to thy teaching. Continue in these things; for in doing this thou shalt save both thyself and them that hear thee" (1 Tim. 4:16).

Another thing I wish to say a word of warning about is, preachers must not let beautiful and weak women lead them into sin. I am sorry to say that it seems like there are some women who take a great liking to preachers, and there are some preachers who seem to be looking for them. Now these women have found out that most of us like nice gifts, and this is the first step they make to test the preacher. In some cases they fail to accomplish their purpose, and the preacher refuses to be attracted by such tactics. Then the preacher is called a fool or accused of not having good sense. But the real fool is the man who falls under the temptation. Paul talked about some who have a "form of godliness, but denying the power thereof: from such turn away. For of this sort are they which creep into houses, and lead captive silly women laden with sins, led away with divers lusts" (2 Tim. 3:5, 6). And in Rev. 22:15 we read, "Without [outside of heaven] are the dogs and the sorcerers, and the fornicators."

Some of our sisters do not like for the preacher to speak much about his wife. I think it is fine to speak of your wife and children occasionally, because a good wife is a protection to her husband. In most churches the preacher is often praised, but hardly a word is ever said about his wife. Why is this? It seems to me she should be praised more than the preacher, because she often suffers more. While her husband is out eating nice dinners and riding in his nice car, she is at home taking care of the children. Such a woman will be blessed, and she ought not be discouraged. She should continue to live a pure, clean life and to be loyal to her husband and help him in his work. Some day these foolish preachers will learn where their protection is.

Visiting Churches in Alabama and Tennessee [1952][35]

On September 30 I carried two of our boy preachers to Tuscumbia, Ala., for the 11 o'clock service. We had a fine hearing. This is where Thomas Rucks[36] preaches and he is doing a great work. A fine donation was given to the school. Percy Ricks[37] has been the life of the cause of Christ in the Tri-cities for over thirty years and all of the white churches are standing behind him and the colored work in this section. To God be the praise, honor and glory. Brother Ricks is also a good preacher. At 3 p.m. we spoke at Russelville, Ala., to a great crowd from the near by towns and communities. Everyone was carried away with my boys. Many shed tears as these boys preached God's word and many encouraging things were said about the work we are doing at Nashville Christian Institute. David Show was in a meeting there, but he was absent on September 30 so the boy and I filled his place. He had a great interest there and he is a great preacher. At 7 p.m. we spoke at Florence, Ala., and also on the radio at 9:15 p.m. Brother Harris[38] has published a good book of sermons. Many of our leading brethren say everyone should have a copy. These sermons cannot be surpassed and will be a blessing to anyone who may read them. His address is 309 South Poplar Street, Florence, Ala. I want every one of our students at Nashville Christian Institute to have a copy. On October 5 I carried two more of our boys to Cookeville, Tenn. At 11 a.m. we preached to a packed house and hundreds were standing out doors, at the Sycamore Street Church (white). Brother Davis[39] is the minister here. At 3 p.m. we were back at Sycamore Street for another service and the crowd was just as great. We were invited to speak at 7 p.m. at the Willow Street Church (white), where Brother Gossett[40] preaches. We were met with another packed house. The donation for the school at both places was great. This will help us to educate the boys who cannot pay their tuition. We have a good many who cannot pay. When our friends give to the school they are assisting us in preparing boys for the greatest work in the world, because preaching the gospel is the only hope for this sin sick world. We were invited to come back. We had a service at the colored church in Cookeville at 10 a.m. This was a great day. To God be the praise, honor and glory. Pray for us."

Meetings in Kentucky and Tennessee [1952][41]

Although it was very late for a tent meeting, interest was very high in the tent meetings at Glasgow, Ky., and Scottsboro, Ala., and some nights we had to have stoves. But the people came to hear the gospel. The white churches at both places are greatly interested in getting the gospel to the colored people and the white people came in great numbers. They were all much impressed with our little boys who preached each night. E. W. Stovall[42] at Glasgow is a great friend to all races and encouraged me much while there. Jack Wilhelm[43] is doing all he can to build up the colored church at Scottsboro. He turned his radio program over to me for two weeks. Many colored people tuned in throughout this section. The church at Scottsboro is sending a little colored boy to our school and the white church at Tyler, Ga., is also sending a fine boy to Nashville Christian Institute. Dan Hooks[44] is doing a great work at Scottsboro and the church loves him. C. L. Caperton[45] of Chattanooga came down to spend several days with us. He is doing great work in the Chattanooga area.

Brethren please remember the school. December 7 is my birthday. If you want to remember me, send a donation to the Nashville Christian Institute. That will please me very much. What you give will be used for the school.

Prepared for Baptism [1952][46]

Many people are immersed when they are not ready for baptism. When one is not prepared for baptism his baptism is of no value to him. When a person is baptized, believing that his sins are already pardoned and that he is already saved, he is not prepared for baptism. God's word teaches, "He that believeth and is baptized shall be saved; but he that believeth not shall be damned" (Mark 16:16). The Bible does not teach that "he that believeth is saved and is baptized because he is saved." But "he that believeth and is baptized shall be saved." When one is scripturally baptized he understands that baptism is for the remission of sins. And when one does not understand this he is not prepared for baptism.

I cannot understand why preachers baptize people and fail to tell them what it is for. Because wherever baptism is mentioned in the Scriptures, the purpose of baptism is also mentioned. I cannot understand why preachers do not teach sinners the purpose and value of baptism. Here is a scripture that few preachers refer to when preaching to sinners. Ananias said to Paul, "And now why tarriest thou? Arise, and be baptized, and wash away thy sins, calling on the name of the Lord" (Acts 22:16). Men and women who desire to be baptized today, should be taught the same thing. They should understand that their sins are also washed away in the blood of Christ, when they are baptized in water. Paul says we were baptized into his death (Rom. 6:3) and in his death he shed his blood, and in baptism we come into contact with the benefits of his blood. He also said we are baptized "into Christ" in this same scripture. There is no salvation out of Christ and we must be baptized into Christ to enjoy salvation. We must know why we are baptized or we are not prepared for baptism. If we ate the Lord's Supper in memory of George Washington and not in memory of Christ, it would be wrong and do us no good. And if we are not baptized for the right purpose our baptism is no good.

Paul said, "Christ also loved the church, and gave himself for it; that he might sanctify and cleanse it with the washing of water by the word" (Eph. 5:25, 26). It is baptism in water, not baptism of the Holy Spirit. Christ commanded the apostles to baptize the people and they could baptize only in water. Only God could baptize people with the Holy Spirit. The Holy Spirit baptism was not given to sanctify or to pardon people. The Holy Spirit came on Pentecost to guide the apostles in preaching the gospel (John 14:26; 16:12, 14; 1 Pet. 1:12). The New Testament was not then written, but now we have the gospel in the New Testament and preachers do not need the Holy Spirit to guide them as the apostles did. In Acts 10 we read that the Holy Spirit came upon the Gentiles to prove to Peter and the church that the Gentiles had the right to be baptized for the remission of their sins, as well as the Jews did (Acts 10:44, 48; 11:15, 18). Cornelius and his household were saved by hearing and obeying the word that Peter preached to them. Acts 11:13, 14). When sinners are taught to hear the gospel (Mark 12:29), believe the gospel (Heb. 11:6), repent of their sins (Luke 13:3), and confess Christ (Matt. 10:32), they are prepared or ready for Bible baptism. Let us search the Scriptures (John 5:29).

Causing Division [1953][47]

It seems like we are living at a time when preachers work hard to build up a congregation for several years, and then wreck it by dividing it and cause hatred and malice to develop among God's people. Our Lord prayed that we all be one that the world might believe that his Father sent him. There is a great wave of division among us today, and the sects that we have fought for years are happy over this alarming condition.

We are taught by the Scriptures to be of the same mind, same judgment, speaking the same thing and let not division be among us (1 Cor. 1:10). And the cause of all this division is over preachers. Preachers are sometimes carried away over seeming success or prosperity. Whenever a preacher attempts to move elders who do not see things as he does, he will surely split the church and create hatred and malice. Whenever a church is divided, it weakens and destroys the spiritual power of the church. Whenever a preacher makes a mistake by dividing a church, he does not want anyone to correct him. This is a shame. The Scriptures teach us to "mark them which cause divisions and offenses" (Rom. 16:17). Brethren, let us remember that the man who splits the church is worse than those who crucified our Lord on the cross. They nailed his fleshly body to the cross and pierced his side, but when a preacher divides the church he is destroying the body of Christ. Christ is "head over all things to the church which is his body" (Eph. 1:22, 23). It is a dangerous thing to destroy the body of Christ. "Know ye not that ye are a temple of God, and that the Spirit of God dwelleth in you? If any man destroyeth the temple of God [the church], him shall God destroy; for the temple of God is holy, and such are ye" (1 Cor. 3:16, 17). Jesus said that "occasions of stumbling should come; but woe unto him, through whom they come! It were well for him if a millstone were hanged about his neck, and he were thrown into the sea, rather than that he should cause one of these little ones to stumble" (Luke 17:1, 2). Brethren, it is a dangerous thing for a man to cause division among brethren and to destroy the church.

When we consider that the church is our Lord's wife, we will not divide it as some of us are now doing. Brethren, let us work hard to keep peace and love in the church. Whenever we find brethren worshiping us instead of the Lord Jesus it is time for us to leave rather than cause division. Brethren please do not stay with a congregation until you cannot get the recommendation of the elders of the church where you last preached. This is your best recommendation wherever you go. When applying for a work, the brethren want to know where you last worked and if you r record was bad there. They will not hire you if they know your record is bad. Let us be careful, brethren. Let us pray for the churches and our brethren who are preaching. "I therefore . . . beseech you to walk worthily of the calling wherewith ye were called, with all lowliness and meekness, with longsuffering, forbearing one another in love; giving diligence to keep the unity of the Spirit in the bond of peace" (Eph. 4:1–3). "But if ye have bitter jealousy and faction in your heart, glory not and lie not against the truth. This wisdom is not a wisdom that cometh down from above, but is earthly, sensual, devilish. For where jealously and faction are, there is confusion and every vile deed. But the wisdom that is from above is first pure, then peaceable, gentle, easy to be entreated, full of mercy and good fruits, without variance, without hypocrisy. And the fruit of righteousness is sown in peace for them that makes peace" (James 3:14–18).

Preparing Young People to Preach the Gospel [1953][48]

The Nashville Christian Institute is struggling hard to prepare young men to bring precious souls to our Lord and to spread the kingdom of God. In America there are thousands of Negroes that have never heard a gospel sermon free of sectarian error. If we can prepare our young men to preach the gospel, the only message that will save men and cause them to live clean, godly lives, we will do a great work. We will also fix their hearts so sectarian teaching will never be accepted by them and cause many who have accepted the doctrines of men to obey the gospel and continue the apostles' doctrine (Acts 2:42). This is what we are doing at Nashville Christian Institute as we teach the Bible daily to all of the students. Many young people who come to our school obey the gospel and we send them back home Christians. Many go back and convert their parents and many young men who have been called to the Army have baptized their fellow soldiers and some of these are now preaching the word. There is no way to estimate the good we are doing and can do as we daily teach these young people the Bible, as they study other subjects also. May God bless you all who are so willingly making this work possible by your gifts. Brethren pray for us.

Letting Our Light Shine [1953][49]

The world is looking for the church that puts religion into practice, or in other words "practice what we teach." Christ said to his disciples, "Ye are the light of the world. A city set on a hill cannot be hid. Neither do men light a lamp, and put It under the bushel, but on the stand; and it shineth unto all that are in the house. Even so let your light shine before men; that they may see your good works, and glorify your Father who is in heaven" (Matt. 5:14, 16). Paul said, "Do all things without murmurings and questionings: that ye may become blameless and harmless, children of God without blemish in the midst of a crooked and perverse generation, among whom ye are seen as lights in the world, holding forth the word of life; that I may have whereof to glory in the day of Christ, that I did not run in vain neither labor in vain" (Phil. 2:14, 16). Now when the disciple of the Lord practices what Jesus taught, he is letting his light shine. When he fails to let his light shine, he becomes a stumbling block and hinders the progress of the church that Christ built. It is a serious thing to hinder the Lord's work.

We cannot hope to convert the world so long as we do not practice Christianity. Christianity is the religion that Jesus planted in the hearts of men. When we drink beer and other intoxicating drinks our light goes out, and we disgrace the church that our Lord bought with his own precious blood. Peter said, "He that would love life, and see good days, let him refrain his tongue from evil, and his lips that they speak no guile: and let him turn away from evil, and do good; let him seek peace, and pursue it. For the eyes of the Lord are upon the righteous, and his ears unto their supplication: but the face of the Lord is upon them that do evil" (1 Pet. 3:10, 12). When men who claim to be Christians fail to live right, they are hypocrites.

In order for us to be the light of the world, we must keep in contact with Christ. Christ is the "generator" that furnishes the light of the world. And we contact the "generator" in baptism. Paul said, "All we who were baptized into Christ Jesus were baptized into his death" (Rom. 6:3). Christ shed his blood in his death, and when we are scripturally baptized, we reach the benefits of his death, and then at once we begin to shine as disciples of the Lord. Then we should begin to practice religion. The Bible tells us that religion is something that we do, it is not something that "we get and cannot lose." James said, "Pure religion and undefiled before our God and Father is this, to visit the fatherless and widows in their affliction, and to keep oneself unspotted from the world" (James 1:27). In order to let our lights shine, we must shun the appearance of evil. We must keep ourselves unspotted from the world. We must shun playing cards, going to the theatre, dancing, and such like, or else our lights will go out. As Christians we must follow in the footsteps of our Lord and stand in the liberty he purchased for us. Paul said, "For freedom did Christ set us free: stand fast therefore, and be not entangled again in a yoke of bondage" (Gal. 5:1).

The Baptism of the Holy Ghost [1953][50]

There is a church known as the Church of God, the members of which claim they are baptized with the Holy Ghost and fire. They are wearing the right name, but their teaching and practice are not according to the Bible. They teach and practice different from the church that was established on the day of Pentecost, the church of God that Jesus built and that began in the city of Jerusalem on the day of Pentecost (Acts 2:1, 47). On that day about three thousand souls were baptized and added to the Lord, and not one of them was baptized with the Holy Ghost. They were too late for the baptism of the Holy Ghost. They heard the noise the Holy Ghost made when it came down on the apostles and on hearing the noise a great multitude gathered and heard the apostle Peter preach the first gospel sermon ever preached by the apostles guided by the Holy Ghost. I want you readers to notice that this sermon was preached after the apostles were baptized with the Holy Ghost. That made the people who heard the sermon too late to be baptized with the Holy Ghost when it came upon the apostles (Acts 2:37, 38). And they not only heard the noise made by the Holy Ghost when he came upon the apostles that day, but they could see him. "There appeared unto them cloven tongues like as of fire, and it sat upon each one of them" (Acts 2:3). And Peter said, "He hath shed forth this, which ye now see and hear" (Acts 2:33). People who claim they are baptized with the Holy Ghost today neither see nor hear anything.

Why do not those who claim to be baptized with the Holy Ghost today preach the same thing the apostles preached, as they were guided by the Holy Ghost on Pentecost? Does the Holy Ghost make people preach a different gospel today? Paul said the man that preached a different gospel, "let him be accursed" (Gal. 1:8). The Holy Ghost baptism was to guide the apostles in preaching the gospel. The New Testament had not been written at that time and a full revelation of the plan of salvation had not been revealed. Before Jesus died he promised the Holy Ghost to guide the apostles into all the truth. In his last speech to the apostles before he was crucified he said, "But the Comforter, which is the Holy Ghost, whom the Father will send in my name, he shall teach you all things, and bring all things to your remembrance, whatsoever I have said unto you" (John 14:26). Christ could not depend upon the frail memory of these men to teach all that he had taught them while he was on the earth. So the Holy Ghost came to bring to their remembrance the things that Jesus had taught them. Again he said in that same speech to his apostles, "Howbeit when he, the Spirit of truth, is come, he will guide you into all truth; for he shall not speak of himself; but whatsoever he shall hear, that shall he speak; and he will show you the things what the Holy Ghost was doing on the day of Pentecost. Just before Jesus ascended he promised the Holy Ghost baptism to the apostles. He said, "For John truly baptized with water; but ye shall be baptized with the Holy Ghost not many days hence" (Acts 1:5). That came on Pentecost, and Jesus called that the baptism of the Holy Ghost. This was promised to the apostles to guide them in preaching the gospel as I have shown. Then years later Peter said that the apostles "have preached the gospel unto you with the Holy Ghost sent down from Heaven" (1 Pet. 1:12).

The apostles never did teach alien sinners to pray for anything. They never danced, rolled at the altar, got religion, or played instrumental music in the worship. The apostles who were baptized with the Holy Ghost taught us to sing, not play, not blow, not pick, and not beat, but to sing (Eph. 5:19; Col. 3:16). People who claim to be baptized with the Holy Ghost claim they get their instruction from David for the use of instrumental music in the worship, but they forget that David was not in the church of God. He never was a Christian. The church had not been built when David lived and Christ had not died for our sins, and people were not called Christians because they were followers of Christ. David lived under a different age, under the law of Moses, not under Christ. We are not following a man who never had the keys of the kingdom and never preached a gospel sermon. The early church continued steadfastly in the apostles' doctrine (Acts 2:42). They did not continue in the doctrine of David.

These people go to Matt. 3:11, 12 to prove that we must be baptized in fire or by fire. But they misunderstand this scripture. John said, "He shall baptize you with the Holy Ghost, and with fire: whose fan is in his hand, and he will thoroughly purge his floor, and gather his wheat into the garner; but he will burn up the chaff with unquenchable fire." The chaff represents the wicked who will be lost, the wheat represents the saved. It is the lost that will receive the baptism of fire. He will clean his threshing floor and burn up the chaff. We are too late for the baptism of the Holy Ghost and too early for the baptism of fire. Thank God for the simplicity of the word.

The Ark and the Church [1953][51]

We read about the flood and the building of the ark in Gen. 6. God found Noah to be a righteous man, and God commanded him to build an ark in which he would be saved from the flood. God gave full instructions to Noah concerning the building of the ark. He was to make it of gopher wood and pitch it within and without. "The length of the ark three hundred cubits, the breadth of it fifty cubits, and the height of it thirty cubits. A light shalt thou make to the ark . . . and the door of the ark shalt thou set in the side thereof" (Gen. 6:15, 16). It was three stories high. When Noah and his wife, his sons and their wives entered the ark, God closed the door. Then the flood came, and all who were not in the ark perished.

Let us remember there was one door, one window, and one kind of wood in the ark. Now the Lord Jesus built his church. As Noah built one ark so Christ built one church. As the window was the source of light in the ark, so the Bible is the source of light in the church. And as there was one door in the ark, so Christ is the door into the church. The only way one can enter the church is through Christ. "I am the way, and the truth, and the life: no one cometh unto the Father, but by me," said Jesus (John 14:6). The ark was built of one kind of wood, so the church is composed of baptized, penitent believers. This is the only kind of material in the church. Those who have not believed, repented of their sins, and been baptized into Christ are not in the church. Remember, God ordered one ark. Just one. And Christ built one church. Just one. The church is the body of Christ (Eph. 1:22), "but now they are many members, but one body" (1 Cor. 12:20). That means there is but one church. We are taught today by some teachers to go to the church of our choice. Where did such teaching come from? I am sure that it did not come from the Bible. We are forced to say it is from the doctrines of men. God never ordered people to pick out the ark to go in to be saved from the flood, because there was only one ark. And God has ordered only one church. Jesus built the church (Matt. 16:18), and purchased it with his blood (Acts 20:28). God picked out the ark and God also picked out the church for man to be saved in. I hope the day will soon come when men will let God pick out the way, and men will stop trying to pick out one to suit them.

God has ordered that men should be baptized and wash away their sins (Acts 22:16). Nearly two thousand years ago God picked out baptism and ordained that men are to have their sins washed away when they are baptized. Men have picked out other ways and means, but only God's way is right. When the Lord arose from the dead he commanded his disciples to go into all the world and preach the gospel to every creature. He said, "He that believeth and is baptized shall be saved; but he that disbelieveth shall be condemned" (Mark 16:15, 16). Concerning those saved in the ark, Peter said, "Which also after a true likeness doth now save you, even baptism, not the putting away of the filth of the flesh, but the interrogation of a good conscience toward God, through the resurrection of Jesus Christ" (1 Pet. 3:21). As eight souls were saved through water, so are we after a true likeness saved by baptism. The waters of the flood separated Noah from the old world, clean of the filth and corruption that was in the world before the flood. So when a man is baptized, he is raised a new creature, raised to walk in a new life. His old sins are washed away in the blood of Christ (Rom. 6:3–11).

Men Love Darkness Rather than Light [1953][52]

The Lord Jesus Christ said, "And this is the judgment, that the light is come into the world, and men loved the darkness rather than the light; for their works were evil" (John 3:19). This statement ought to be a warning to every Christian, because when a Christian goes back into the world, he goes back into darkness. Christ said, "Let your light shine before men; that they may see your good works, and glorify your Father who is in heaven" (Matt. 5:16). When a Christian fails to let his light shine, he also fails to glorify God. Again the Lord said, "Ye are the light of the world. A city set on a hill cannot be hid. Neither do men light a lamp, and put it under the bushel, but on the stand; and it shineth unto all that are in the house."

Today our homes are lighted with electricity, but we must press the button to get the light. So it is in getting light in the church or house of God. We must touch the button, and that button is Christ. Without contact with Christ, there is no light.

We must know how to turn the light on or we will never come out of the world of darkness. If you were visiting in a home where you had never been before, you would not know where to find the button that turned the light on. But laying down on the floor, rolling and mourning would not give you light. Some one would have to tell you where the button is. It is in baptism. We must contact Christ in water baptism. In baptism we are buried with him and raised with him (Rom. 6:3, 4; Col. 2:12). We are baptized into Christ (Gal. 3:27). There is no salvation out of Christ. In Christ we find salvation and become the light of the world.

But when Christians fail to live right and serve the Lord faithfully, they put their light under a bushel and again walk in darkness. They walk in darkness when they play cards, gamble, go to the theaters, drink beer, dance, and such like (Gal. 5:16–21). These things will put out the Christian's light and cause the world to lose confidence in him. These are the things that hurt the influence of the church with the world. If we do not live better lives than men of the world, we are no better than they are. How then can we influence them to become Christians? "Put to death therefore your members which are upon the earth: fornication, uncleanness, passion, evil desire, and covetousness, which is idolatry; for which things' sake cometh the wrath of God upon the sons of disobedience: . . . put them all away: anger, wrath, malice, railing, shameful speaking out of your mouth: like not one to another; seeing that ye have put off the old man with his doings, and have put on the new man, that is being renewed unto knowledge after the image of him that created him" (Col. 3:5, 10). Here is also a scripture from the apostles that I would like for all Christians to read often, so they would not be guilty of putting their light under a bushel and walking in darkness. "Therefore let us also seeing we are compassed about with so great a cloud of witnesses, lay aside every weight, and the sin which doth so easily beset us, and let us run with patience the race that is set before us, looking unto Jesus the author and perfecter of our faith, who for the joy that was set before him endured the cross, despising shame, and hath sat down at the right hand of the throne of God. For consider him that hath endured such gain saying of sinners against himself, that ye wax not weary, fainting in your souls" (Heb. 12:1, 3). That man who refuses to follow this teaching is walking in darkness and there is no light in him. "They who practice such things shall not inherit the kingdom of God" (Gal. 5:21).

Trouble in Michigan [1953][53]

The meeting in Detroit, Mich., closed July 29. For nearly two weeks the crowds were great. Our brother, O. L. Throne [*sic*],[54] made a public confession of his sins. He has been accused of being the cause of division in Detroit, which has affected the whole brotherhood. Brother Throne [*sic*] showed a Christian attitude in making his confession. I have great regard for any man who will confess his sins. I hope all are willing to forgive him and forget the past and press on to greater things in the kingdom. Let us pray for our brother. He is a useful and capable gospel preacher. The Cameron Avenue Church sponsored this meeting. A. C. Holt preaches for this church. It was a pleasure to work with him.

An Expression of Gratitude [1953][55]

For over fifty-five years the Gospel Advocate and the Firm Foundation have introduced to the churches and encouraged our leading Negro preachers. They have caused the white churches to call us to establish thousands of churches in the Southland of America and some parts of the West, East, and North. Had it not been for these great papers, the brotherhood would not know that such great evangelists as S. W. Womack, G. P. Bowser, R. N. Hogan, Luke Miller, John R. Vaughner, F. L. Thompson, A. L. Cassius, Sutton Johnson, and hundreds of other great Negro preachers lived. These men owe a debt of gratitude to these two great papers because they have endorsed us and informed the white brethren of the South about us. They have always accepted and published our reports and for all this free advertisement we are thankful. These papers also encouraged the white churches to call the Negro evangelist to establish churches all over America. Thank God. We thank God for David Lipscomb and G. H. P. Showalter,[56] who were instrumental in encouraging the brethren to call us to preach to my race in the years passed. Although Brother Lipscomb has passed on to his reward, Brother Showalter yet lives. What a blessing these men have been with their pen. The editors that have followed Brother Lipscomb have continued his good work among my people. I thank God for all of the writers of these great papers. We also owe a great debt of gratitude to the great Christian schools and colleges that have also encouraged us.

Press On [1954][57]

As we are about to enter a new year with its blessings and its disappointments, we must press on to the mark of the high calling in Christ Jesus our Lord. We must never forget the Lord is watching over his children day and night, and he listens to their cries. This encourages us to press on. Jesus once told his disciples to consider the lilies of the field, how they toil not, neither do they spend, yet the Father in heaven cares for them. He also told them to consider the little sparrow flying from limb to limb and how the Father takes care of them. Consider how much greater you are than these, and this will encourage you to press on. What a blessing to have someone to carry your troubles and to protect you from your enemies. He has promised to make them our footstool. So let us press on.

God only watches over his children who trust him. One must be born of the water and Spirit to become one of his children. He must believe and be baptized unto the remission of his sins and then God adds him to his church. Then the child of God must press on unto death, because there is a crown of life laid away for all his faithful children. So let us press on, ever looking to Jesus who promised to return and take his children to the place he is gone to prepare. Brethren, let us press on.

Examine Yourselves [1954][58]

The apostle Paul said, "Try your own selves, whether ye are in the faith; prove your own selves" (2 Cor. 13:5). Again he said, "Let each man prove his own work" (Gal. 6:4). I am sure as we enter the new year we should all carefully examine ourselves that we may be able to see ourselves as we really are. Sometimes we think we are living pure, godly lives, but by close examination we will find we need to lay aside some weights that we may run the Christian race with patience. The word of God teaches us to "lay aside every weight, and the sin which doth so easily beset us, and let us run with patience the race that is set before us, looking unto Jesus the author and perfecter of our faith" (Heb. 12:1, 2).

We also need to examine our lamps and see if they are under a bushel. When we are at a card table playing cards or at some party dancing our lights are under a bushel. And sometimes by close examination we will find that we have no oil. It matters not how good we are living we should examine ourselves daily. The Lord said he would come as a thief in the night. So we must always be ready for we know not the day nor the hour when our Savior will return. Let us also examine ourselves on the matter of giving. Do we give as the Lord has prospered? Do we give cheerfully and liberally? The word of God taught us to give on the first day of the week and to give bountifully, because the Lord loves a cheerful giver. When we give cheerfully and bountifully we will have no regrets at the end of the year when we examine ourselves on this subject. God also commands us to live religion. He does not tell us to get religion. He said that "pure religion and undefiled before God and the Father is this. To visit the fatherless and widows in their affliction, and to keep himself unspotted from the world" (James 1:27). The question is, are we doing this?

Sometimes when we are fixing to make a long trip we have our car checked. We tell the attendant at the filling station to check everything, because we are fixing to make a long trip. Well, the Christian should check himself for he also is fixing to make a long trip as he enters a new year. We check our cars because we do not want to take a chance and we should not take a chance about our salvation. We want the attendant to have a gauge when he checks our tires. We don't want him to guess at how much air he puts in our tires. So the Christian wants a gauge when he examines himself. And that gauge is the word of God, not a manual or a creed written by a man. Never let a preacher or anyone check you who does not have the word of God as his gauge.

As we go through the year we should remember to examine ourselves daily and to pray without ceasing that we may please our Lord and glorify him in our bodies (1 Cor. 6:20).

The Doctrine of Men [1954][59]

The doctrines of men are dangerous because they cause people to be divided and confused. It was the purpose of Christ's coming into the world to make us all one in him (Gal. 3:27; John 17:21). He prayed that we all might be one that the world might believe the Father sent him. In order for us to be one, Jesus wants us all to search the Scriptures (John 5:39), so we could all speak the same thing and that there would be no division among us.

When we think seriously about the many ways that man has introduced to the world to make Christians or to be saved, we can readily see that one cannot be saved unless we all obey the teaching of Christ (2 John 9). When we all follow the teaching of Christ we will all do the same thing in order to be saved in Christ. But we must all be taught the same thing in order to get into the church of Christ.

Baptism puts us into Christ. "For we are all sons of God, through faith, in Christ Jesus" (Gal. 3:26). There is no salvation out of Christ. We are sons of God through faith in Christ. "For as many as are baptized into Christ did put on Christ" (Gal. 3:27). "Or are ye ignorant that all we who were baptized into Christ Jesus were baptized into his death?" (Rom. 6:3). Paul said we are saved "through the washing of regeneration and renewing of the Holy Spirit" (Tit. 3:5). It is impossible to get into Christ without being washed in water baptism. In water baptism our sins are washed away (Acts 22:16), and we are born again (John 3:5).

When we are taught the pure gospel we travel the same way and understand God's word alike and there is no division and we are in the one church that Christ built (Matt. 16:18). At the judgment all nations will be judged out of one book and the same word will judge us in the last day.

I hope this article will cause someone to think on these things and be saved. There is too much confusion caused by false teaching, and men are led away from the truth. Let us all study the word of God that we all may be one in Christ. This is my prayer.

Things That Are Dangerous [1954][60]

Sometimes as we travel the highway we hit a dangerous spot before we see it, because we are not watching as we should watch. It sometimes causes serious damages to the car and to the ones in the car. So it is in the church. We hit dangerous spots and one of the most dangerous spots is division among brethren. This is sometimes caused by the preacher fighting false doctrines. Some members of the church do not like for the preacher to fight false doctrine and some do like it. Some do not like for the preacher to call the names of the sects around us, and they go to the elders and ask them to "fire" the preacher if he doesn't stop calling the names of the sectarian churches. And if the elders refuse to let the preacher go, they split off or divide the church and go down the street a little ways and start another congregation. Do they love the sects more than they love their own brethren? This is a disgrace to the cause of Christ and it is causing the sectarians to stand off, the Methodist and Baptist, etc., and laugh while our brethren crucify the Lord afresh by division in the church (Heb. 6:6). When a number of brethren divide the body of Christ, they are worse than those who crucified the Lord on the cross. The Jews crucified his fleshly body and the Roman soldier divided his flesh with the spear, but when brethren divide the church they divide and crucify the spiritual body of Christ (1 Cor. 12:12). This work is of the devil. James said, "If ye have bitter jealousy and faction in your heart, glory not and lie not against the truth. This wisdom is not a wisdom that cometh down from above, but is earthly, sensual, devilish. For where jealousy and faction are, there is confusion and every evil deed. But the wisdom that is from above is first pure, then peaceable, gentle, easy to be entreated, full of mercy and good fruits, without variance, without hypocrisy" (James 3:14–17).

If gospel preachers would fight this evil it would cease, but some of us are so anxious to get a place to preach we endorse division. Then they call us to preach it soft and pleasing to our sectarian friends, so our brothers and sisters can bring their sectarian friends and kinfolk where their feelings will not be hurt. Brethren, sometimes we seem to forget that God commanded Abraham to leave his kinfolk and his country and to go into a land that he would give to him. We seem to forget that our Savior once taught his lesson so strong until many left him. He never asked them to remain, but he did ask his disciples if they wished to go also (John 6:66, 67). Brethren and sisters in Christ, please let the people or sects go and stay united and never divide the church. And let us encourage the preacher to fight the sectarians and the false doctrines they teach and call their names so they will know whom we are fighting. This, however, must be done in love and with the spirit of our Lord. They named themselves, why should they be offended when we call them by their names? When Jesus came to the grave of Lazarus he called him by his name, because he didn't want all the dead to get up. Jesus called the sects by their names when he preached about them. He never one time hinted at them. He called their names. Read. Matt. 25.

Brethren, let us be steadfast, unmovable, always abounding in the work of the Lord (1 Cor. 15:58), and let us fight the good fight of faith and lay hold on life eternal (1 Tim. 6:12). Let us watch and pray and not divide God's people. Pray for me.

A Trip to Texas [1954][61]

On my trip to Texas I carried two fine little boy preachers with me. We stopped at Port Arthur, Texas, and had a great day there. This church was established by the Sixth Street Church (white) twenty-five years ago and the members are very grateful to them. This church now numbers over four hundred and they have been for some time self supporting. They recently remodeled their building and it is beautiful. Luke Miller[62] spent over fifteen years with this church and he is loved by all of the members, white and colored, for his great work. Since that time John O. William and O. L. Aker[63] have labored with this church.

From here we went to Texas City and held a three weeks' meeting under a tent. Several nights were real cold but the interest increased. Two were baptized and four restored. The church in Texas City (white) financed this meeting and attended in large numbers. W. M. Carter is the minister of the colored church and Brother Rodgers is the minister of the white church. He encouraged us greatly while there. We went next to Houston for a tent meeting for two weeks. On the first Lord's Day morning we preached at the Fifth Ward Church (colored) where Jesse Burson[64] preaches. They have just completed improvements on their building, costing about $40,000. Brother Burson is a great worker in the kingdom of our Lord. On Sunday March 14, at 3 P.M., we began a meeting under the tent with the Montgomery Road Church, where L. Brown is doing a great work. The white church where Otha D. Fikes[65] preaches invited me to hold this meeting financed by them. Four were baptized and six restored. Sometimes there were over fifteen hundred present and at times there were more white people than colored people present. The white brethren bought over two hundred pounds of meat to be barbecued so we could have a dinner on the ground on Lord's Day. Such demonstrations as this will convince the world that the spirit of Christ prevails in the church of Christ. Christ fed five thousand one time.

Some Great Meetings [1954][66]

The meeting in Huntsville in May started off with high interest. About thirty years ago I established this wonderful church and they have the greatest attendance of any colored church in that city. While there two white churches turned their radio program over to us and this astonished the colored people of Huntsville. The white brethren attended the meeting in great numbers, and many colored brethren came from villages and cities for miles around. I have held many meetings there but this was the best attended meeting. Robert Butler[67] is preaching for this church. He and his wife are respected by both the colored and white brethren for his good work. There were four baptisms and several restored. They gave a great contribution to Nashville Christian Institute and encouraged the boy preachers with me. Christian education is a blessing to the church. In June I was in a meeting in Beamsville, Ontario, Canada. People came from many parts of Canada, Florida and other far away states. The interest was good from the beginning. There are no colored people living there and this was a great experience for all of us. There was no unpleasantness or bad feeling. Thank God. I had two little boy preachers with me and everyone admired them. They gave a good contribution to the Nashville school. There were fifteen baptisms at Smithville and Beamsville. No colored people live at Smithville. Our audiences and baptisms were all white people. A few colored people came over from New York. We are invited back for next year and we appreciate this. We made many friends for the school while there.

The Light of the World [1954][68]

Nearly two thousand years ago Jesus taught his followers to be the light of the world. We who are followers of the Lord today should remember that people must be lighted or led to our Lord by our lighting the way. Some years ago we were in our car one night and suddenly our lights went out. It was terrible. The driver found it difficult to keep us in the middle of the road. A man driving another car saw us in trouble and stopped to see if he could in any way assist us. I told him to drive slow and let us follow him into Franklin. He gladly consented to do this. Now the reason we wanted to follow him was he had a light. He was a perfect stranger to us, but he had a light. So you see, when we let our light shine people will follow us. We should always remember that while traveling the highways we must have lights. The law demands it. Also the law of God demands that we let our light shine on the highway to heaven.

Sometimes we do things that are not wrong in themselves, but they cause someone to stumble. So don't stubbornly continue doing things that make others stumble. Paul said, "If meat causeth my brother to stumble, I will eat no flesh for evermore that I cause not my brother to stumble" (1 Cor. 8:13). Sometimes the company we keep causes our light not to shine. So try to avoid this kind of company and keep unspotted from the world. I have baptized people who were the only Christians in the home, but by letting their light shine the whole family was led to Christ. The more faithful you are the greater your influence is and your light will shine brighter day by day. All men respect and admire a real Christian who lets his light shine anywhere and at any time. An electric light will shine in the basement, in the attic, in the kitchen or in the parlor. In fact it will shine anywhere. So it matters not where we may be, we should let our light shine, because the world needs light. The word of the Lord is a lamp unto our feet and a light unto our path. The world needs light, so let us shine.

Brother Keeble's Birthday [1954][69]

This to remind my many friends and friends of Nashville Christian Institute, that I will be seventy-six years old on December 7. Last year many friends gave gifts to the school on my birthday. Many of my friends have suggested that my birthday be an annual occasion when friends of the school will send a donation to the school. I have put so much of my best years into the school, and it would make me happy for you to remember the school on my birthday. Send your donations to A. C. Pullias,[70] care of David Lipscomb College, Nashville, Tenn. Brother Pullias is treasurer of Nashville Christian Institute. Every gift will be acknowledged. Remember your gifts to the school will help us train young men to preach the gospel. Your gifts to the school will continue to do good long after the Lord calls me from the labors on this earth to my reward above.

Thank God for This Opportunity [1955][71]

I am thanking my friends who so kindly remembered the Nashville Christian Institute on December 7, my birthday. I was seventy-six years old on this date and your liberal response has made it possible for us to continue the great work of preparing young ministers to evangelize among over three million Negroes in America. These fine workers will soon be on the field with the word of God, bringing thousands to our Lord and spreading God's kingdom. I wish to thank all the Nashville churches for sending so many nice pies, cakes, fruits and other good things to make it easy to care for all who attended our lectureship this year. And thank the churches all over America for sending all kinds of bedding to make it comfortable for our students during these cold nights.

I wish I could tell the whole brotherhood of all of our problems, because many would respond to our needs if they only knew what a struggle we are having to keep up with our monthly expenses. And we thank God daily for our many, many friends. Please pray for the Nashville Christian Institute. The address of the school is 801 Twenty-Fourth Avenue, North, Nashville 8, Tenn. Please send your contribution to Athens Clay Pullias, who is the treasurer of the school.

The Automatic Age [1955][72]

In this day our homes are run automatically. We press a button and cook our meals. Just press a button and the biscuits start cooking and you can set it at a certain point and it will "kick off" so the biscuits will not be burned. Our automobiles are run automatically. We one time had to start our cars by cranking them, and sometimes get our arms broken. But now we press a button or turn on a key and the car starts automatically. No car today has a crank in it unless it's the driver. Everything in the home is run by a switch, except the children.

Sometimes man thinks he has discovered something new, but this automatic system began in the Garden of Eden when God created man out of the dust of the earth and breathed into him the breath of life. Man became a living soul, so the first man was an automatic machine. When the children of Israel were delivered from bondage they were led automatically by a pillar of cloud by day and a pillar of fire by night. All this was automatically done by God. When they came to the Red Sea God automatically parted the sea, Israel passed over but the enemy was destroyed. In the process of being born again, God automatically changes man from one state to another. Man is sometimes puzzled because he cannot see how God does this. Jesus told Nicodemus one must be born of the water and the Spirit. Sometimes we press a button in our homes and the light comes on. Jesus taught in the Sermon on the Mount that God's children are the light of the world. But we cannot become the light of the world until we touch the button that causes the light to shine. That is when one is baptized into Christ. When we touch the button we become the light of the world, new creatures, have our sins washed away, sanctified and become members of the church of Christ.

The Name [1955][73]

This subject has long been a source of much religious trouble. It has caused division among people who profess to be Christians. The sectarians believe that the name is not important, just so one is born again.

On the day of Pentecost (Acts 2:38, 42) about three thousand were baptized in the name of Jesus Christ. We see from this text that it was essential that they be baptized in this name in order for their shins to be remitted. They were commanded to be baptized in the name of the man they had crucified, in the name of the man they buried, and the man that tasted death for every man. As bad as they had hated this man, Jesus Christ, they now had to be baptized in his name to be saved.

We also read, "And in none other name is there salvation: for neither is there any other name under heaven, that is given among men, wherein we must be saved" (Acts 4:12). Refusing to accept the name of Christ they set at naught the stone which the builders had rejected, but which had become the head of the corner. This shows how important the name of Jesus Christ is. John the Baptist did not baptize in the name of Jesus Christ, and I am convinced that churches today that Jesus did not build cannot baptize in the name of Christ. Only the Lord's church has the right to do this. Furthermore, the church that Jesus Christ bought with his blood should wear his name. In Matt. 16:18, Jesus said, "Upon this rock I will build my church." It is his church and his church should wear his name. When we become members of the church we need not worry, for we know that it will never be rooted up. It is blood bought, rock bottom and Holy Ghost filled. Thank God.

Preachers Should Be Examples [1955][74]

If preachers knew that they are watched by the people where they labor, they would be more careful in their way of living. For example, if the preacher is a liberal giver the whole church will give liberally. But it is sad to say that many preachers are the poorest givers. Yet we teach others to give bountifully and the pitiful thing about it all is, when the church gets where it can hardly pay him and take care of other expenses, he begins to rebuke the church for not giving more. And he is the cause of them not giving bountifully, by not giving bountifully himself. I am writing this article trusting that it will cause us to see that the preacher hinders the church to give liberally, and he should be an example to them in liberal giving.

If a preacher is a theater goer and a card player, he won't see man of the members at prayer meeting or Bible study. The church today is too often filled with worldliness and all kinds of corruption. Christians are like a pure, fresh egg. When a fresh egg is cracked you will find the yellow and white not mixed. But when it becomes impure the yellow and the white will be found mixed. So it is with Christians when they live pure lives, they do not mix with the world. But when they mix with the world they become impure and no one can tell them from the world. God tells us to come out from among them and be separate and God will receive us.

Christians are called the light of the world and the salt of the earth. But no one can let their light shine at a card table, in a theater or at a drinking party. When Christians do such things they cover up their light with a bushel. Paul teaches us in Gal. 5:21, if we practice such things we shall not inherit the kingdom of God. We are to lay aside every weight and the sin that doth so easily beset us and run with patience the race, looking unto Jesus the author and perfecter of our faith. Let us all try to prevent our liberty in Christ becoming a stumbling block to those who are weak. Let us work while it is day.

Nashville Christian Institute [1955][75]

We are about to finish our new dormitory and recreation hall at Nashville Christian Institute. We now appeal to our many friends who have helped us for years to also help us furnish these buildings. It will cost us $20,000 to do this properly. We want to get in the new buildings before winter sets in. Our old dormitory is very cold in the winter and very uncomfortable for the boys. We have about eighty boys in the dormitory and some of them have no father and mother. Some are making fine students for the ministry. I carry two or three boys with me on my tours, in the interest of the school and brethren everywhere are astonished at their ability to preach the pure gospel of Christ.

We hope to have our opening by December 1, if it is the Lord's will. Please send us a donation soon, whether large or small, to Nashville Christian Institute. . . .

The Gospel Advocate [1956][76]

For nearly fifty-five years the Advocate has been reporting my work and caused the brethren all over the brotherhood to call me for meetings. During this time thousands of my race were brought to our Savior and many congregations have been established. Also hundreds of gospel preachers have been trained and developed into useful servants of our Savior. Among these are John Vaughner and Luke Miller. I have always thanked God for these great men and many others. I will always be thankful to the Advocate for their unselfish attitude toward me and my race. The present management has also supported me greatly and encouraged the Nashville Christian Institute for years. In the past sixteen years thousands have been taught the Bible daily and many have developed into fine young gospel preachers and are preaching today for some of our best congregations. Thank God.

Christian education is a great blessing to my race, and we thank God for churches that are doing such great mission work among all people regardless of their nationality or color. I am so glad the gospel is to be preached to every creature. I find that my race is thirsting after truth as never before and many parents desire to send their children to a Christian school. If they were able they would. I hope some day we can get the brethren and sisters to establish a scholarship fund to help the child who desires to get a Christian education. Our youth of today is facing some serious problems. They need the gospel. Christianity is the only hope of the world today and something must be done to save our children from sin. Right now is a great opportunity for the churches of Christ and I hope the brethren and sisters throughout the brotherhood will help us in our school work. And in this way save our youth. One of our fine boys has just closed a two weeks' meeting at the school with several baptisms. The harvest is great and the laborers are few. Let us work while it is day. Many of our boys preached while in the Army and converted people on the battlefield. Some came back home Christians and some preaching. There is power in the gospel. . . .

Sound Doctrine [1956][77]

Paul said to Titus, "Speak thou things which befit the sound doctrine" (Titus 2:1). This means that our preaching and conversation must become sound doctrine. When we allow ourselves to destroy the influence and character of our fellow men, we are doing something that does not become sound doctrine. Many of us take delight in slaughtering our brother in Christ. This ought not to be.

A good many times we go to places to preach and we start off trying to see if the church is sound in the doctrine, and to see if the regular preacher is sound or comes up to our standard. I am often asked if I believe in certain things. When they ask these questions they are trying to see if I am sound in the doctrine. I always tell them I believe the apostles' doctrine and I stand on it. Some of my best friends have told me when I became connected with the Nashville Christian Institute I ceased to be a sound gospel preacher. But when I began to travel with my little boys, the brethren who once said this school connection made me unsound, now say I am sound in doctrine. When they hear these boys preaching they know that I am doing the right thing in training them. But they misunderstood what I was doing. After a demonstration with the boys they were convinced.

A few years ago when I held a meeting in one of our cities, one of the brethren told the regular preacher at that place that if he allowed me to take a collection during that meeting, he would never help him in that work again. But I asked the congregation one afternoon to give a contribution to the school and when the offering was counted they found a check for $100 from the man that didn't want the collection taken. After hearing the boys preach that afternoon many of the brethren were convinced that I am a sound gospel preacher.

We must always speak the things that befit sound doctrine. When Peter refused to preach the gospel to the Gentiles he had to be converted. After God converted him on the house top he became a sound gospel preacher (Acts 10:1, 34). He converted the first Gentiles to become Christian. But he became unsound again in Antioch and Paul had to rebuke him to his face. Peter today is a good pattern for a sound gospel preacher to follow.

We are also taught to use sound speech that cannot be condemned. And to follow a patter of good works we must also be sound enough in doctrine in practice to teach men to follow us. We should not bite and devour one another (Gal. 5:15). The church gradually commits suicide by hating one another. We must be so sound in doctrine that when we are persecuted for righteousness we will rejoice and be exceedingly glad (Matt. 5:11, 12). We should prove all things and hold fast to that which is good (1 Thess. 5:21). We will then take the word of Christ. Brethren, let us have that love that hides a multitude of sins and that will make us love our enemies. When Peter denied his Lord, Jesus had enough love in his heart to forgive him and allow Peter to preach the first sermon on Pentecost. We would have told Peter, that we meant to let him preach that first sermon but after he sinned we changed our mind. But Jesus let him preach it. Thank God.

A Meeting in New Mexico [1958][78]

I was in a meeting at Carlsbad, N.M. June 8–20. The audiences grew from the beginning. Brethren, both white and colored, came for miles around each night. Three were baptized and two restored. Berry Minor[79] is doing a great work there. The white brethren are supporting this great man of God. His faithful wife is a real preacher's wife. This is one reason why he enjoys so much success in his work. This was my third meeting at Carlsbad. I was blessed to have my wife with me and also Percy Ricks, my brother-in-law, and his wife. Erma Jackson is also a sister of my wife, and they spent almost a week with us in the meeting. They came from Tuscumbia, Ala. Don't forget Nashville Christian Institute. I hope more churches will send students to the school this fall. This is a fine way to do missionary work. We need, so badly, more preachers to carry the gospel to a hungry world. Please help us to increase our enrollment. The cost is $40 a month. Pray for us.

Nashville Christian Institute [1959][80]

Nashville Christian Institute has opened with one of its largest enrollments, and one of its best faculties. President Willie T. Cato is making a great impression on our great brotherhood. He is appreciated by all for his great Christian spirit. We are expecting this to be one of the best years for the school.

We have eighty boys in the dormitory and over half of them plan to be preachers of the gospel. Many of them are not able to pay their tuition and we hope that all who read this report will want to make a liberal contribution monthly to help us meet our expenses and keep these boys in school. We would hate to have to send some of them home because brethren failed to help them. We need more sound gospel preachers well prepared to go out into the world to proclaim the word. Won't you help these young men to secure an education and prepare themselves to preach the gospel of Christ? We have had to turn some away because they were not able to pay their tuition and we could not help them. Think on this please. As President Emeritus I am still traveling in the interest of the school. It is an inspiration to work with Brother Cato in this great work. He often has me to come into his office to pray. And we believe that thousands all over the country are praying for us. Don't forget to send a check to Nashville Christian Institute, 801 Twenty-Fourth Avenue, North, Nashville, Tenn.

Traveling to the Northeast [1959][81]

I am eighty-one years old and feel fine. The future looks bright, thank God, and we press on. I spent October in Jacksonville, Fla. Twenty-eight responded to the gospel call, and the churches were greatly edified in this area. Walter Cox, the minister, worked night and day. He is greatly encouraged by the white brethren in that city. When they complete their building it will be one of the best among our brethren. From Jacksonville I went to Washington, D.C., for a mass meeting. We preached in the building of the white brethren to about 1,500. One responded. Brother Greer is doing a good work there. I preached also one night in Philadelphia in the building of the white brethren with Brother Jack Myers. He preached in the first service and I preached next. Brother Myers was very kind and nice to me. While there I also visited the school at Villanova and spoke there. Brother Harold Thomas is the president.[82] We next visited New York City and a two weeks' meeting. Two were baptized. Brother Coffman[83] and Brother Pat Boone[84] attended the services. Brother Boone led the singing of four songs and we were proud to have them visit our services. The white brethren in Washington and New York City plan to have me back in the summer for a month at each place. The people at both places seem hungering for the bread of life. The harvest is indeed ripe and the laborers are few. Let us all work while it is day, for the night will soon come. Please remember Nashville Christian Institute during the next year.

Marshall Keeble. (Photo courtesy of Abilene Christian University Office of University Relations.)

Andrew M. Burton. (Photo courtesy of the Disciples of Christ Historical Society.)

Richard N. Hogan, a native of Arkansas, emerged as a prominent preacher in African American Churches of Christ. Hogan was both inspired and admired by Keeble. (Photo courtesy of Patsie Lovell Trowbridge.)

David Lipscomb (1831–1917), a white supporter of black evangelists. Through the pages of the *Gospel Advocate,* Lipscomb shaped the theological perspectives of African American Churches of Christ. (Photo courtesy of the Disciples of Christ Historical Society.)

James L. Lovell (1896–1984), a native Tennessean and renowned religious editor in Churches of Christ, one of many white supporters of Keeble. Lovell often organized preaching campaigns in the western United States for Keeble, R. N. Hogan, and other black evangelists. (Photo courtesy of Patsie Lovell Trowbridge.)

Preston Taylor (1849–1931), a former slave from Louisiana, emerged as an affluent and influential entrepreneur in Nashville during the early twentieth century. Taylor also preached for the Disciples of Christ and baptized Keeble into that fellowship in 1892. (Photo courtesy of the Disciples of Christ Historical Society.)

Chapter 6

The Global Evangelist: Keeble in the 1960s

Civil unrest and social disorder unsettled Keeble's land through the turbulent decade of the 1960s. A century after the Civil War, the "place" of the black man in the United States remained an open question. The proliferation of sit-ins, marches, riots, boycotts, and protest demonstrations demanded for the black man a place of equality in American society. And while the passage of the Civil Rights Act of 1964 and the Voting Rights Act of 1965 stirred in African Americans glimmers of hope, the violent response of white racists sought to dash blacks' optimism. The horrific bombing of the Sixteenth Street Baptist Church in Birmingham, Alabama, which killed four young innocent girls; the death of reformer Medgar Evers in Jackson, Mississippi; the bludgeoning of Viola Liuzzo, a white proponent of the civil rights movement; the depraved murder of three civil rights workers, James Chaney, Andrew Goodman, and Michael Schwerner, in Neshoba County, Mississippi; the violent death of Jimmie Lee Jackson in Alabama; the assassination of Malcolm X; and the martyrdom of Martin Luther King Jr.—all murderously demonstrated the implacable resistance of many white southerners to the social and political changes sweeping the country in the post–World War II era. At the same time, other whites, who drew back personally from such mayhem, quietly acquiesced in the ferocity of racism's more brutal enforcers.[1]

Marshall Keeble remained virtually silent concerning these chaotic and troublesome events because he focused his attention on the spiritual plight of African Americans, not their social condition. In the early 1960s, Keeble traveled abroad for the first time to Europe, Asia, and Africa. The generous monetary gifts of white friends and supporters financed his dream missionary trip come true. Upon returning from his dream trip, Keeble wrote and published his experiences in a book, *From Mule Back to Super Jet with the Gospel*. In this informative volume, Keeble not only chronicled his excursions abroad but also interjected his personal experiences about preaching campaigns in the United States. While traveling, preaching, and baptizing in foreign lands, he further offered moral instruction to Christians in America, advising, "Give the preacher the praise and the encourage he deserves. Don't freeze the preacher. He's got the hottest message in the world." This chapter contains the full-length text of his foreign excursions as well as a statement from Keeble lamenting the closing of the Nashville Christian Institute in 1967.

From Mule Back to Super Jet with the Gospel [1962][2]

In the summer of 1960, my good friends all over the country sent me on a missionary journey to Africa with Lucien Palmer. This was an unbelievable experience to me. Since going on this trip into foreign lands, I am strengthened spiritually, and I can never thank my friends enough for what it has meant to me. It is a long way from Mule Back, the way I rode when I was a boy in Marshall County, to traveling by Super Jet, the way we went in 1960. I was never in a jet before, and it looked as if we were on our way to met Him right then. There were 165 people in that big super jet plane.

I came back from my trip full of new experiences. And yet some of them felt like old experiences to me. When I saw those women in Bethlehem carrying water on their heads in earthen jars, it took me back to the times I saw my mother walking tall with a bucket on her head; bringing back water from the spring down below the meetinghouse on Jackson Street in Nashville, Tennessee, where I worship.

One of the most wonderful things about this missionary journey was the chance it gave me to visit the Holy Land, the place the maps call Jordan and Israel. It's holy because that's the place where the Savior was born and lived and died for us. It was a marvelous thing to be able to walk the streets of Bethany and Jerusalem where He walked. All my life when I read about those places, I imagined just how it was. They were real to me. But now that I have gone and seen them for myself, they are even more real. I have been there. And I want you to know about some of the places Brother Palmer and I saw and the things that happened to us.

The first stop we made was London. We landed there on the Lord's Day in time for worship. We started looking for the church and when we found it, it was a small church; and to my surprise, one of the boys[3] who graduated from my own Nashville Christian Institute was helping to lead in that assembly. The Army had him over there, but he was also using his opportunity to work in the church of our Lord.

The brethren from the church at Aylesbury showed us all over London. We saw everything. We saw London Bridge, the Tower of London and the Queen's House, Buckingham Palace. It was a big square house with a fence around it. And every day at 11:30 there is the Changing of the Guard. These men, dressed up in red coats and big hats that came almost over their eyes, ride up on horses to take over their duties for the afternoon from the guard who have been there all morning. Those were smart horses. They looked like they had more sense than their riders.

We saw Big Ben on top of the Parliament Building. You're never the same after you've seen and heard Big Ben. We saw many interesting things in London. It was very odd to see all of the drivers going on the wrong side of the street. Our visit to England would not have been complete without seeing No. 10 Downing Street, Westminster Abbey, Picadilly [sic] Square and Scotland Yard.

After we left London we flew to Paris. The missionaries there gave us a moving and kind reception. I preached one night in Paris, and I was glad to meet the brethren there, and see the good work they are doing.

In Paris, one of the strange things was the side walk cafes. I never thought I would eat at one of those places, eat right out on the sidewalk, and they charged us extra for eating outdoors. We visited many places in Paris and I especially like Arc De Triumphe [sic], Eiffel Tower and the Palace of Versailles, this palace cost eighty million dollars.

Then we went to Rome, Italy. We met with the church in Rome, and there I preached with an interpreter for the first time. He was the fifteen year old son of a colonel in our armed forces stationed in Italy. This family is very zealous for the church. The young man made me feel comfortable, since boys have been a specialty of mine for so many years.

Rome is one of the most interesting and historical cities in the world. It has been the center of the Roman Catholic faith for almost two thousand years. But I know that the law was to have gone out of Zion, and the Gospel of the Lord was to have gone forth from Jerusalem.

In Rome, the missionary's wife showed us around. She took us to the old Mamertine Church, built on the location of the prison where Paul was held while he awaited his execution. The dungeon is a circular room fifteen feet in diameter and under twenty-two feet of solid stone. Here is where Paul wrote Colossians, Ephesians, Philippians, and other letters to the young churches. "Brother Keeble," someone asked me, "how did you know it was the prison where Paul was?" When I bought a ticket to Rome, how did I know I was going to Rome? They said the ticket was to Rome. How do you know you are a Christian? Paul said, "If any man love God, the same is known." Again he said, " I would not have you ignorant, and "These things are written that you might know." And I felt that I was standing in the dungeon of the man who wrote those things to the churches at Colosse, Ephesus, Philippi, and other cities. Paul was a knowing Christian. He said, "I know in whom I believe." There was no doubt in his mind, and why should I doubt that this is the place?

We also saw St. Peter's Cathedral and Vatican City, the home of the Pope. His Palace has one thousand one hundred rooms. The thing that impressed me most about St. Peter's Cathedral was the large bronzed statue of the Apostle Peter. He was in a sitting position, and the tourists have literally kissed off his big toe. I am wondering what Peter would have said about this, since he said to the man who fell down to worship him, "Stand up, for I myself am a man."

I was moved when I entered the Coliseum, and my thoughts turned to the many Christians who met death, for their faith, when thrown to wild beasts. The catacombs, the underground caves where many early Christians lived and worshipped, were another reminder of those tragic times under Roman rulers. The old Roman Wall, the Road to the South, and the Roman Forum also point to the destruction of this once powerful and rich kingdom.

We were especially interested in the areas where the 1960 Olympic games were to be held, since a young lady from Tennessee, a student at A&I State College here in Nashville, was to compete in the meet. (She won.)[4]

One of the strange things in Italy is the way they tell time. The clocks run from midnight to midnight, or from one to twenty-four hours. It sounded very strange to ask the time of day and have them answer, "Seventeen minutes to thirteen, or, "Our plane will leave at fourteen forty-five o'clock for Cairo, Egypt."

In Cairo we ate our breakfast on the balcony of the Hotel Semaramis, looking out over the Nile River. We had time in Cairo to see the museum where there is a great collection of things which were found in King Tut's tomb, all the things the early Egyptian thought he needed for his trip into the other world. These things are more than fourteen hundred years older than the time of Christ and are very interesting. I didn't doubt that these were buried with King Tut. I think the man who doubts these things is looking for an excuse to doubt.

Soon we left Cairo for Beirut, Lebanon. We were only there overnight but we had a beautiful view of the Mediterranean Sea from our hotel window. The next morning we set out by car for Jerusalem, a distance of about two hundred or two hundred fifty miles south. We passed through the cities of Damascus and Ammon and Jericho. The thought of the road to Damascus just overwhelmed me because that was the road where Paul heard our Lord and was struck blind. That is where Paul's whole life was changed.

The road to Damascus and the Jericho Road made me feel so overcome with joy that I could walk these roads I had read about so often. Most of this was hilly dry land and I came to understand what our Lord meant when He said, "I will not leave thee desolate." There were white houses on the hillsides as well as many tents and cave openings and quite a few apple trees. At one place on the road we saw a camel so loaded that he looked like a walking haystack. We saw many people riding donkeys, and otherwise living much as the people lived in Jesus' time. Camels and donkeys are used extensively with farming saw well as other types of work. The members of the famed Royal Jordanian Camel Corps patrols the desert areas of the country on camel back, safeguarding the land from intruders.

The only way to go inside of Old Jerusalem is to go to Lebanon, as we did, and go from Beirut. If you go to Israel first, which is most direct and most natural, you are barred from going into the Old City and the Holy Land. The hatred between Jews and Arabs, who hold Jordan and the Old City of Jerusalem, is so great that there is no traffic from Israel, although the Israeli border cuts across part of the New City of Jerusalem. Many tourists have been disappointed by trying to enter the Holy Land and Jerusalem through Israel, only to be barred at the very gates of the Old City.

We made the trip from Beirut to Jerusalem by car, passing many large mountains, one of the most famous being Mt. Hermon. Much of the country was dry and desolate and our impression along the way was rocks, rocks, rocks. There were immigration and custom offices as we passed from Lebanon to Syria and from Syria to Jordan in our car. We saw many Arab refugees, and were impressed by the conditions of the people generally, which showed that many of them were still living under conditions much as they must have been in the first century. One of the really touching things was to see the refugee camps. These Arabs had come out of Israel by the thousands when the Jews took over the country.

Around Jericho, in the rich Jordan valley, we saw many trucks loaded with oranges, bananas and other fruits. This territory is famous for its fruits and vegetables.

As we neared Jerusalem, I was moved to discover how clearly the Bible records the geography of the region. It is all just the way the Bible describes it. When the Bible says East, it means East; and when it says West it means West. If it says up, it means up, and if it says down, it means down. Going down to Jericho is down hill all the way from Jerusalem. And you go up to Jerusalem just the way the Bible says. Anyone who knows a thing about God's geography knows he is there!

When we got to Jerusalem, we couldn't find the church. In fact, we realized the church was not there. We lamented this greatly. We knew our plans to establish the work on the Israeli side in the near future; but couldn't help thinking how sad it is that no missionary was planning to come and settle in Jordan. Brother Palmer and I had our worship service alone. Both of us were moved to tears as we remembered the death of our Lord while we worshipped in the Old City.

We stayed at the American Colony Hotel, and our guide was Mahmoud Khamis, a Moslem. He is well known for his ability as a guide and for his good knowledge of the Bible. He studied English at the University of Jerusalem and speaks five languages well. His service as interpreter for Arabs and Americans in both world wars has also helped to develop his unusual ability to hold the interest of any tourist who visits his country. He was particularly attentive to us; especially, I think, because he had received a telephone call from the States about us. Even though he had guided many famous Americans, such as Adlai Stevenson,[5] he had never talked long distance by telephone to America, about visitors who were coming. We felt as if we had received the finest guided tour this dedicated guide had ever given.

I have been asked if I could understand any of the languages in the Holy Land. No. But I was interested in finding out about the language our Lord spoke. It was Aramaic. I understood the language of the Lord better when I learned that the word we translate "uttermost" in the Bible is the Aramaic word for "speck." I see now more clearly what the Lord meant when He said the Gospel was to begin in Jerusalem, then to Judea and Samaria and to the uttermost parts of the earth. As long as there is one little speck of the world which has not heard about our Lord, we have work to do. Sadly I realized more fully how negligent we have been in doing this command of our Lord to carry the gospel to every speck of the earth.

In Jerusalem you literally walk by faith. We walked the streets He walked, and saw the things He saw. There were many things which I am sure were exactly as they were in Jesus' day. We saw people riding on donkeys like the one He rode into Jerusalem a short time before His crucifixion. And we saw men carrying water in goat skins slung across their backs. We saw the old walls that marked the location of Solomon's temple.

One of the most sacred spots near Jerusalem is the Mount of Olives. This is a large rounded hill about a mile long, outside the gates of Jerusalem. It is separated from the city by the deep, narrow Kidron Valley, which is also known as the Valley of Jehoshaphat. The Bible speaks of it as "a Sabbath day's journey" from Jerusalem. This is where Jesus went in the evening to pray, when other people went to their homes. You remember He said, "Foxes have holes, and the birds of the air have nests; but the Son of man hath not where to lay his head" (Luke 9:58). Then, Luke 21:37 tells us that, "in the daytime Jesus was teaching in the temple and at night He went out and abode in the mount that is called the Mount of Olives."

It was from the little village of Bethpage on top of the Mountain that Jesus rode the borrowed colt down the slope and into the city of Jerusalem. After the Lord's Supper in the upper room, Jesus and the eleven went out to the Mount of Olives. Brother Palmer and I walked all over this mountain, because we wanted to be sure that we were stepping in His steps; and we felt very close to our Lord there.

At the foot of the mountain is the Garden of Gethsemane. Here he prayed in agony while his disciples fell asleep. We saw the large, flat rock where Peter, James and John are said to have slept while he prayed. There are many old olive trees in the garden. These trees are twisted and hollowed with age, but they still bear fruit, reminding everyone who looks at them that one never gets too old to bear fruit for the Lord. And it was here that Judas came and placed the kiss of betrayal on his cheek, which was the signal to take him. Thirty pieces of silver, approximately fifteen dollars, is mighty cheap to sell the Lord, but sometimes we sell him for much less.

Jesus' tomb is near here, and his ascension took place somewhere on the Mount of Olives. So this mountain is connected with our Lord in very special ways. As we walked over its slopes and in the garden of Gethsemane, I relived all those events in his life. Climbing those slopes was hard for an old man, but I did not want to miss a step of it. It was a most moving experience, and it is impossible to tell you what it is like and how I felt.

In one of the mosques at the top of the Mount of Olives the attendants took off our shoes and we went inside. This mosque, like all of the others, had no furnishings or seats of any kind. Mohammedans when worshipping sit on the floor oriental style, or kneel. The fixtures and decorations are most elaborate, gold ceilings, gold chandeliers, colored glass and beautiful mosaic. Our guide took out his prayer rug and knelt facing Mecca. The Moslems are a very devout people, and five times a day they are called to prayer by their priests, who go up into tall towers all over the city of Jerusalem to call the faithful to prayer.

When our guide had finished praying to Allah, I asked him if I could pray too, and he said I could. How happy I was to pray to God, through the blessed name of Jesus, in this fine old mosque. When we finished, I could see he was greatly moved for there were tears in his eyes.

The top of the Mount of Olives gives a fine view of the City of Jerusalem, looking across the Valley of Jehoshaphat. From here we looked toward the West and saw where Joshua stood and commanded the sun and moon to stand still that there might be more time for him to win a victory on the battlefield of his God. This is where Jesus stood and made His lament for Jerusalem: "O Jerusalem, Jerusalem, thou that killest the prophets, and stonest them which are sent unto thee, how often would I have gathered they children together even as a hen gathereth her chickens under her wings, and ye would not!" (Matt. 23:37).

From the Mount of Olives it is possible to see many of the landmarks inside the walls of the Old City, such as the "Dome of the Rock." This Dome looms over the city. It is part of one of the two Arab mosques on the grounds where the temple of Solomon once stood. Inside one of these is "The Rock." This is nothing more than the top of Mt. Moriah. The top if this particular mountain projects itself into the center area of the mosque, and over it is the Dome of the Rock. It was on Moriah that Abraham prepared to sacrifice his son, Isaac.

The west wall of the Temple was for centuries the wailing place of the Jews. To a Jew the greatest joy was to be able to worship in the Temple area. But they were shut out by the Arabs, who controlled the area. So each Friday from 2:00 P.M. until late at night the Jews came to weep for the Temple which had been destroyed, and to pray for the coming of the Messiah, and the reestablishment of Jerusalem. This old wall as near as they could come, and they leaned against it and wept. Today the

Wailing Wall is silent, because there is not a single living Jew in the entire old city of Jerusalem.

On Friday our guide took us to visit the Church of the Holy Sepulchre, which is built on the hill believed to be Calvary. We began by going to the House of Caiaphus and to Pilate's hall. Climbing the many steps leading from the courtyard of Caiaphus' house to the hall where Jesus was tried was hard for an eighty-two year old man. Brother Palmer asked me if I wanted to stop and rest. But I wanted to continue on, I wanted to feel the steps of the Lord as he went to his trial. It was most impressive. There on those steps, near where Peter denied his Lord, it was a painful thing to examine myself, and to ask if I would have been any more loyal to my Lord than was Peter.

We left the spot where Jesus was tried, spat upon and crowned with thorns, and we took the path which led to Calvary. The priests were making their regular Friday march along this path, the path which Jesus took to his crucifixion, carrying his own cross. This is called the Via Dolorosa, or way of sorrow. Walking slowly in this sad procession, we thought of the many sufferings which our Lord endured before He was finally nailed to the cross and lifted up.

I don't think I would have been able to bear to relive these things in my heart if I had not remembered Jesus' own words: "And I, if I be lifted up from the earth, will draw all men unto me." There is power in the old gospel.

We had the privilege of going into the grave where Christ was laid, into the tomb where my Savior lay. I asked if I could pray, and I prayed. I stood there and cried. It was a powerful feeling, something I can't explain. Its vine covered tomb in a garden was the most impressive thing we saw in Jerusalem. Somehow, we felt that this was the place.

Bethany is a short rip outside of Jerusalem beyond the Mount of Olives. This is where Jesus often stayed in the home of His friends Mary, Martha and Lazarus. A church has been built over the site of their simple home. It was to Bethany that Jesus came when He was weary of the crowds. I am happy that I went into this home from which Mary and Martha ran to him, to meet Him after their brother Lazarus was dead. I was glad to go there and see the grave where Lazarus was buried. Jesus called to him. And how did he call him? By his name, "Lazarus, come forth." (And that's the way he calls his church, by his name.)

What a thrilling experience it was to stand in the identical spot and relive in my mind the very scene that the Bible plainly declares took place here! I wish you could have been there too.

The home of Simon, the leper, was also at Bethany. It was here the woman washed the feet of Jesus with her tears, dried them with her hair and anointed his feet with precious ointment.

Bethany is also on the road to Jericho. A little farther along the same road, halfway between Jericho and Jerusalem we came to the Inn of the Good Samaritan which recalls Jesus' parable of the man who fell among thieves. And we saw the caves where robbers used to hid, waiting for the unprotected traveler to come along.

On this same road is a sycamore tree, the traditional place where Jesus told Zacchaeus to "Come down." And he calls us to come down too. We must be humble. That servant, who would be great in his kingdom, must be least, and servant of all.

Near Jericho is the place where Jesus was baptized in the river Jordan. The Mountains of Temptation are here, too, where our Lord spent forty days fasting and praying after His baptism. When we came to this spot on the river we saw people dipping up water and putting it in bottles to take back home. We just hope and pray that these people know the Word of the Lord has recorded why John was baptizing at this place, "because there was much water there."

The Jordan flows into the Dead Sea. We went around on the south side where we saw the openings of the caves where the Dead Sea Scrolls were found. I was interested to learn that one of the leaders of this expedition was from Dyersburg, Tennessee. The guide and I sat on a small covered pavilion looking out over the Dead Sea, while Brother Palmer went swimming.

There is no river in all the world surrounded by so many sacred memories as the River Jordan, especially at the spot where Old Jericho stood. Moses stopped on the east side of the Jordan when he left Egypt. Here is where Moses handed over the staff of leadership to Joshua. And here also is where Joshua took the city of Jericho with his armies and his trumpets.

This is where the conquest of Canaan began. Near here Moses died on the top of Mt. Pisgah. The lives of both Elisha and Elijah are associated with the River Jordan. Saul was made king here. God allowed battles to be fought in these surrounding plains which decided the course of the lives of His chosen people. Here is where John the Baptist preached his first sermon. And above all, it is where Jesus was baptized by John the Baptizer. Some of Jesus' disciples were called to follow him at this location. The guide pointed out many sacred sites, and each time he would say, "This is the traditional place," or "This is the traditional spot." I wondered why he kept saying traditional, and then I remembered that he was a Moslem, and not a follower of Christ. Through the use of the word traditional, the devil was trying to sow doubt in the hearts of them that heard him. The devil works in many ways to destroy our faith, but I know that our God is able to preserve and keep those places, that we might be encouraged. I'm just as sure that I walked where Jesus walked, as I am that he is now at God's right hand making intercession for those who trust him.

When we visited Bethlehem, of course we wanted to see the place of our Savior's birth. The Church of the Nativity has been built over the stable where Jesus was born. It is one of the oldest churches in existence. My memories of the simple manger, which the Bible says was where Jesus was laid when he was born, overshadowed the gold and jeweled decorations that man has added here. There is a silver star set in the marble floor of the church. Through a hole in the center of this star you can see the original rock floor of the stable. I was reminded of the Star of the East which led the wise men here. And I thought of Christ's people, living stones in His kingdom. What a thrilling day, for me to be in Bethlehem. How I was filled with joy to be in the very cradle of Christianity, where Christ, the Word of God, became flesh and dwelt among men.

Bethlehem is a few mile south of Jerusalem. Only a littler farther south of Bethlehem is the city of Hebron, associated with Abraham and the Old Testament fathers. Hebron is one of the oldest cities in the world, and I did not doubt this one bit after being there. On the outskirts of Hebron are the Oaks of Mamre, where Abraham pitched his tents and where he bought a family burial place. Can you imagine how I felt when I stood under the Oaks of Mamre and thought that here or near here, the angels announced to Abraham that he should have a son named Isaac?

On the road to Jerusalem we saw the tombs of Abraham and Sarah, Isaac, Jacob and many others; all located here in rocky caves, which have not been entered since the Crusades. The Crusaders built a small Moorish building over Rachel's tomb. The graves are cut out of solid rock and the bodies were wrapped in linen in ancient times and laid in the stone compartments, stacked on top of one another like dresser drawers. The well where Jesus had the conversation with the Samaritan woman is near these tombs. What a wonderful experience to review what our Lord said to this woman, "He that drinketh of the water that I shall give him shall never thirst."

When we got back to Jerusalem, we had come to the end of our stay in the places associated with both the Old and New Testaments. And if everything we saw while we were in the Holy Land was man made, the ground that we walked on was God made. My Lord's feet made footprints in that soil, and for over sixty-five years I have been trying to walk in the steps of the Savior. "Trying to walk in the step of the Savior" is one of my favorite songs, and oh, how I enjoy singing it with my brethren. All the things we did in Jerusalem and the surrounding country were just a getting ready for our missionary trip to Africa. Because we had left the United States in order to obey our Lord's command, to take His gospel to the uttermost parts of the earth, to lift Him up to the native Africans of Nigeria. I was sorry to leave the places where I had felt so near to my Lord, but I was glad to be going to do what I felt He intended me to do. So we turned our eyes from Jerusalem toward Nigeria.

We drove by car to Beirut and left Lebanon by plane on June 28. We did not go directly to Nigeria, but passed through Athens, Greece, and returned to Rome before turning South to Kano, Nigeria, and finally to Port Harcourt. One of the great sights as we crossed Africa was seeing the Sahara Desert from our plane. High over the desert we ran into a snow storm. Snow and ice collected on the wings and windows of our plane. I was anxious. Then I remembered how God had asked Job if he had considered the value of the snow. How wonderful it was to turn my mind to the nitrogen and other valuable properties of snow, sent by God's hand—I was no longer afraid.

The missionaries met us at Port Harcourt, and we went by car about eighty miles into the bush, to the Bible College at Ukpom, and a little later to the Bible College at Onitcha Ngwa. This missionary visit to Africa was the real purpose of our trip and I was anxious to see the extent to which the work had progressed. Ukpom Bible College is in the middle of the bush country of Nigeria. The campus is composed of twenty acres and six buildings. About sixty to seventy students are enrolled each year and all are studying to be gospel preachers. The school started in 1954.

At Onitcha Ngwa, in Iboland, there is another Bible College just like the one at Ukpom which was established in 1957. These schools have been and are doing much to get local gospel preachers prepared to preach to the natives. At present there are over three hundred fifty congregations in Nigeria and new ones are being established almost every week. The missionaries have done a great job in spreading the kingdom but probably their greatest work is in the training of native evangelists.

Nigeria has no free public schools like we have in the United States. Almost all the schools in the country are operated by private agencies, most of them church groups. The government is glad to cooperate with these schools when they meet certain conditions. The schools then become eligible for government grants. Because of this cooperative spirit in Nigeria, it is undergoing an orderly and peaceful transition to new ways.

Members of the church of Christ, under the Nigerian Christian School Board, conduct eleven village schools near Ukpom. Fourteen preachers who are graduates of the Ukpom Bible College teach Bible to the two thousand five hundred children who attend these village schools. These schools also employ about eighty-five Christian teachers. Ukpom Bible College has become the training center for future leaders of the church, business and government.

In order for the government to approve a private school the village must provide land, and build an adequate building, and must find a qualified person to be approved by the government as the manager of the school. Nigerian parents, like American parents, want an education for their children; and there has been a great demand for managers to establish and run these village schools. Ukpom Bible College has helped to supply this need. Nigerian schools under the church of Christ are dependent on Christians from everywhere, for the support of the gospel preachers who bring them the message of the Bible.

There aren't many places where you can get a bargain these days. But here is one place you can get one. For just $60 you can sponsor a class of thirty boys and girls, so they will get one hundred eighty hours of Bible training. For $2 you can pay the tuition for one boy or girl for a whole month.

The first converts were made through a correspondence course sent out by Lawrence Avenue Church of Christ in Nashville, Tennessee, in 1947. This course was designed for G.I.'s, but C. A. O. Essien,[6] a native Nigerian heard of it and requested this course. He was baptized and became the life blood of the work with his people. From 1947 to 1952 about sixty congregations were established—all of them before the arrival of a full time missionary from the church in America. Brother Essien died in the summer of 1959. I visited the grave of this fine soldier of the cross, and rejoiced that I could do honor to his memory.

Bush country was not a new experience to me, because sixty-five years ago I preached in a wild and little settled area like this, under a brush arbor. People came down the road from outlying places, carrying their lanterns. These lanterns were the only light they had. It was this way when I was young, and it is this way now in the bush country of Nigeria.

When I was preaching in Africa I had to have an interpreter. After a few minutes I caught on that I had to talk slower. It slows a fast man down, preaching with an interpreter on either side. I remembered Peter on the Day of Pentecost. This sermon was preached, and every man heard in his own tongue. We had about eighty-eight baptisms altogether while we were there.

Once when there was a large number of people to be baptized, they told me there were many wild beasts around this watering place, a herd of elephants, wild animals of all kinds, snakes, crocodiles. I had come through that one time before. Once when I was preaching and baptizing in Hillsboro River near Tampa, Florida, I looked up and saw an alligator. I didn't bother the alligator and the alligator didn't bother me.

On one occasion while I was in Africa, I spoke to an audience of about two thousand, imagine two thousand native Africans, many bare footed, scantily dressed, babies in their arms, but they came to hear about Christ. Some accepted, and came so fast that Brother Palmer[7] wondered if they understood what they were doing. He asked them, "Do you understand what you are doing?" Their answers proved that they did.

There were people running into the water to be baptized. They ran. After getting in the water, they ran. That is the gospel that is so powerful and quick that it saves. That is the word of God.

Everywhere I preached these people received the gospel with joy. It's a wonderful thing for a preacher to see the word of God take hold of a man. In order for the preacher to do his best, you got to back him up. Give the preacher the praise and the encouragement he deserves. Don't freeze the preacher. He's got the hottest message in the world. He just needs somebody to fan him.

During the time we were in Africa, we took part in Bible classes with the students at Ukpom and Onitcha Ngwa, and we joined with them in the Lord's Day worship. We also met with the Ukpom village chiefs and village council representatives.

Some of our time was spent going through the bush country to the little villages within a radius of seventy-five miles from Ukpom. As we drove and walked, we often saw little altars set up beside the road to pacify different gods. These people of the different tribes have not been taught about the one true God. They believe that the rivers and the animals all have spirits and they are afraid of these spirits. They make a little altar and bring an egg, and old hat, or a chicken to place on the altar as a gift to the spirits. These are really sacrifices. But they're aimed in the wrong direction. I wonder if we Christians, in our Christian nation, would give a chicken to the Lord, if we had only one chicken? These altars made me think of what Paul told the people of Athens. He said, I perceive you are a very religious people; you have built many altars; and I see you have one to the unknown god. This is the One I want to tell about. Paul used what he saw to preach them the gospel message. We are the ones who will be held responsible for those who do not know.

I taught in the Nigerian Christian Village Schools in some way every day while I was there, and I was always well received. I preached in the church buildings and in the open air meetings both day and night. Once we met together with about twelve congregations present. I held Lord's Day morning service at Ikot Usen, where the work was started in Nigeria, and nineteen were baptized there. A welcome was held for us in the school building and several hundred people attended. There was a big program by the local people, with visiting dignitaries present. Then we turned the afternoon into a preaching service, and fifty-five were baptized.

One of the things Brother Palmer and I did was to help conduct a lectureship in Iboland. Students came from many surrounding villages. A few had bicycles. A bicycle to them is what he finest automobile is to us. One of their sayings is a bicycle makes you many men. This useful possession is polished after each ride, every bit of dust must come off. With pride of ownership and devotion, he spends hours shining this valuable means of transportation. Altogether we spent three weeks in Nigeria, there of the most memorable weeks in my life.

Among the many interesting things I saw there were the open air markets, there are no stores like we have. The men and women came on market day from miles around, most of them walked, carrying fruits and vegetables and trinket on their heads, to sell. Everything was spread out on the ground, the meat and everything else right out in the open. And great crowds of people came to buy. They came to market every fourth day. These people do not have calendars, clocks and watches like we do. They determine time and seasons by the sun and the moon. I was told that they are never late for an appointment, never get the days mixed up, and they know exactly the day, the month and the year. Just how they do this, I did not find out, but it seems to beat our way of getting to places on time. I was reminded how Paul used to preach in the market place.

Nigeria is a long way from the United States. And its ways are a long way from ours. This especially is true in the back country, away from the European built cities. There is no electricity and very few gasoline motors. The grass in front of the buildings at the Bible schools, twenty acres of it, is cut by hand with grass shears.

We received many gifts in many places. The students at the Bible College gave us a farewell party which was also attended by government dignitaries in the area. At this festival they made us promise to come back. I was given a robe and made and honorary chief. The walking cane of authority was passed over to me by the Paramount Chief. I am honored to be an African chief.

A Christian can't go to Africa without being reminded of our Lord's commission. The native people carry water in pots made of mud. And I thought how we Christians are earthen vessels, water pots of our Lord. Are we carrying the water of Life to the thirsting people of this world?

Another thing that is needed in Nigeria is hospitals. There are very few hospitals. When someone gets sick, four friends put him on a stretcher and carry him on their heads to the nearest hospital, which may be many miles away. All the stretcher bearers trot in rhythm, so the sick man won't be jostled about too much. Sometimes the hospitals are just too far away for sick people to get there. The church ought to have a hospital in this country. Jesus said, "Go out into the uttermost parts of the world and preach the gospel." Preaching and teaching may be the first parts of our commission. But Jesus also told his disciples to heal.

As Christians we are supposed to pray without ceasing. The Moslem knows you need to pray. It is tragic that people like the Moslems who do not believe in Christ as the Son of God have more zeal than those who are Christian.

Colossians 3:16 tells us, "Let the word of Christ dwell in you richly in all wisdom, teaching and admonishing one another in psalms and hymns and spiritual songs, singing with grace in your hearts to God." In Nigeria it interested me to hear the hymns and psalms sung in three languages at once.

Such Christian fellowship I have never seen. Our whole journey was a witness to the fellowship that Christians share with other Christians. I am convinced, by the way they welcomed us, that the fellowship with us greatly strengthened the Christian faith in Nigeria. Brother Palmer knows the work well there, and he was directly responsible for establishing six of the Nigerian village schools. I was very fortunate to be able to go to Nigeria with Lucien Palmer. There is a great need for more Christian workers in Nigeria, and we should support them with our prayers and gifts. A feeling of Christian fellowship was evident as we met other Christians all along the way to and from Nigeria, in Rome, Paris, and London.

Before I close I want to tell you about the final Lord's Supper which Brother Palmer and I shared on this trip. Our last Lord's Day together found us thirty-three thousand feet in the air, above the Atlantic Ocean, on a Super Jet. Brother Palmer had forseen [sic] this and he had provided the loaf and fruit of the vine. That was a most precious occasion to remember. I now know more fully that when God gives a command he will not hinder obedience. "Providentially hindered" is man made.

Two or three can meet with our heavenly Father. Even one Christian must not forsake the request that was made by our Lord, "Do this in remembrance of me." John on the Isle of Patmos was in the spirit on the Lord's Day, and the windows of heaven were opened to him.

Now that I am home I think of what one Nigerian preacher said in one of his prayers. "Lord help me to believe what I've been preaching." That sounded strange at first, but after thinking it over, I know he is right. All of us need to believe what we have been preaching, believe it so much that we are ready to live by it. And, if it be the Lord's will, I plan to return with Lucien Palmer, to further the work of the church in the bush country of Africa.

Will you pray for us to this end?

Nashville Christian Institute to Close [1967][8]

It's been a long time since I started training boys and girls at Nashville Christian Institute. Since that time Sister Keeble and I have loved, worked, and given our lives to see this work done. We plan to continue to help young people.

If we continue to help young people here at Nashville Christian Institute, we face many problems. The problems are increasing. Accreditation, this is a must. Everywhere I go, my people ask about this. Use to be, we didn't know about this; so we didn't ask.

We need more ground. The State tells you that you have to have so many acres. We don't have acres; we have a few city lots that we have recently bought. We must have a new building. Everybody wants to live in a new house now, so we've got to have one here at the school. We have bought some new equipment, but we sure need more.

Our teachers are important in our work. Our teachers have never been paid like most other teachers, but they have kept teaching. Some would leave for more money. Right now our teachers' salaries are less than half of the amount paid public school teachers. That tells you why they would leave.

Our enrollment is getting smaller each year. My people are now flocking to the finer schools which are now open to all races. These schools are closer to them, so they don't have to ride the bus. They can go free; you know we like things that don't cost nothing.

If we continue to operate as a school, we must spend several million dollars. This would include a new location. This would have to be big enough for a new elementary and a new high school building. Even if we did this, we don't know whether the public would appreciate it enough to give to help us, or send us their children. They may say "Well we've got the same thing right across the street."

Brother A. M. Burton was always interested in my race of people, he loved everybody but he always helped me and my people. While Brother Burton was still living, he appointed some men from the Board and the President of our school to study our needs, our problems, and how we could best serve the Negro boy and girl. After spending months looking at our work and examining all the facts as well as seeing the many needs that we have, the committee recommended to the Board that the Nashville Christian Institute close its doors at the end of the school term. That will be June 2, 1967. They also recommend that everything the school owns should be sold and the cash be put into the A. M. Burton–Marshall Keeble Scholarship Fund of the David Lipscomb College Foundation. That's a fund that Brother Burton started before he died. He wanted to help Negro boys and girls get a college education. Praise God for such a man.

While Sister Keeble and I regret to see Nashville Christian Institute close her doors, we wholly support what we thought had to be done. We live in a new day. We must be a part of that new day, there is no other way.

I shall continue to work in behalf of Christian education everywhere. Especially, I want to work for the A. M. Burton–Marshall Keeble Scholarship Fund. You know, I'd want to do that because that's got my name.

Since the action has been taken by the Board, Jackson Street church of Christ here in Nashville has given $1,000 to the A. M. Burton–Marshall Keeble Scholarship Fund. That's the congregation where I have been a member all my life. The Liberty City church of Christ in Miami, Florida has given $550 to this fund. I'm asking all of you who are concerned about my race of people to help the most promising of these young people get a Christian education at David Lipscomb College. These talented young people need to be prepared to serve God.

No one could regret the closing of our school more than sister Keeble and I, but we must change. Times have changed, so please accept this change. Please throw your help behind it. Please give to the A. M. Burton–Marshall Keeble Scholarship Fund. Please help us find deserving Negro boys and girls to educate.

Chapter 7

The Importance of Trained Ministers

One of Marshall Keeble's most unforgettable experiences occurred in 1927 in Jackson, Tennessee, where a Baptist minister, three Methodist preachers, and a Pentecostal leader attacked him from all sides. "Five sect preachers attacked the things that I taught; but when I took the Book of books and proved what I taught, they were defeated in their undertaking. . . . These men did all they could to check the impression the truth was making on the people." One of the Methodist preachers, probably a Bible and Greek instructor at Lane College, challenged Keeble, who, like Booker T. Washington, downplayed the significance of biblical languages before an audience who knew virtually nothing about Greek (see note 8 of this chapter). Keeble, however, never forgot that experience, and in the years after it happened he mentioned it several times. He understood that his own limited education was a liability—not an asset. The documents that make up this chapter, then, reveal a man passionately concerned about education, a man of genuine humility, and a man eager to see young aspiring black ministers better equipped for the preaching ministry.

Paradoxically, in the 1950s Church of Christ schools and colleges controlled by white Christians across the South frequently invited Keeble to address their lectureship crowds. Yet they never allowed his black students from the Nashville Christian Institute or any blacks to enroll until the early 1960s. On the one hand, Keeble spoke frankly, forthrightly, and at times with a tone of indictment. On the other hand, the black evangelist-educator never directly challenged the segregation that permeated the schools and congregations claiming to be Christian. This posture of accommodation marked Keeble as distinct from many other important black preachers in Churches of Christ such as Samuel Robert Cassius, George Philip Bowser (1874–1950), Richard Nathaniel Hogan (1902–1997), and others. Keeble believed that only the support of white Christians could ensure the success of efforts to educate young black men, so he softened or even stifled any animosity he might have felt.

"The Church among the Colored"[1]
Lecture, February 23, 1950, Abilene Christian College

This is one occasion that I am at a loss to find words to express my gratitude and appreciation to Brother Morris[2] for inviting me to have a part in this great program. I feel my unworthiness and unfitness for such a great occasion. I have prayed continuously to God to give me strength and power to guide me in whatever way that he thinks is best, or rather knows best, that I might say just those things that are appreciated and that are essential and necessary, on an occasion of this kind. I feel that in the common expression, I feel that right at this time I am "on the spot." That's the way I feel. Nevertheless, we may have just a little enjoyment, a little laughter, but all of us sincere. I think sometimes the trouble with the church is we carry too long faces in order to appear sincere. That don't count. So I am glad to have the privilege to be here.

When Brother Morris first wrote me, I had an engagement at Los Angeles for about a month or 45 days, but when I got that call I cancelled that meeting and decided I would go to Los Angeles at some future time, that this was more important. Some of you might differ with me leaving off a religious work, godly work, to come and lecture on an occasion of this kind for a material matter. I don't see it that way. I see that I came that I might help in a great cause that the Negro preacher would be better qualified to go to Los Angeles. They have done a fine job, but there is something needed that all of them do not have and this meeting is for the purpose of giving to us just what we need to meet these intellectual giants that strut up and down the country and challenge the church of Christ. You are responsible for it. You can either prepare us or you can let them slaughter us. Take your choice. It's up to you. Or you can turn around by silence and indifference help them to slaughter us. You can—you know how to do that.

Now then, Dr. Young[3] not only is a doctor, he is a great doctor; has a great record and has made a great record in Dallas—not only in Dallas—throughout the United States of America Dr. Young is known. But he has time to be an elder, church of Christ. He has time to take off from his work that he is needed to do and help to foster a cause or to lead us in a cause that will develop a race that is badly in need of civilization. I expect if we had any way of checking on Dr. Young on his stay up here, materially speaking, thousands of dollars have been lost. That's the way you look at a man to find out whether he means it or not. Thank God for him. He has been an inspiration to me. The church where he is an elder has helped our school for six or seven years, and six hundred dollars a year. The Board of Trustees of the Southern Bible Institute[4] has established the policy of soliciting funds from individuals only, not from church treasuries. Gentlemen, let's not get excited, brethren and sister, about helping the school. All these missionaries you heard talked about that's over yonder doing a great work, we are all praying for them. You hear Brother Morris and you hear Brother Pullias[5] and you hear Brother Tiner[6] and you'll hear Brother Hardeman[7] tell you they are students of ours. Aren't we proud of them? I know you are. These presidents have a right to say they are their students. They have sat at the feet of the faculties where they are presidents. They have a right to claim them. And the church has a right to claim the whole thing. You know, I would like to have a few amens. Little as you think of it we are retarding the progress of the church trying to be quiet, trying to be up to date and modern and the preacher don't know when he has said anything that suits anybody. We are afraid we will go sectarian that it's just as bad to pull off a bridge as to back off. After you get through, you're off. It's a great pleasure to see these great men like Brother Morris, Brother Young and the whole faculty of this school behind this movement. David Lipscomb College's being behind the Nashville Christian Institute is the reason we have made the progress we have. When we run out of a teacher or need one we know where to borrow one. He will be there in about half an hour and take the class in charge, and competent and prepared to do it. Abilene Christian College is right behind this movement, a greater thing they have never undertaken in their life. And it is a great thing, and one thing I am proud of that the president and the college, all the members of the faculty I don't believe are ashamed of it. I really believe the whole thing is a hundred per cent behind Brother Morris. I do, I do. And God is leading us.

I tell you what happened to me. I was holding a meeting once at a place and there was a colored man that happened to have finished college, had some advantage of me intellectually, and he knew that he had it because you could tell from our discussion in the language that I was using that I was short, and the verbs that I was splitting and the adjectives that I was bursting. He could tell that I was unprepared intellectually to stand before him and he attempted to take advantage of me. And here's what he said. When I quoted Acts 2:38, he got up right in the audience and asked me, "What is the Greek on that?" He knew that I knew nothing about Greek. What's the Greek on that? I stood there puzzled, didn't know what to say about it, and didn't want the cause of Christ to suffer, but he had me. This thought came to me, and I was proud of it. I said everybody in this audience that knows Greek lift their hands. I looked around and I saw nobody's hand up. I turned around to this great preacher and I said, "What's the need of discussing Greek? Nobody out there knows it," and I got away with him and felt sorry for him.[8] But this institution that Brother Young is the chairman of the Board of Directors, [and they] are trying to prepare young men that can meet that problem. After a while you'll ask for that in your audience and about half your audience raises their hand and you're in it. But I got by with that. I am a little afraid that the young men coming on behind me will not be able to make it that way, so it is up to you and it's up to our colored brethren that are doing everything they can; it will be very feeble, but they will do the best they can. The colored man can pay for anything if you put it on a small enough basis. Make the installment payment small enough and we'll buy this whole city of Abilene.

I don't want to forget one young man who deserves a lot of praise and a lot of credit in this institution goes up or down. Brother Kirkpatrick[9] deserves a lot of praise. He was chosen by the Board to travel around and inform the churches and the brethren and I know he has a hard job. I know he met some that didn't want his message and he met some that accepted him warmly. I meet them, but I never get offended. I go back again; if you don't mind on a second trip, I am accepted. Don't ever be disheartened. Just continue to trust God in a problem of this kind. Brother Young said that at first he was opposed, he was opposed to this. Why, that's natural. He had his privilege to be so. And many of you may be opposed to it now. That's the reason this meeting is here, to knock the opposition out of you! If we can introduce enough facts or enough things for you to think on, by this time next year you may be with Dr. Young, or opponent no longer. There was a time that the white brethren over this country opposed holding meetings for the colored people because they feared they were too spasmodic. I have had white brethren to tell me that we ought to have done this 20 years ago, Keeble, but we thought your people were excitable and spasmodic and this would not appeal to them. Thus, we didn't offer it to them. But when they called me, or called for another colored preacher and the colored man responded they forgot, they forgot if they ever did know, that the gospel can take the dance out of a man, stop him from dancing, pull him out from under a mourner's bench and set him up on a seat. That's all they need. But look how long the colored man suffered with a misunderstanding and a misconception of the white man.

The same is true today. Somebody said the southern problem and the northern problem. When you meet my brethren in Christ in the north, in the south, in the east, in the west there is no problem. My brethren in Christ today, white, are looking out every way possible to bring the Negro to Christ, north, south, west and east. I see no problem. Only thing I see is the world. And if the young man needs preparing to carry it, let's establish an institution where he can get the preparation, where he can be prepared, where he can be able to meet these intellectual giants that come out of these sectarian colleges. I don't have nothing to boast about, but I'm just bragging a little. Now then, somebody is worried about whether a mixed faculty will work. That has come up and naturally it would come up; some white people on the faculty and some colored, will that work? Gentlemen, if its work in a sectarian school, it ought to work in a school where everybody is a Christian. It works in sectarian schools. Fisk University, a congregational school, had a white president and a white people on the faculty for the last 75 years and we have more spirit of Christ than they had, I think. Don't get excited, it's God working trying to lift the people that have been possibly misled. And now your hearts are running out for them. The very spirit of Christ is in your heart or you wouldn't be interested in us. It's the interest of the church of Christ that has missionaries in Africa; it's the interest of the church of Christ in America that sent Brother McMillan[10] and all the missionaries to Japan after they had stabbed us in the back. That's fine. That's the spirit of Christ. I believe these missionaries have forgotten the attack at Pearl Harbor. The gospel of Christ will knock out of us all the prejudice and malice we have against any man. It will knock it out. And when it hasn't done so, we haven't absorbed enough of the spirit of Christ. Gentlemen, I must appeal to you. This has been my experience for the last 50 years, working with both races, and the colored people are anxious to be led.

I was holding a meeting at Hopkinsville, Kentucky, and the white preacher met me when I came down on the Pan American—a lot of colored people standing on the platform. When this white man grabbed both of my grips and put them in the car and me following along behind him, it excited the Negro in Hopkinsville and he couldn't understand that. This white brother was trying to make me welcome and show me that they were behind me a hundred percent, that was all, get me ready for the messages I had planned to deliver; letting me know that I had friends in Hopkinsville. That was what he was trying to do. Made a good job of it. Carried me on to where they had selected for me to stay, told the lady here's the man. He tried to tell her what kind of a character I was and not to be any ways uneasy; he'll act right. So many of us don't. I ate at that home and then I said to this preacher, "I would like to go over there where you are putting up the tent at." He said, "Well, come on." I got over there and about 20 white brethren were putting up the tent, driving stobs, wet with perspiration in August; not a colored man on the ground. Well the colored people were interested. They walked over there and they said, "What is this?" They said, "It is going to be a meeting." "Well, who's gonna do the preaching?" He said a colored man. "Well, how come you all are putting it up?" He didn't understand it; the white brethren understood it. And then a white man walked up to me and he said this to me. I thought he was a brother of the church of Christ when I first met him, but he asked me this question: "You gonna do this preaching here?" I said, "Yes sir." He said, "Well, there's no need of you preaching to your people. Why you're not a nation. The gospel is not for you all, it's the nations, and you're not a nation." He said something there. I don't really know now what I am. There you are, I don't know. Really to tell you the truth I know I'm not an African. I know that. But what are you, Keeble? I'm a

The Importance of Trained Ministers

natural born American. I was born in America and I am proud of the fact because it is the greatest country in the world. It's the richest country I the world. We are lending money now to everybody. We are feeding the world, ain't that right? Sure! Amen. America, who wouldn't be proud of the fact that he's an American? Who wouldn't? A man that isn't proud that he's and American he needs to get off somewhere and be examined. Something is wrong with him, mentally, my friends. He said the gospel is to all nations and you all are not a nation. "Well," I said, "what are you gonna do about Mark? Mark said go preach the gospel to every creature. So if I happen not to be a nation, I'm creeping around her." And that man couldn't answer that question. He walked right on off and never said another word to me and left the ground. The white brethren said, "Keeble, we're glad you handled that that way. He has been here after us all day," after the white brethren all day trying to discourage them.

I want to tell the colored people that are present here today if you are saved in heaven and you happen to recognize Mark, when you get there, shake hands with him. Ain't that right? Why? He's the only one that included all. Thank God for Mark. If I ever meet him, I'll say, "Mark, you took care of all of me." Thank God. Matthew said "nations," Luke said "nations," Mark said "creatures." And we wouldn't know today that baptism saves us if Mark hadn't told us. Matthew didn't say that it saves, just told us what to baptize in, what name; Luke just tells us it starts at Jerusalem and he quits, but Mark says it's for "every creature." That includes the whole world anybody that is eligible to believe the gospel has got sense enough to understand it according to Mark; he's eligible. Gentlemen, I'm proud of Mark.

And we're going over now to the tenth chapter of the book of Acts and show you what misunderstanding does—misunderstanding. Peter was down at Joppa. He had the keys of the kingdom, but he misunderstood how to use them. He had let about 3,000 in on the day of Pentecost, he walked and talked with Jesus, he was on the mountain of transfiguration with him, he heard him say "go teach all nations," but yet Peter misunderstood that commission. He misunderstood it and when he get down to Joppa he refuses to go preach to the Gentiles whom the Jews looked upon as dogs. He said I'm not going. God carried him up on a housetop and performed a vision there, a miracle you might call it, or whatever you want to call it. A net was let down knit at the four corners containing all kind of fowls and four footed beasts of the earth and creeping things, rather, of the earth. And there was in that net, no doubt, a hog cause he is four footed. The [Seventh-Day] Adventists ought to read that and see that they can eat him now. God told Peter to slay and eat, and Peter stood up there on the housetop and told God he wasn't gonna eat it. When he got through with him, he was willing to eat everything in the net. Why did he eat it? He said what I've cleansed, I've cleansed, and don't you even call it common or unclean. That settled that. Peter didn't argue any more, came down off of the housetop and he finds six Jewish brethren that he brought there with him, they were down there waiting for him to come down. There were some other men there waiting for him to tell him they want him at Caesarea Philippi, at Cornelius' house, and they went up there.

Now I'm fixing to tell you something that ain't written now. Just what I'm fixing to say isn't written, but it is inferred. I'm reading now between the lines, I'm fixing to. Those six Jewish brethren went along with Peter, they didn't see the transaction on the housetop; they were not up there. Consequently, they don't know what happened. When Peter came down, no doubt they objected to going along with Peter. But Peter might have prevailed with them and got them to go on down there. It appears to me that there was a little discussion between them as they went on up there by the way the language reads. They trodded along, it is possible, that some of them said, Now Peter, I'll go along with you but I'm not going to have a thing to do with them, they're not in it no how. Now Peter said, come on, something might happen to change your mind.[11]

That ain't written, now don't you all go home and look for that. That ain't in there nowhere. That's what the Baptists ought to do when they're calling for mourners. They ought to say come on to the mourner's bench, but it ain't in the Bible nowhere, come on. Then the man would know whether to go or not. The same way the Methodist when he's fixing to sprinkle. Tell the man to let you sprinkle some water on his head but it ain't in the Bible, and then he would know whether to be silly enough to sit there. Now somebody says, Brother Keeble, that's the only objection we have had of you for years, you call names. But Jesus calls them, he calls them, and I don't think a better preacher lived. I don't think so. He called them, he called them. And when you find preachers dodging these names, it's a little dangerous; it's a little dangerous to dodge these names. Now the only way I would suggest that you call a name or you fight another man's doctrine, always wrap your message up so he can receive it. I you were to go to a store tomorrow, say for instance to buy meat, or steak or something, and the man just handed it to you without wrapping it up, without wrapping it up, would you carry it dangling on out of the door? Wrap your messages up with love. Let the individual see that you're telling him because you love him and your messages will be well taken. I've never run a man off yet. If I did, he came back. You can tell them, you can tell them, but you must show to him that you are interested in his should and you're not doing it with malice neither with prejudice, nor hatred in your heart, and he will take anything you tell him. Why you can call a man a liar just straight out liar, if you know how to call him it! And if you don't know how to call him that, I would advise you not call him that. So, therefore, names don't hurt nothing; names help the gospel because the man knows you're not hinting at him.

You know, we have a lot of brethren today said now, when they stand in the pulpit and I have been sitting in the audience many times—I know what the preacher wanted to say, you could almost see him wanting to say it—almost. He said, you sectarians, there you are, there you are, and the denominational world—

The Importance of Trained Ministers

well that do sound good. But, brother, you don't get far. The man you're talking about doesn't consider himself what you called him. So you missed him completely. If you had said, Brother Baptist, and you could call him that without any violence to the Scripture, Ananias called Saul brother before he baptized him, so you don't hurt nothing—don't get excited, it won't hurt—that's the way you do it, and you call him that. Jesus walked up to the grave of Lazarus and he called him by his name. But why did he call him by his name? If he hadn't called him by his name everybody in the cemetery would have got up. He called him by his name and Lazaarus came out of the grave and Jesus told those that were standing by to just loose him; he didn't have the power to get up. You didn't have power to raise him, but you can loose him. Whatever you can do, God wants you to do it. And that you can't do, impossible, He'll do it for you. That's the reason I believe in telling a man who you are talking about.

I was preaching in Los Angeles, California, about 20 years ago. There was a young white man in the audience—I talked about every church I could think of. I called every name imaginable that entered my mind, but I hadn't missed this young man's church. Did you know he wouldn't sit down when I said be seated? He remained standing. He was about six feet, weighting over 200 pounds, in the middle of the tent—he said, "What about my church?" There's a man mad because I missed his church. There you are. It doesn't hurt, brethren, to call names. I looked at him, I said, I didn't know a thing about the Latter Day Saints—he says "I'm a Latter Day Saint." I said, "What are you? Latter Day Saint?" I hadn't said nothing about them because I didn't know nothing about them. I didn't know enough about their doctrine for me to discuss that, so I was puzzled as to how to answer that and I asked him again, "What did you say?" I understood him at first. I'm thinking now while he is giving me his next answer, I had the answer for him, or rather his next question, I had my answer ready. I said, "You say Latter Day Saint?" He said, "Yes, Sir." I said, "You're too late." You're too late—too late! And when I told him that he sat right down. Did you know that that answer satisfied him? And the next night when the invitation was extended he came walking down the aisle and was baptized at the Central Church of Christ in Los Angeles. He was baptized that night; I went right on over, I wanted to see him baptized. And when he came out of the water and got dressed, I met him and shook his hand and congratulated him for not being ashamed of the gospel, and he said, "Brother Keeble, I don't stay in nothing late"—nothing too late—nothing too late! Gentlemen, it's wise to give these people an answer, if you got it, of some nature. It'll help a man; help him to see the light of the gospel of Christ if you call his name. That young man never would have obeyed the gospel had he not stood up and told me what he was. It doesn't hurt, it doesn't hurt, it doesn't hurt.

Now, I know this; Dr. Young is about all I know here that'll bear me witness on this. Somebody else might do it, but Dr. Young knows that many cases

that he had had needed to be operated on, but he doesn't advise an operation right suddenly. He advised first precaution, see if we can scatter that, see if we move it through some other process. I hate to cut. No preacher here likes to stand up and cut on people; if he can preach the gospel and scatter it, why he'd like to do it, and if not take the Sword of the Spirit and cut it out, perform the operation. And that's what men and women ought to be willing to be cut on, with the word of God, until they are stripped of everything that might prevent them from entering the eternal city. And then again, Cornelius' case. When Peter preached to Cornelius and the Holy Sprit came down upon these Gentiles for the first time, Peter turned around and says this: "Who can forbid water? Don't that sound like they had had an argument? Don't that sound like an argument happened there? Can you all forbid water? You fussed about coming up here to preach to these Gentiles. You argued with me all the way up here. Now can you forbid water? Don't you see the Holy Ghost coming on them like it did us Jews down at Jerusalem? Can you kick on it now? It looks like, brethren, that's between the lines. Is that right? Something must have come up or he wouldn't have used that language. And then Peter said, now, now, we know that God is no respecter of persons, but in every nation he that feareth God and worketh righteousness is acceptable with him.

I'm closing with this. A few days ago in our chapel one of our students sent up there by the Rossville church of Christ—paid his tuition—might be some members of that church here, but they'll be glad for me to tell this, a fine example for other churches that want to help the unfortunate boy. This boy was sent up there and they paid his tuition for four or five years—$270 a year—furnished him clothes, that white church done that. I've never been there, but, this boy stood in chapel the other day and preached the gospel and 22 students came stepping down the aisle and they were baptized for the remission of their sins. That's a nice point there for Christian education. That's a nice place to tell you that you needn't to get scared of helping the school. I got something, ain't I, brethren? Now then, if that ain't missionary work, if that wasn't missionary work, after dismissal some of you all tell me what that was. And that isn't the first time. I've preached there one time at the school when I was in, and 22 came forward and five of them were teachers. Now, somebody said, "Oh, oh, had teachers not members of the church!" Brother McMillan is going to experience this. He is going to find that the colored man that's qualified won't want to teach for the salary that the Board authorized pay. You'll run into that, Brother McMillan. We ran into it. Our colored brethren and sisters said no. I can get so-and-so; I'm not going to teach for that small amount, and that forced us out there to get a Baptist, and to get a Methodist and finally got a Catholic as principal of the school. Now there all of you look at me excitable. I told this at Dallas. Brother J. W. Dunn[12] was sitting in the audience, and when I said these teachers were not members of the church of Christ he turned right red, right red, he didn't like it, he didn't like it, and he didn't like it. But when I said I baptized all of them, Catholic

The Importance of Trained Ministers

and all, the whole thing have been baptized, Brother Dunn said, "Hire some more of them!" Don't get excited. You preach the gospel, you can handle that fellow, hear the gospel every day. Ain't nobody can stand it every day, every day, every day, every day! There ain't nobody. He'll either have to quit or obey it. Now then, they were baptized. The principal was a Catholic at that time. And I wish to say to you, my friends, that the gospel has power.

Brother J. W. Brents,[13] one of the best Bible teachers we have in the brotherhood, has been on our faculty now for about six or seven years, on our faculty. He says it is the greatest work he has ever done in his life, and there isn't a greater missionary in our brotherhood than J. W. Brents. He hasn't done anything but missionary work since he has been in the ministry. But he says, this is his greatest work. That man ought to know what he is talking about with the experience he has had. And you brethren ought to take his word for it and not question him. That's the trouble with the church of Christ now; we try to question one another. You know, my friends, and not only that, a lot of these students that obeyed the gospel were girls that sit at the feet of Sister A. R. Holton[14] every day. When these girls heard this boy preach why they were ready for the gospel of the godly woman that teaches them in the classroom every day. So that little boy didn't have much to go to get them to come out. They were already softened. My friends, you have to learn. And I don't think there's a greater Bible teacher, now I don't mean no harm, Brother Morris, I don't mean a bit of harm, but I don't think you've got a better teacher than Sister Holton. You've got good teachers all right. Now, I don't mean a bit of harm by that. Ain't nobody a better friend to me than Brother Morris, but I've got to let him know what we have in our school on our faculty is equal to anybody in the brotherhood. Now you all don't know this. Sister Holton and Brother Holton and Brother S. H. Hall[15] and Brother Goodpasture[16] who teaches quite often in our school and comes out, and I'll tell you another thing about Brother Goodpasture, he preaches better for us than he does at his own church. Yes, sir. I'll tell you what Brother Goodpasture said one day. He preached for us one day and the students looked like they were taking his messages so good and taking it down, and when he did stop, he said, "This is closer to heaven than I've been in my life." Brother he wasn't joking, the tears were in his eyes, and it was the way we received his message. Not a greater man among us that B. C. Goodpasture, but he hadn't had nobody to stimulate him that way. You know Babe Ruth. Babe Ruth used to knock home runs. Why he had a right to knock them. He wasn't that much better than any of the rest, but the rest of them were not able to get their fans to back them up like Babe Ruth. When he started after the bat they commenced yelling. Who couldn't knock a home run? If you all were to yell right now I could knock one. Just ain't nobody to do it.

I am in sympathy for the gospel preacher in the church of Christ. Why? He stand up to preach in a Frigidaire. The congregation sits out there and try to free[ze] him. Some good pious brother just looks like a cake of ice looking at him. When I find one trying to freeze me I don't look at him no more. I want to say a word to the young gospel preacher. Don't get discouraged when they try to freeze you, cause they know a little more than you do and you're just making your first effort of all and they'll try to freeze you. But don't get excited, you'll make it. I want to tell you what to do. When you see one trying to freeze you, you do like you do with your modern Frigidaire, turn on your defroster. That's right. That's right. I've got a defroster on you all this evening; that's the reason you're smiling and encouraging me. You started in here freezing, but I have you defrosted.

I hope and pray that the day will come when we all can see this school headed by Brother McMillan and also endorsed by Dr. Young as the chairman of the Board of Directors, one of the greatest colleges in the world, educating boys and girls of the Negro race and preparing them to get out and meet anybody that rises up against the church of Christ. And these men will rejoice and when they are in their graves, beneath the sod, they will live in the hearts of these young men that go out and preach the gospel to a lost and dying world. Brother Morris and the faculty of this school will live on into the hearts of these boys and girls when they go out into the fields in foreign lands, they will live on and on in the hearts of these boys long after they have deceased.

I now conclude with this thought. May the grace of God dwell in your heart and may the grace of God cause you to look upon no race as being inferior, but let's make him what he ought to be and lift him on a higher plane that Jesus can bless you and give you a crown that fadeth not away.

A Prepared Ministry [1952][17]

After preaching the gospel for over fifty-five years I am able, I think, to tell you tonight some problems that I have met that prove to be handicaps to me.

The first thing I discovered in my early ministry was that my schooling was very limited, but I was able to read books of sermons written by our educated brethren,[18] who write to these papers and they will never know what they have meant to me in preparing me to meet these intellectual giants who defy the church of Christ, and overthrow the faith of many of us.

I am still reading articles in these papers written by brethren, who graduate at our great colleges, and these articles have prepared me and enabled me to meet educated men, whom I have debated with and the people thought I defeated them. I was debating, but I want you brethren who are educated to know that it was you that won the debate, and I am proud of the colleges that prepared you, so I could read your articles in our papers, and read your books of sermons.

You brethren who head these great schools will never know what a blessing you are to the church. I have flown here from West Palm Beach, Florida, to say a few words concerning what you have meant to me for nearly sixty years, and I want you to know that you are proving to the world that the church of Christ is as well prepared educationally as they are. And I thank God daily for these great Christian Colleges and high schools. I love to meet these godly men and women who have sat at the feet of these great Christian College professors.

I feel proud and happy every time I walk on the campus of these schools and colleges, because they are blessings to the New Testament Church. I am told great scholars translated the Bible and gave it to us in the English language, so the whole world is blessed by these learned men.

Sometimes we buy peanuts and we are asked, "Do you want them shelled?" And we say, "Yes," because we are too lazy to shell them. So years ago these great scholars shelled the Word of God for the world, and we who are not scholars are not jealous of those who shelled the Bible for the world. And now we have it in our own language. What could I do if it wasn't shelled, or translated? Oh! How thankful we all are to the scholars.

I find that the most of our highly educated brethren are very meek and humble. Brother G. P. Bowser worked for over forty years trying to build a school for the colored boys and girls. He sowed the seed in our hearts, and as a result we have the Nashville Christian Institute, and Southwestern College, whose president is on this rostrum with us tonight. So we see that Brother Bowser's efforts were not a failure. For years he was the best educated man among us; and we thank God today for G. P. Bowser.

S. W. Womack worked with Brother Bowser because they discovered we needed prepared men for the ministry of God's Word. So we will always be indebted to these great, godly men.

To prove to you all that we need prepared men among us, to meet our enemies here is what happened about thirty-five years ago in a meeting I was conducting at Martin, Tennessee.[19]

A Methodist preacher who was highly educated asked me what the Greek on Acts 2:38. He knew I didn't know any Greek. So I had to get around him by asking the crowd a question. I asked them if there was anyone in the crowd that knew Greek, and I found that there was no one who knew Greek. And then I turned to the Methodist preacher and stated, "What is the need of discussing Greek, when no one in the crowd understands Greek?" That was all I could do to meet his effort to overthrow the truth, and mislead someone. As a result I baptized some of the leading colored people.

Brethren, you can see that the colored brethren need schools that can prepare them for the ministry of God's word, and lift up the church of Christ.

The theme for the lectureship is "The New Testament Church." The New Testament church among the colored brotherhood is begging for more encouragement and assistance to our schools that are struggling for existence, so we can prepare our ministry to meet any attack that our educated enemies might make upon the New Testament church.

Since I have been traveling with our boy preachers, many brethren are being convinced that Christian education is the great need of the New Testament church.

Our Board of Directors is asking the brethren and sisters all over the brotherhood to send donations to the Nashville Christian Institute on my birthday, December 7, 1952. This will be for the school. I will be 74, and have preached the gospel 55 years, thank God. Brethren don't forget us in your prayers, because we mean to spread the New Testament church among the fifteen million Negroes living in America.

Humility [1953][20]

Our Savior was born in humble surroundings, among the cattle, but he was the Savior of the world, and now the world must hear Him and obey Him, who once lay in a stable.

The Bible teaches us to humble ourselves under the mighty hand of God, and He will exalt us. I hope the day will come when we can possess the spirit of humility that every child of God must have in order to be successful worker in the kingdom of our God.

Meekness and humility are the elements we need to fertilize our hearts, so the Word of God can grow in our hearts and bring forth fruit to the glory and honor of our Lord.

Moses, who was reared in the king's palace, humbled himself. And desiring to please God, rather than to enjoy the pleasures of sin for a season, by being humble, he was permitted to lead the Children of Israel out of Egyptian bondage. And as long as he remained humble he was successful, and blessed. And as long as he was humble and meek, God was pleased and blessed all of his work. But when he became exalted, he trusted in himself and struck the rock. This was because he lost control of himself and lost that meek and humble spirit. And for this cause he missed the Promised Land.

Many preachers are failing today, and hindering the Cause of Christ because they don't have the spirit of humility and meekness.

Our Lord remained meek and humble until He finished His work on earth. And we must remain meek and humble until we complete our labors on earth. We should hunger and thirst after the spirit of humility, so we will be a living example to the world, and be able to lead many to Christ, and God's kingdom will spread and Jesus be lifted up until God be all praise, honor, and glory!

The Life of the Preacher [1955][21]

I am afraid that too many of us are too careless about living what we preach, and we don't realize that most of the troubles we are having in the Churches today are caused by talking too much about your fellow preacher and this is caused by hatred. So many times we go into places to preach and are asked about the preacher who used to labor at a certain place, and we start off telling everything hurtful that we can think of just to destroy him, and if we know anything good about him we are careful to not mention it. All of this is with an idea of building up ourselves by destroying others. What a pity. We should remember to do unto others as we would have them do unto us, because all of us want nice things said about us.

I appreciate this opportunity of calling my preaching brethren's attention to this terrible habit, and I hope my advice will cause us who are guilty of this habit to stop it. From now on look for things complimentary to say, not about preachers only, but everybody. You form the attitude of knocking everybody, and preachers should be the last to form this un-Christlike disposition.

Brethren, let us remember that if we bite and devour one another, we will be consumed by one another. So many of us are hindering the cause we love best, because everyone looks for preachers to be living examples. The Apostle Paul lived what he taught so much he invited the Church to follow him because he was a follower of Christ, great example. It was Christ who said, "by this shall all men know that you are my disciples of you have love for one another." And we should all remember that love will hide a multitude of sins. It was God who gave His Son for a sinful world, because His love hid a multitude of sins.

Oh! If we had more of the love of God in our hearts, we would not destroy our brother for whom Christ died. Always look for that which is good and not bad, and to do this we must have pure hearts, because Christ taught "Blessed are the pure in heart," and "rejoice when we are falsely accused," and "rejoice and be exceeding glad." Watch and Pray!

Notes

Introduction

"The Magic Negro" in Churches of Christ, 1914–1968

1. Christopher John Farley, "That Old Black Magic," *Time,* Nov. 27, 2000, 14. Other examples of the presence of the "Magic Negro" in contemporary movies can be seen in the 1990 movie *Ghost,* in which Oda May Brown (played by Whoopi Goldberg), a black spiritualist, helps Sam Wheat (Patrick Swayze) protect his girlfriend Molly Jensen (Demi Moore) from the evil scheme of Carl Bruner (Tony Goldwyn). The 1999 movie *The Green Mile,* based on a Stephen King novel, cast John Coffey (Michael Clarke Duncan) as a man with supernatural powers of clairvoyance and healing. Coffey heals Paul Edgecomb (Tom Hanks) of his severe bladder infection and exorcizes brain cancer from the warden's wife, yet the Magical African American Friend displays childlike qualities. In the 2000 movie *Remember the Titans,* the MAAF is Coach Herman Boone (Denzel Washington), who befriended the Bigot with a Heart of Gold (BHG), Coach Bill Yoast (Will Patton).

Additionally, in the 2003 comedy *Bruce Almighty,* God (Morgan Freeman) humbles himself as a janitor, displays his divine powers, and teaches egotistical Bruce Nolan (Jim Carrey) a lesson in humility. For further scholarly discussion of the Magic Negro in contemporary movies, see Rita Kempley, "Movies' 'Magic Negro' Saves the Day—But at the Cost of His Soul," *Issue* 49, available at www.blackcommentator.com (accessed Mar. 1, 2007); Gayle R. Baldwin, "What a Difference a Gay Makes: Queering the Magic Negro," *Journal of Religion and Popular Culture* 5 (Fall 2003):1–18; and Heather J. Hicks, "Hoodoo Economics: White Men's Work and Black Men's Magic in Contemporary American Film," *Camera Obscura* 18 (2003):27–55.

For examples of Hollywood executives giving black actors saintly roles, suggesting that "the black man is too good to be true," see K. Anthony Appiah, "'No Bad Nigger': Blacks as the Ethical Principle in the Movie," in *Media Spectacles,* ed. Majorie Garber, Jann Matlock, and Rebecca L. Walkowitz (New York: Routledge, 1993),

77–90. Special thanks to Tobin Shearer, a friend and scholar at Northwestern University, for introducing me to the "magic Negro" concept.
2. J. W. Brents, "Sowing and Reaping," *Gospel Advocate* 73 (Oct. 15, 1931):1300.
3. E. N. Glenn, "Keeble in California," *Christian Leader* 47 (May 16, 1933):7.
4. Ruth Hailey, telephone interview with author, Jan. 24, 2007. Hailey, who heard the black evangelist preach in West Tennessee, never forgot an expression of Marshall Keeble, who while preaching turned to his song leader, Fred Lee, and said, "Now ain't that right, Lee?" Lee would respond, "That's right Marshall, preach on."
5. Louis R. Harlan, *Booker T. Washington: The Wizard of Tuskegee, 1901–1915* (New York: Oxford Univ. Press, 1983).
6. Floyd H. Horton, "Praises Keeble's Work," *Gospel Advocate* 80 (Nov. 10, 1938):1068. Annie C. Tuggle, *Another World Wonder* (n.p., n.d.), 61, made a similar observation: "Under such pressure as this, Bro. Keeble was as brave as a lion and as humble as a lamb. They were not able to resist the wisdom and the spirit by which he spake."
7. John Dollard, *Caste and Class in a Southern Town* (Garden City, N.Y.: Doubleday, 1949), 173, 257.
8. S. H. Hall, "The West End Church of Christ and the Keeble Revival, Atlanta, Georgia," *Gospel Advocate* 73 (Oct. 8, 1931):1250
9. O. C. Lambert, "From the Wide Harvest Field," *Firm Foundation* 52 (July 2, 1935):6.
10. Marshall Keeble, "From the Wide Harvest Field," *Firm Foundation* 52 (Sept. 10, 1935):6.
11. Marshall Keeble, "From the Wide Harvest Field," *Firm Foundation* 52 (Oct. 1, 1935):6.
12. Willie T. Cato, *His Hand and His Heart: The Wit and Wisdom of Marshall Keeble* (Winona, Miss.: J. C. Choate, 1990), 14.
13. Glenn, "Keeble in California," 7.
14. S. H. Hall, "The Death of Sister Keeble," *Gospel Advocate* 75 (May 4, 1933):429.
15. Marshall Keeble, "News and Notes," *Gospel Advocate* 75 (Feb. 2, 1933):119.
16. J. E. Choate, *Roll Jordan Roll: Biography of Marshall Keeble* (Nashville: Gospel Advocate, 1974), 70–73.
17. Glenn, "Keeble in California," 7.
18. Marshall Keeble, "Keeble to be Here," *Gospel Advocate* 83 (Dec. 25, 1941):1242.
19. For the potent impact that both Womack and Campbell had on Keeble, see Edward J. Robinson, "'The Two Old Heroes': Samuel W. Womack, Alexander Campbell, and the Origins of Black Churches of Christ in the United States," *Discipliana* 65 (Spring 2005):3–20.
20. Glenn, "Keeble in California," 7.
21. A. M. Burton, "The Jackson Street Meeting," *Gospel Advocate* 56 (May 21, 1914):556.
22. Marshall Keeble, "Among the Colored Folks," *Gospel Advocate* 62 (May 27, 1920):532.
23. Glenn, "Keeble in California," 7.
24. Ibid.
25. Ibid.

26. Marshall Keeble, "Sowing and Reaping," *Gospel Advocate* 76 (May 17, 1934):482. See also Marshall Keeble, "Sowing and Reaping," *Gospel Advocate* 76 (May 31, 1934):529.
27. Wilbur J. Cash, *The Mind of the South* (New York: Alfred Knopf, 1941).
28. The following books are exemplary of the useful and insightful works on Marshall Keeble's remarkable life: B. C. Goodpasture, *Biography and Sermons of Marshall Keeble, Evangelist* (1931; reprint, Nashville: Gospel Advocate, 1966); Arthur Lee Smith Jr., "A Rhetorical Analysis of the Speaking of Marshall Keeble" (masters thesis, Pepperdine Univ., 1965); Forrest Neil Rhoads, "A Study of the Sources of Marshall Keeble's Effectiveness as a Preacher" (Ph.D. diss., Southern Illinois Univ., 1970); Choate, *Roll Jordan Roll;* Cato, *His Hand and His Heart;* Tracy L. Blair, "For a Better Tomorrow: Marshall Keeble and George Philip Bowser, African-American Ministers" (master's thesis, Middle Tennessee State Univ., 1996); and Darrell Broking, "Marshall Keeble and the Implementation of a Grand Strategy: Erasing the Color Line in the Church of Christ" (master's thesis, East Tennessee State Univ., 2003).

    The term "Jim Crow" originated in 1832, when a popular white entertainer, Thomas "Daddy" Rice, observed an African American street performer sing and dance in Baltimore, Maryland. The black man's song went:

    > Wheel about, turn about,
    > Do it jus' so,
    > An' every time I wheel about
    > I jump Jim Crow.

    Rice became so enamored with the black man's performance that he added it to his own act. Whites initially applied the term "Jim Crow" jokingly to all African Americans, but by the end of the nineteenth century it was used to refer to the laws passed in the South to segregate black people in transportation, housing, and other aspects of daily life. See Sharon Harley, Stephen Middleton, and Charlotte M. Stokes, eds., *The African American Experience: A History* (Englewood Cliffs, N.J.: Globe Book, 1992), 212–13; and Leon Litwack, *Trouble in Mind: Black Southerners in the Age of Jim Crow* (New York: Vintage Books, 1998).
29. Cato, *His Hand and His Heart,* 18. What was true for Keeble was equally true for other black evangelists in Churches of Christ. Samuel Robert Cassius (1853–1931), a predecessor of Keeble, observed in 1922, "I have had to win my way through religious prejudice in my own race, and race prejudice among the brethren of my own faith." Cassius, "My Trip to the East," *Christian Leader* 36 (June 20, 1922):12. See also Edward J. Robinson, *To Save My Race from Abuse: The Life of Samuel Robert Cassius* (Tuscaloosa: Univ. of Alabama Press, 2007), 164.
30. For books that illuminate Keeble's childhood and adolescent worlds, see Nell Irvin Painter, *Exodusters: Black Migration to Kansas after Reconstruction* (New York: Alfred A. Knopf, 1977); Howard N. Rabinowitz, *Race Relations in the Urban South, 1865–1890* (New York: Oxford Univ. Press, 1978); Leon F. Litwack, *Been in the Storm So Long: The Aftermath of Slavery* (New York: Harper and Row, 1988); and Faye Wellborn Robbins, "A World within a World: Black Nashville, 1880–1915" (Ph.D. diss., Univ. of Arkansas, 1980). For an informative treatment of the Freedmen's

Savings Bank, see Barbara P. Josiah, "Providing for the Future: The World of the African American Depositors of Washington, DC's Freedmen's Savings Bank, 1865–1874," *Journal of African American History* 89 (Winter 2004):1–16.

31. Over an eighteen-month period, the Jubilee Singers raised forty thousand dollars for the construction of Jubilee Hall. See Andrew Ward, *Dark Midnight When I Rise: The Story of the Jubilee Singers, Who Introduced the World to the Music of Black America* (New York: Farrar, Straus, and Giroux, 2000).

32. C. Vann Woodward, *Origins of the New South, 1877–1913* (1951; reprint, Baton Rouge: Louisiana State Univ. Press, 1997), 211–12; Rayford W. Logan, *The Betrayal of the Negro from Rutherford B. Hayes to Woodrow Wilson* (1954; reprint, New York: Da Capo Press, 1997); C. Vann Woodward, *The Strange Career of Jim Crow* (New York: Oxford Univ. Press, 1966); Howard N. Rabinowitz, *The First New South, 1865–1920* (Arlington Heights, Ill.: Harlan Davidson, 1992), 140–41.

33. John Hope Franklin and Alfred A. Moss Jr., *From Slavery to Freedom: A History of African Americans* (1947; reprint, Boston: McGraw, 2000), 385; David Chalmers, *Hooded Americanism: The First Century of the Ku Klux Klan* (New York: Doubleday, 1965); Raymond Allen Cook, *Fire from the Flint: The Amazing Careers of Thomas Dixon* (Winston-Salem, N.C.: John F. Blair, 1968); Kathleen M. Blee, *Women of the Klan: Racism and Gender in the 1920s* (Berkeley and Los Angeles: Univ. of California Press, 1991); Nancy Maclean, *Behind the Mask of Chivalry: The Making of the Second Ku Klux Klan* (New York: Oxford Univ. Press, 1994). Race riots were not confined to the South, however. See Philip Dray, *At the Hands of Persons Unknown: The Lynching of Black America* (New York: Modern Library, 2002), 254–56.

34. Marshall Keeble, "Four Years of Evangelistic Work," *Gospel Advocate* 61 (Jan. 9, 1919):41; Robbins, "World within a World," 287; Choate, *Roll Jordan Roll,* 21; Louis R. Harlan, "The Secret Life of Booker T. Washington," *Journal of Southern History* 37 (Aug. 1971):393–416; Louis R. Harlan, *Booker T. Washington: The Making of a Black Leader, 1856–1901* (New York: Oxford Univ. Press, 1972); Harlan, *Booker T. Washington: The Wizard of Tuskegee;* and Don Haymes, "Marshall Keeble," in *Encyclopedia of the Stone-Campbell Movement,* ed. Doug Foster, Paul M. Blowers, Anthony L. Dunnavant, and D. Newell Williams (Grand Rapids, Mich.: Eerdmans, 2004) (hereafter cited as *Encyclopedia of the Stone-Campbell Movement*), 441–42.

35. Marshall Keeble, "From the Brethren," *Gospel Advocate* 67 (Apr. 9, 1925):354. See also Michael O. Emerson and Christian Smith, *Divided by Faith: Evangelical Religion and the Problem of Race in America* (New York: Oxford Univ. Press, 2001), 132. When R. N. Hogan (1902–1997), a Keeble contemporary and an influential black preacher in Churches of Christ, was asked whether he thought A. M. Burton was a racist, he answered, "Yes I do. Because if he was not he would not have given me a room in the basement." See Calvin H. Bowers, *Realizing the California Dream: The Story of Black Churches of Christ in Los Angeles* (n.p.: Calvin H. Bowers, 2001), 277.

36. Blaine A. Brownell, "Birmingham, Alabama: New South City in the 1920s," *Journal of Southern History* 38 (Feb. 1972):21–48; Dan T. Carter, *Scottsboro: A Tragedy of the American South* (Baton Rouge: Louisiana State Univ. Press, 1969); and Clarence

Norris and Sybil D. Washington, *The Last of the Scottsboro Boys: An Autobiography* (New York: G. P. Putnam's Sons, 1979).

37. Goodpasture, *Biography and Sermons,* 18; Marshall Keeble, "Jesus, Misunderstood," (Nashville: David Lipscomb College Annual Lectureship, 1948), 126. For a thorough treatment of black Americans' transition from the Republican party to the Democrat party in the 1930s, see Nancy Weiss, *Farewell to the Party of Lincoln: Black Politics in the Age of FDR* (Princeton, N.J.: Princeton Univ. Press, 1983).

38. Members of the "Black Cabinet" included Harold L. Ickes, a former president of the NAACP Chicago branch, Robert L. Vann, editor of the *Pittsburgh Courier,* and Mary McLeod Bethune, founder-president of Bethune-Cookman College. Franklin and Moss, *From Slavery to Freedom,* 429–31, assert, "Roosevelt's black advisers differed from their counterparts in previous administrations in that they were placed in positions of sufficient importance that both the government and the African American population generally regarded the appointment as significant. They were not people whose relationship with the government was nebulous and unofficial. They were oath-bound servants of the citizens of the United States, although they could not be described as policy makers."

39. Ibid., 507.

40. Numan V. Bartley, *The Rise of Massive Resistance: Race and Politics in the South during the 1950s* (Baton Rouge: Louisiana State Univ. Press, 1969); Nadine Cohodas, *Strom Thurmond and the Politics of Southern Change* (New York: Simon & Schuster, 1993); Steven F. Lawson, *Black Ballots: Voting Rights in the South, 1944–1969* (New York: Columbia Univ. Press, 1999); Taylor Branch, *Parting the Waters: America in the King Years* (New York: Simon & Schuster, 1988); Pete Daniel, *Lost Revolutions: The South in the 1950s* (Chapel Hill: Univ. of North Carolina Press, 2000).

41. Marshall Keeble, "The Church among the Colored," in *Abilene Christian College Bible Lectures* (Austin, Texas: Firm Foundation, 1950), 156.

42. Marshall Keeble, "Among the Colored Brethren," *Gospel Advocate* 93 (June 21, 1951):399.

43. Gary Holloway and John York, eds., *Unfinished Reconciliation: Justice, Racism, and Churches of Christ* (Abilene, Texas: Abilene Christian Univ. Press, 2003).

44. Peter J. Paris, *The Social Teaching of Black Churches* (Philadelphia: Fortress Press, 1985), 1, has noted that African American churches tend to fall in one of two categories: compensatory (which focus on the world beyond this world or the "otherworldly") or political (which focus on issues of social injustice). Because of Marshall Keeble's pervasive influence and the antipolitical theology that they imbibed from their white mentors, most African American Churches of Christ fell into the former category. For other important studies on this dichotomy, see Carter G. Woodson, *The History of the Negro Church* (1921; reprint, Washington, D.C.: Associated Publishers, 1985); E. Franklin Fraizer, *The Negro Church in America* (New York: Schocken Books, 1964); and C. Eric Lincoln and Lawrence H. Mamiya, *The Black Church in the African American Experience* (1990; reprint, Durham, N.C.: Duke Univ. Press, 1992).

45. Gene C. Finley, ed., *Our Garden of Song: A Book of Biography of Song Writers of the Church of Christ and Articles and Other Items of Interest of Our Worship in Song* (West Monroe, La.: Howard, 1980), 174–76.
46. In light of H. Richard Niebuhr's five typologies of Christian ethics, Keeble (at least publicly) assumed a "Christ against culture" posture. See Niebuhr, *Christ and Culture* (1951; reprint, San Francisco: HarperCollins Publishers, 2001), 45–82.
47. Cato, *His Hand and His Heart*, 18.

Chapter 1
The Sufficiency of the Church: Keeble in the 1910s

1. Tolbert Fanning, "The Lord's Treasury," *Gospel Advocate* 3 (Mar. 1857):69. See also Bill J. Humble, "The Missionary Society Controversy in the Restoration Movement (1823–1875)" (Ph.D. diss., Univ. of Iowa, 1964). Keeble's first known article to be published in the *Gospel Advocate* appeared under the heading "Meetings in Tennessee and Mississippi," *Gospel Advocate* 57 (Nov. 11, 1915):1150–51.
2. Marshall Keeble, "Among the Colored People," *Gospel Advocate* 58 (May 11, 1916):482–83.
3. "Campbellite" was a term of derision applied to Churches of Christ. The term reflected the theological influence of Alexander Campbell (1788–1866) on the worship practices and organizational structure of Churches of Christ.
4. This statement reveals that Marshall Keeble, like most black preachers in Churches of Christ in the early twentieth century, depended solely on the generosity of white Christians to evangelize African Americans.
5. Andrew Mizell Burton (1879–1966) was the most important white Christian philanthropist in the history of African American Churches of Christ. He funded all of Keeble's evangelistic tours in the United States and beyond.
6. G. Dallas Smith's Bible drill were Bible study lessons were published by the Gospel Advocate Company in Nashville, Tennessee, and designed to increase students' knowledge of the Bible.
7. Marshall Keeble, "Among the Colored People," *Gospel Advocate* 58 (June 22, 1916):638.
8. Probably the preacher or overseer for the fledgling black congregation in Mount Pleasant, Tennessee.
9. That Keeble's first wife, Minnie Womack, served as the song leader suggests that there were not enough men equipped to serve as worship leaders. In the same year, when an inquirer asked G. P. Bowser whether women could lead prayer in the worship service when men were present, the editor of the *Christian Echo* answered, "There is no Scripture forbidding her praying in public." G. P. Bowser, "Questions," *Christian Echo* (Oct. 1916):4.
10. Annie C. Tuggle (1890–1976) was a native of Tennessee who converted to Churches of Christ in 1908. Tuggle's autobiography appears in *Another World Wonder.*
11. Marshall Keeble, "Among the Colored People," *Gospel Advocate* 59 (Jan. 25, 1917):93.

12. Keeble realized the necessity of submitting monetary reports, not only to reveal his accomplishments but also, more important, to demonstrate credibility and integrity. Church historian Earl I. West has correctly noted that "not to give these [detail financial reports] would cast suspicion on their integrity and damage their support." See Earl I. West, *The Search for the Ancient Order* (3 vols.; Indianapolis: Religious Book Service, 1949–79), vol. 3:309.
13. Marshall Keeble, "Among the Colored Folks," *Gospel Advocate* 59 (Aug. 2, 1917):751.
14. The Highland Church of Christ in Louisville, Kentucky, was led by Elmer L. Jorgenson (1886–1968), a staunch supporter of domestic and foreign missions.
15. Marshall Keeble, "Among the Colored Folks," *Gospel Advocate* 60 (Aug. 29, 1918):835.
16. Nicolas Brodie Hardeman (1874–1965) was one of the most influential educators and evangelists in twentieth-century Churches of Christ. See David H. Warren, "Nicholas Brodie Hardeman," *Encyclopedia of the Stone Campbell Movement*, 380–81.
17. Marshall Keeble, "Four Years of Evangelistic Work," *Gospel Advocate* 61 (Jan. 9, 1919):41.
18. With these statements Keeble confirmed his opposition to missionary societies. Like Tolbert Fanning and other white leaders in Churches of Christ, Keeble believed that the church was the only authorized institution to engage in evangelism.
19. Marshall Keeble, "Among the Colored Folks," *Gospel Advocate* 61 (Mar. 13, 1919):261. The "two old heroes" in this article refer to Samuel W. Womack (1851–1920) and Alexander Campbell (1862–1930), cofounders of the Jackson Street Church of Christ in Nashville, Tennessee. See Robinson, "Two Old Heroes," 1–20.
20. A black evangelist who preached for Churches of Christ in Mississippi and Tennessee.
21. A white evangelist in Churches of Christ and editor of the *Christian Leader* for several years.
22. Marshall Keeble, "An Interesting Report," *Gospel Advocate* 61 (June 12, 1919):572–73.
23. Nathan and his wife Frances Cathey were grandparents of Richard N. Hogan (1902–1997), an influential black preacher in Churches of Christ. See R. N. Hogan, *Sermons by Hogan* (Austin, Texas: Firm Foundation, 1940), vii; Tuggle, *Another World Wonder*, 63–64.
24. A native of Hardeman County, Tennessee, D. J. Bynum preached in Mississippi and Tennessee before planting a black congregation in Detroit, Michigan, in the 1930s. Tuggle, *Our Ministers and Song Leaders of the Church of Christ* (Detroit: Annie C. Tuggle, 1945), 31; Tuggle, *Another World Wonder*, 64–65.
25. Tom H. Busby (1882–1970), a black preacher in Churches of Christ, was born and reared in the state of Arkansas. His preached for congregations in Tennessee, Alabama, Arkansas, Mississippi, Missouri, and Michigan. See Tuggle, *Our Ministers and Song Leaders*, 28; T. H. Busby, "Get Acquainted," *Christian Echo* 35 (Dec. 5, 1940):7; and R. N. Hogan, "Brother T. H. Busby Passes," *Christian Echo* 68 (Sept. 1970):1.
26. Alexander Bagby Lipscomb (1876–1940) was David Lipscomb's nephew and an editor for the *Christian Leader*.
27. Edwin Alexander Elam (1855–1929) was a preacher and writer for Churches of Christ in Tennessee.

28. J. C. McQuiddy (1858–1924) was a pacifist and publisher of the *Gospel Advocate*. See Richard T. Hughes, *Reviving the Ancient Faith: The Story of Churches of Christ in America* (Grand Rapids, Mich.: Eerdmans, 1996), 147–49.
29. David Lipscomb (1831–1917) was the most influential leader in Churches of Christ in the South immediately after the Civil War. Here Keeble acknowledged the indebtedness of both white and black Christians to Lipscomb's work. See Robert Hooper, *Crying in the Wilderness: A Biography of David Lipscomb* (Nashville: David Lipscomb College, 1979).
30. Marshall Keeble, "Among the Colored Folks," *Gospel Advocate* 60 (Feb. 14, 1918):162–63.
31. Minnie Keeble.
32. Robert Keeble.
33. "Digressivism" or "progressivism" referred to members of the Stone-Campbell movement (Disciples of Christ) who "digressed" from the "pure gospel" by worshiping with instruments of music and by evangelizing through missionary societies.
34. Elisha Granville Sewell (1830–1924) was a well-known writer for the *Gospel Advocate* and preacher for Churches of Christ in Middle Tennessee.
35. The black preacher in Tennessee. See note 19.
36. This statement attests that the *Gospel Advocate*, first published in 1855, exerted potent influence on the minds of black leaders (Womack and Campbell) who laid the theological foundation upon which African American Churches of Christ were built.
37. Perhaps Marshall Keeble I.
38. Theolphilus Brown Larimore (1843–1929) was an evangelist and educator in Churches of Christ.

Chapter 2

If It Were Not for the White Christians: Keeble in the 1920s

1. Alexander C. Campbell, "Work among the Colored People," *Gospel Advocate* 51 (Dec. 2, 1909):1523.
2. Samuel Robert Cassius, "I Have Kept the Faith," *Christian Leader* 36 (Jan. 31, 1922):3; Marshall Keeble, "Among the Colored Folks," *Gospel Advocate* 62 (Mar. 4, 1920):235.
3. Keeble, "Among the Colored Folks," *Gospel Advocate* 62 (Mar. 4, 1920):235.
4. Keeble worked on the assembly line of the Ford Motor Company in Detroit, Michigan. See the next article.
5. Marshall Keeble, "Among the Colored Folks," *Gospel Advocate* 62 (May 27, 1920):532.
6. Marshall Keeble fathered five children with first wife Minnie Womack. It is unclear whether this boy was Clarence Keeble, who later died tragically after touching a high-voltage wire, or Robert Keeble, who passed away in 1964. See Cato, *His Hand and Heart*, 4.
7. Alexander Bagby Lipscomb (1876–1940), Joe McPherson (1877–1918), Samuel Fletcher Walten Smith (1858–1930), Samuel Parker Pittman (1876–1965), and Filo

Bunyan Srygley (1859–1940) were white leaders in Churches of Christ in Middle Tennessee and were editors (or frequent contributors) to the *Gospel Advocate*.

8. Black members of the Jefferson Street Church of Christ pulled away from the Jackson Street Church of Christ as early as 1918. Even though the details of the church conflict are nebulous, the Jefferson Street congregation evolved into what is now the thriving Schrader Lane Church of Christ, Nashville, Tennessee.

9. Marshall Keeble, "A Great Man Gone," *Gospel Advocate* 62 (July 29, 1920):744–45.

10. Henry Clay, a Civil War veteran, a resident of Silver Point, Tennessee, and a black minister in Churches of Christ, collaborated with Samuel W. Womack for several years. See Tuggle, *Another World Wonder*, 54–55.

11. Annie C. Tuggle mentioned a Calvin Dowell, a resident of Nashville, an understudy of A. C. Holt, and an aspiring minister. See Tuggle, *Our Ministers and Song Leaders*, 51.

12. Marshall Keeble, "Among the Colored Folks," *Gospel Advocate* 62 (Oct. 21, 1920):1039. Keeble's remarks here show that he won many black converts to Churches of Christ because white Christians often used their influence as merchants and entrepreneurs to bring their African American employees to the black evangelist's meetings. Keeble met and converted Lonnie Smith through the efforts of "Pop" Richardson and M. A. Dye, white grocery store owners in St. Petersburg, Florida. Smith later emerged as a preacher, song leader, and church planter in Texas and other southern states. See Choate, *Roll Jordan Roll*, 62.

13. There were two schools associated with the Stone-Campbell movement in Henderson, Tennessee: West Tennessee Christian College, founded in 1885, and Georgie Robertson Christian College, which existed from 1897 to 1907. A board of trustees purchased the latter school from the founders and renamed it Freed-Hardeman College in 1919. A. G. Freed (1863–1931) was N. B. Hardeman's former teacher. See Mark A. Hamilton, "Freed-Hardeman University," *Encyclopedia of the Stone-Campbell Movement*, 344.

14. Marshall Keeble, "Among the Colored Folks," *Gospel Advocate* 63 (Jan. 20, 1921):78.

15. Keeble here voiced a concern echoed by other black evangelists. Samuel Robert Cassius, a black itinerant preacher in Churches of Christ, chided white believers who worked "overtime trying to convert Africa, China and Japan, and Cuba, and the rest of the Islands of the Sea" but neglected African Americans in their local communities. Domestic evangelism was just as important as foreign missions. See Cassius, "Out on the Firing Line," *Christian Leader* 44 (July 29, 1930):12.

16. Marshall Keeble, "Among the Colored Folks," *Gospel Advocate* 63 (July 14, 1921):678–79. Like most southern cities in the early twentieth century, Birmingham, Alabama, was rigidly segregated. In this racially stratified milieu, Keeble collaborated with white Christians to advance the "pure gospel" among African Americans. Keeble's racial posture was markedly different from Baptist minister-politician Fred Shuttlesworth, who imbibed a "combative spirituality." See Andrew M. Manis, *A Fire You Can't Put Out: The Civil Rights Life of Birmingham's Reverend Fred Shuttlesworth* (Tuscaloosa: Univ. of Alabama Press, 1999), 24.

17. W. C. Graves was either the preacher or an elder at the West End Church of Christ in Birmingham, Alabama.
18. Marshall Keeble, "Among the Colored Folks," *Gospel Advocate* 63 (Sept. 15, 1921):911. Joe McPherson (1877–1918) was a white mail-carrier and preacher for Churches of Christ in Nashville.
19. Here Keeble referred to the three-week 1914 meeting in Nashville, which A. M. Burton helped organize, during which McPherson preached, and during which twenty-seven people received baptism. See A. M. Burton, "Among the Colored People," *Gospel Advocate* 56 (May 21, 1914):556; and Robinson, "Two Old Heroes," 3–20.
20. Marshall Keeble, "Among the Colored Folks," *Gospel Advocate* 63 (Dec. 1, 1921):1177.
21. Utica, Mississippi, located in Hinds County, was home to a Pentecostal group known as "Spot or Wrinkle Folks." See William H. Holtzclaw, *The Black Man's Burden* (1915; reprint, New York: Negro Universities Press, 1970), 90. According to Holtzclaw, a resident and educator in the Utica community, this new group "was sweeping everything before it in our neighborhood." For more biographical information on Holtzclaw, see Arnie Cooper, "'We Rise upon the Structure We Ourselves Have Builded': William H. Holtzclaw and Utica Institute, 1903–1915," *Journal of Mississippi History* 45 (Feb. 1985):15–33.
22. Probably A. C. Carter, a well-liked deacon in the black Baptist Church in Utica. "Deacon Carter was an influential man in the community. Not only was he a deacon of the Baptist Church, which had about four hundred members, but he was respected by everybody, white and black alike." See Holtzclaw, *Black Man's Burden,* 82.
23. C. P. Jones and Charles H. Mason (1866–1961) collaborated and organized the Church of God in Christ in 1897. This Pentecostal (or Holiness) Church grew rapidly initially in parts of Tennessee, Alabama, and Mississippi. In 1921, Jones, who was living in Jackson, Mississippi, stressed that "men should live absolutely pure lives, without spot or wrinkle." Jones was doubtlessly the "pastor" who came to investigate Keeble's doings in Utica. See Holtzclaw, *Black Man's Burden,* 90–91. See also Milton C. Sernett, ed., *African American Religious History: A Documentary Witness* (Durham, N.C.: Duke Univ. Press, 1999), 314–24.
24. William H. Holtzclaw, a student of Booker T. Washington at the Tuskegee Institute in Alabama, organized the Utica Institute in Hinds County in 1903. By the time Keeble visited Utica in 1921, Holtzclaw's school had increased to a couple of hundred students. Holtzclaw, *Black Man's Burden.* See also Neil R. McMillen, *Dark Journey: Black Mississippians in the Age of Jim Crow* (Urbana: Univ. of Illinois Press, 1990), 93–95.
25. Marshall Keeble, "Among the Colored Folks," *Gospel Advocate* 64 (Jan. 19, 1922):64.
26. Marshall Keeble, "Preaching in Oakland, Cal.," *Gospel Advocate* 66 (Apr. 17, 1924):383.
27. D. C. Allen, an obscure African American preacher from Texas, began preaching in Oakland, California, in 1902 until his death in 1942. Samuel Robert Cassius followed Keeble's visit and reported limited results. Cassius, "Being Led of the Spirit," *Christian*

Leader 38 (Oct. 14, 1924):12. For other references to D. C. Allen, see J. W. Jackson, "The Gospel to the Colored Race," *Firm Foundation* 11 (Aug. 27, 1895):4; W. Halliday Trice, "Oakland Colored Church Free of Debt," *Christian Leader* 53 (May 1, 1939):18; Marshall Johnson, "Departed," *Christian Echo* 37 (Dec. 5, 1942):5; and Stephen D. Eckstein Jr., *History of the Churches of Christ in Texas, 1824–1950* (Austin, Texas: Firm Foundation, 1963), 200.

28. Samuel Robert Cassius had traveled to California as early as 1902, and he helped his son, Amos Lincoln Cassius (1889–1982), establish the Compton Avenue Church of Christ in 1922. See Bowers, *Realizing the California Dream*.

29. Theophilus Brown Larimore (1843–1929) and Emma Page Larimore (1855–1943) were influential educators, humanitarians, and colaborers in white Churches of Christ. See Douglas A. Foster, "Emma Page Larimore" and "Theophilus Brown Larimore," *Encyclopedia of the Stone-Campbell Movement*, 452–53.

30. Marshall Keeble, "From the Brethren," *Gospel Advocate* 67 (Apr. 9, 1925):354.

31. Marshall Keeble, "From the Brethren," *Gospel Advocate* 67 (June 18, 1925):594. Keeble's meeting in Greenville, South Carolina, left behind a fledgling black congregation, but it fizzled out because of lack of leadership. Through the diligent efforts of Wilton H. Cook, a spiritual grandson of Keeble, the congregation was revived and evolved into what is now the I-85 Church of Christ in Greenville. See J. Edward Meixner, *History of the Church of Christ in Greater Greenville, S.C.* (n.p., 1978), 33–34.

32. In order to comply with Jim Crow mandates, Keeble always allowed white leaders to baptize white seekers. Keeble understood that a white man (especially a white woman) submitting to baptism at the hands of a black minister was unacceptable in the segregated South.

33. Marshall Keeble, "From the Brethren," *Gospel Advocate* 69 (Jan. 27, 1927):91. At the beginning of each new year, Keeble consistently conducted a two-week meeting for his home congregation, the Jackson Street Church of Christ in Nashville, Tennessee.

34. This was probably Keeble's first experience of preaching the "pure gospel" on the radio.

35. Samuel Henry Hall (1877–1961), an influential white leader in Churches of Christ, did much to encourage and support black evangelists.

36. Marshall Keeble, "Our Messages," *Gospel Advocate* 69 (Apr. 21, 1927):368.

37. Keeble never insisted that people coming from the "digressives" (or members of the Christian Church or the Disciples of Christ) be rebaptized; they were viewed as "estranged brethren." See David Edwin Harrell, *The Churches of Christ in the Twentieth Century: Homer Hailey's Personal Journey of Faith* (Tuscaloosa: Univ. of Alabama Press, 2000).

38. Marshall Keeble, "From the Brethren," *Gospel Advocate* 69 (Oct. 13, 1927):978–79.

39. Bishop Isaac Lane (1834–1937) led black Methodists away from the predominantly white Methodist Episcopal Church, South, in 1866 and helped form the separate Colored Methodist Episcopal (CME) Church. See Othal Hawthorne Lakey, *The History of the CME Church* (Memphis: CME Publishing House, 1985); and Lincoln and Mamiya, *Black Church*, 62–63.

40. Marshall Keeble, "Report of Work," *Gospel Advocate* 71 (Jan. 10, 1929):48. Keeble's most important work was not as a church planter but as a trainer and mentor for young men whom he baptized. Even though the editor is uncertain about the specific identity of twelve preachers whom Keeble baptized in 1928, he is certain that one of those preachers was Shelton T. W. Gibbs I (1898–1976), who after converting from the African Methodist Episcopal Church to Churches of Christ gave a couple of his sons and grandsons to the preaching ministry of black Churches of Christ. See Tuggle, *Our Ministers and Song Leaders,* 62; and R. N. Hogan, "Goodbye to a Great Servant" *Christian Echo* (Aug. 1976):7.
41. Marshall Keeble, "The Lakeland Meeting," *Gospel Advocate* 71 (Mar. 14, 1929):261.
42. Marshall Keeble, "From the Brethren," *Gospel Advocate* 71 (Sept. 19, 1929):908–9.

Chapter 3

Disseminating the Bread of Life: Keeble in the 1930s

1. Brents, "Sowing and Reaping," 1300.
2. Marshall Keeble, "Notes," *Christian Worker* 17 (July 9, 1931):5.
3. Marshall Keeble, "Sowing and Reaping," *Gospel Advocate* 74 (Jan. 28, 1932):124.
4. Marshall Keeble, "Work in Florida," *Gospel Advocate* 72 (June 12, 1930):574.
5. Luke Miller (1904–1962) was a convert of Marshall Keeble and a noteworthy evangelist among African American Churches of Christ. See Luke Miller, *Miller's Sermons* (Austin, Texas: Firm Foundation, 1940), 4–7.
6. Marshall Keeble, "From Brother M. Keeble," *Gospel Advocate* 72 (Aug. 21, 1930):816.
7. Marshall Keeble, "Report of M. Keeble," *Gospel Advocate* 73 (Jan. 8, 1931):44–45.
8. Marshall Keeble, "A Report," *Firm Foundation* 48 (July 14, 1931):7.
9. Marshall Keeble, "A Report," *Christian Worker* 17 (Dec. 10, 1931):3.
10. Marshall Keeble, "From the Field," *Christian Worker* 21 (Sept. 26, 1935):5. The church Keeble established in Tyler is now the North Tenneha Church of Christ.
11. Harvey Scott was the white minister for what is now the West Erwin Church of Christ in Tyler, Texas.
12. Lonnie Smith was a black convert of Keeble's from Florida.
13. Marshall Keeble, "Keeble at Bowling Green," *Gospel Advocate* 78 (Aug. 13, 1936):788.
14. Marshall Keeble, "Among the Colored Brethren," *Gospel Advocate* 79 (Mar. 4, 1937):211.
15. An African American minister in Churches of Christ.
16. An African American minister in Churches of Christ.
17. Marshall Keeble, "Keeble in Florida," *Gospel Advocate* 80 (Feb. 17, 1938):163.
18. Marshall Keeble, "Keeble in Alabama," *Gospel Advocate* 80 (June 23, 1938):586.
19. An African American preacher from Florida whom Keeble converted.
20. Marshall Keeble, "Brother Keeble Reports," *Gospel Advocate* 80 (Sept. 8, 1938):852.

21. A white leader in Churches of Christ who preached in Mississippi and Tennessee.
22. Marshall Keeble, "Reports Home Meeting," *Gospel Advocate* 81 (Feb. 23, 1939):189.
23. Marshall Keeble, "Many Heard Keeble at Gadsden," *Gospel Advocate* 81 (Aug. 10, 1939):754.
24. Marshall Keeble, "The Outlook," *Christian Echo* (Oct. 20, 1939):6.
25. A reference to Matthew 15:14.

Chapter 4
I Mean to Wear Out on the Battlefield: Keeble in the 1940s

1. Unlike black preachers in Churches of Christ such as Samuel Robert Cassius, who viewed the word "nigger" as an insult, Keeble had no misgivings about using the word. Here Keeble used the word to insult another black man, perhaps reflecting his own black self-hatred. Additionally, Keeble was not offended when whites called him "nigger." In a recorded interview with J. E. Choate, the black evangelist stated, "Don't never get mad about being called a 'nigger.' If you do, you are resenting him [the white man]." See J. E. Choate, Interview with Marshall Keeble, Tape 2 (Disciples of Christ Historical Society, Nashville, Tennessee). For a thorough and scholarly discussion of the controversial word "nigger," see Randall Kennedy, *Nigger: The Strange Career of a Troublesome Word* (New York: Vintage Books, 2003). For Cassius's deep aversion for the word "nigger," see Robinson, *To Save My Race from Abuse*, 31–33, 123.
2. Marshall Keeble, "Jesus, Misunderstood" (Nashville: David Lipscomb College, Annual Winter Lectureship, 1948), 2:123. Keeble likely had in mind his experiences in Jackson, Tennessee, where professors from Lane College "attacked me one night and attempted to show the crowd that I was teaching false doctrine." See Marshall Keeble, "From the Brethren," *Gospel Advocate* 69 (Oct. 13, 1927):978.
3. For a good historical sketch of the Nashville Christian Institute, see Sara Harwell, "Nashville Christian Institute," *Encyclopedia of the Stone-Campbell Movement*, 552.
4. Marshall Keeble, "Brother Keeble Reports," *Gospel Advocate* 82 (Mar. 21, 1940):286.
5. A convert and student of G. P. Bowser, Alonzo Jones (1890–1942) preached for several years for a black Church of Christ in Chattanooga, Tennessee. See Tuggle, *Our Ministers and Song Leaders*, 84; Tuggle, *Another World Wonder*, 43–57.
6. Born near Belfast, Tennessee, A. C. Holt converted to Churches of Christ at an early age. He later emerged as a reputable educator and preacher among African Americans Christians in Tennessee, Georgia, Michigan, and New York. See Tuggle, *Our Ministers and Song Leaders*, 72–73.
7. Dennis M. English, a native of Hickman County, Tennessee, ministered to black congregations in Detroit, Michigan; Nashville, Tennessee; Valdosta, Georgia; and Memphis, Tennessee. See Tuggle, *Our Ministers and Song Leaders*, 54–55.
8. A Keeble convert from Florida, John R. Vaughner later emerged as one of the most effective preachers and church planters in the history of African American Churches of Christ. See Tuggle, *Our Ministers and Song Leaders*, 151.

9. A native of Florence, Alabama, F. L. Thompson converted to Churches of Christ in 1931 after relocating to Nashville, Tennessee. In addition to serving as an editor for the *Christian Counselor,* a paper published by African American leaders under the auspices of the *Gospel Advocate,* Thompson planted congregations in Tennessee, Georgia, Florida, Maryland, and Alabama. See Tuggle, *Our Ministers and Song Leaders,* 143.
10. Marshall Keeble, "Need More Like Him," *Gospel Advocate* 82 (Mar. 28, 1940):304. Filo Bunyan Srygley (1859–1940), a brother of Fletcher Douglas Srygley (1856–1900), served as an influential editor of the *Gospel Advocate.* See Terry J. Gardner, "Fletcher Douglas Srygley and Filo Bunyan Srygley," *Encyclopedia of the Stone-Campbell Movement,* 698.
11. Marshall Keeble, "The Outlook," *Christian Echo* (May 5, 1941):6.
12. Amos Lincoln Cassius (1889–1982) was an effective leader and preacher among black Churches of Christ. See Robinson, *To Save My Race from Abuse,* 82–85, 161–62.
13. R. N. Hogan (1902–1997), a native of Arkansas and a disciple of G. P. Bowser, was one of the most talented preachers in the history of African American Churches of Christ. Hogan established several congregations across the country and did some of his most evangelistic work in southern California. See Bowers, *Realizing the California Dream;* and Edward J. Robinson, "R. N. Hogan," *Encyclopedia of the Stone-Campbell Movement,* 401–2.
14. A reference to John 9:4.
15. Marshall Keeble, "A Great Opportunity," *Gospel Advocate* 86 (May 18, 1944):341.
16. Marshall Keeble, "Students Are Baptized," *Gospel Advocate* 86 (Dec. 28, 1944):855.
17. Marshall Keeble, "Encouragement Letter," *Christian Echo* 40 (June 20, 1945):3. G. P. Bowser (1874–1950) established the *Christian Echo* in 1902. As his health declined, Bowser delegated editorial responsibilities to his young protégés.
18. Fannie Bowser (c. 1869–1947). See R. Vernon Boyd, *Undying Dedication: The Story of G. P. Bowser* (Nashville: Gospel Advocate, 1985), 20, 99.
19. Marshall Keeble, "Nashville Christian Institute," *Gospel Advocate* 89 (June 26, 1947):452.
20. Marshall Keeble, "Nashville Christian Institute Commencement," *Gospel Advocate* 91 (June 30, 1949):402.
21. Alonzo Rose (1916–1992) was baptized into Churches of Christ in 1940 by Dennis M. English and soon emerged as one of the most gifted preachers in the history of African American Churches of Christ. Rose groomed four of his sons to be preachers in Churches of Christ: Marshall Keeble Rose, Jimmy Rose, Floyd Rose, and Richard Rose. Sylvia Rose, a daughter of Alonzo, served as a choir directress at Southwestern Christian College for many years, and she composed several melodious and meaningful hymns, including "Restore My Soul," "Holy Spirit," and "Mansion, Robe, and Crown." See Tuggle, *Our Ministers and Song Leaders,* 130.
22. After graduating from Fisk University in 1928, Otis H. Boatright, a native of Haywood County, Tennessee, preached for the Jackson Street Church of Christ in Nash-

ville and served as principal for the Nashville Christian Institute. See Tuggle, *Our Ministers and Song Leaders,* 9–20; Tuggle, *Another World Wonder,* 138–40.

Chapter 5
This Is Bible Religion: Keeble in the 1950s

1. Goodpasture, *Biography and Sermons,* 26–27. The best current study on black preaching in Churches of Christ remains Michael W. Casey, *Saddlebags, City Streets, and Cyberspace: A History of Preaching in the Churches of Christ* (Abilene, Texas: Abilene Christian Univ. Press, 1995), see especially chapter 10.
2. Goodpasture, *Biography and Sermons,* 38.
3. Hughes, *Reviving the Ancient Faith.*
4. Marshall Keeble, "Among the Colored Brethren," *Gospel Advocate* 92 (Dec. 14, 1950):814–15.
5. Marshall Keeble, "Among the Colored Brethren," *Gospel Advocate* 92 (Dec. 28, 1950):842.
6. Here Keeble followed the pattern set by the Jubilee Singers, who toured the United States and Europe in the 1870s to garner funds to help sustain Fisk University. See Ward, *Dark Midnight When I Rise.*
7. Marshall Keeble, "Among the Colored Brethren," *Gospel Advocate* 93 (Jan. 11, 1951):30–31.
8. Marshall Keeble, "Among the Colored Brethren," *Gospel Advocate* 93 (Jan. 18, 1951):47.
9. Marshall Keeble, "Among the Colored Brethren," *Gospel Advocate* 93 (Feb. 1, 1951):78–79. Here Keeble proffers an example of his rejection of culture. For an example of the "Christ against Culture" typology imbibed in Tertullian, the Mennonites, and Leo Tolstoy, see Niebuhr, *Christ and Culture,* 45–82.
10. Marshall Keeble, "Among the Colored Brethren," *Gospel Advocate* 93 (Feb. 8, 1951):94–95.
11. Marshall Keeble, "Among the Colored Brethren," *Gospel Advocate* 93 (Mar. 8, 1951):158–59.
12. Marshall Keeble, "Among the Colored Brethren," *Gospel Advocate* 93 (Apr. 12, 1951):238.
13. Marshall Keeble, "Among the Colored Brethren," *Gospel Advocate* 93 (Apr. 19, 1951):253–54.
14. Marshall Keeble, "Among the Colored Brethren," *Gospel Advocate* 93 (Apr. 26, 1951):269.
15. Keeble first preached in Birmingham, Alabama, in 1921. In another article in 1921, Keeble said that white Christians in Birmingham paid his boarding fare with a Baptist family whom he never identified. Nevertheless, Keeble's meeting yielded forty baptisms, including a "little band of what are called 'sanctified' people." See Keeble, "Among the Colored Folks," *Gospel Advocate* 63 (July 14, 1921):678–80.
16. Marshall Keeble, "Among the Colored Brethren," *Gospel Advocate* 93 (May 17, 1951):317–18.

17. Marshall Keeble, "Among the Colored Brethren," *Gospel Advocate* 93 (June 21, 1951):399.
18. Marshall Keeble, "Among the Colored Brethren," *Gospel Advocate* 93 (June 28, 1951):413–14.
19. Marshall Keeble, "Among the Colored Brethren," *Gospel Advocate* 93 (July 26, 1951):478–79.
20. Marshall Keeble, "Among the Colored Brethren," *Gospel Advocate* 93 (Aug. 16, 1951):527.
21. Marshall Keeble, "Among the Colored Brethren," *Gospel Advocate* 93 (Sept. 6, 1951):574–75.
22. Marshall Keeble, "Among the Colored Brethren," *Gospel Advocate* 93 (Sept. 20, 1951):606–7.
23. Marshall Keeble, "Among the Colored Brethren," *Gospel Advocate* 93 (Nov. 22, 1951):751.
24. Marshall Keeble, "Among the Colored Brethren," *Gospel Advocate* 94 (Jan. 24, 1952):62–63.
25. Marshall Keeble, "Among the Colored Brethren," *Gospel Advocate* 94 (Feb. 28, 1952):142–43.
26. Marshall Keeble, "Among the Colored Brethren," *Gospel Advocate* 94 (Mar. 13, 1952):174–75.
27. Marshall Keeble, "Among the Colored Brethren," *Gospel Advocate* 94 (July 3, 1952):437–38.
28. Vanderbilt Lewis was born in Mississippi in 1913. After enrolling in the Nashville Christian Institute in 1941, Lewis began preaching. Upon graduating from Pepperdine University, he served Churches of Christ in Texas, California, and Oklahoma. See Batsell Barrett Baxter and M. Norvel Young, eds., *Preachers of Today: A Book of Brief Biographical Sketches and Pictures of Living Gospel Preachers* (Nashville: Christian Press, 1952), 202.
29. Keeble, "Among the Colored Brethren," *Gospel Advocate* 94 (July 3, 1952):437–38.
30. Alvin Shirley Simmons was born in Guthrie, Oklahoma, in 1933. After graduating from the Nashville Christian Institute in 1952, Simmons served churches in Tennessee, New York, and Ohio. See Baxter and Young, *Preachers of Today* 1:401.
31. Edward Washington McMillan (1889–1991), a native of New Baden, Texas, served as president of Southwestern Christian College from 1950 to 1967.
32. Marshall Keeble, "Among the Colored Brethren," *Gospel Advocate* 94 (July 24, 1952):486.
33. Marshall Keeble, "Among the Colored Brethren," *Gospel Advocate* 94 (Sept. 11, 1952):598–99.
34. Marshall Keeble, "Among the Colored Brethren," *Gospel Advocate* 94 (Sept. 18, 1952):615–16.
35. Marshall Keeble, "Among the Colored Brethren," *Gospel Advocate* 94 (Oct. 30, 1952):711–12.
36. Thomas Wandell Rucks, a native of Florence, Alabama, was born in 1896. After receiving baptized by John T. Ramsey, Rucks served congregations throughout Alabama. See Baxter and Young, *Preachers of Today* 1:296.

37. Percy E. Ricks was born in 1894 in Tuscumbia, Alabama. After being baptized by his grandfather George Ricks (1838–1908), a former slave and the first black man to own property in Alabama, Percy preached for three decades for the High Street Church of Christ in Tuscumbia, Alabama. See Tuggle, *Our Ministers and Song Leaders,* 58–59; and Ervin C. Jackson, "George Ricks," *Encyclopedia of the Stone-Campbell Movement,* 652.

38. John Harris converted from Catholicism to Churches of Christ in 1948 and emerged as a powerful preacher and prolific writer for African American Churches of Christ. See Baxter and Young, *Preachers of Today* 1:151.

39. Perhaps O. Jennings Davis Jr., a native and resident of Middle Tennessee. See Baxter and Young, *Preachers of Today* 1:96.

40. Robert Carl Gossett, a native of Hickman County, Tennessee, began serving the Willow Street Church of Christ in Cookeville, Tennessee, in 1949. Baxter and Young, *Preachers of Today* 1:137.

41. Marshall Keeble, "Among the Colored Brethren," *Gospel Advocate* 94 (Nov. 20, 1952):766.

42. Elden William Stovall, a native of Rives, Tennessee, served congregations in Texas, Tennessee, and Arkansas before moving to Glasgow, Kentucky, where he conducted a weekly radio program. See Baxter and Young, *Preachers of Today* 1:329.

43. Jack Petty Wilhelm was born in Scottsboro, Alabama, in 1930. The Scottsboro case, in which two white girls accused nine black boys of rape, strained race relations regionally and nationally. In an era of racial strife, Wilhelm seemingly worked for peace. For biographical information on Wilhelm, see Baxter and Young, *Preachers of Today* 1:370.

44. A black preacher from Montgomery, Alabama, who attended the Nashville Christian Institute in 1944. See Tuggle, *Our Ministers and Song Leaders,* 78.

45. A black preacher who converted to Churches of Christ in 1930 after hearing Marshall Keeble. See Tuggle, *Our Ministers and Song Leaders,* 36–37.

46. Marshall Keeble, "Among the Colored Brethren," *Gospel Advocate* 94 (Nov. 27, 1952):782–83.

47. Marshall Keeble, "Among the Colored Brethren," *Gospel Advocate* 95 (Mar. 12, 1953):158.

48. Marshall Keeble, "Among the Colored Brethren," *Gospel Advocate* 95 (Apr. 9, 1953):222–23.

49. Marshall Keeble, "Among the Colored Brethren," *Gospel Advocate* 95 (Apr. 16, 1953):238.

50. Marshall Keeble, "Among the Colored Brethren," *Gospel Advocate* 95 (May 7, 1953):286.

51. Marshall Keeble, "Among the Colored Brethren," *Gospel Advocate* 95 (July 9, 1953):437–38.

52. Marshall Keeble, "Among the Colored Brethren," *Gospel Advocate* 95 (Sept. 10, 1953):590.

53. Marshall Keeble, "Among the Colored Brethren," *Gospel Advocate* 95 (Oct. 1, 1953):645.

54. Probably Orum Lee Trone Sr., who was born in Birmingham, Alabama, in 1915, baptized by Dennis M. English in 1928, and preached for churches in Pontiac and Detroit, Michigan. See Tuggle, *Our Ministers and Song Leaders,* 146; and Baxter and Young, *Preachers of Today* 1:349.

55. Marshall Keeble, "Among the Colored Brethren," *Gospel Advocate* 95 (Oct. 22, 1953):710–11.

56. G. H. P. Showalter (1870–1954) owned and edited the *Gospel Advocate* in the early twentieth century. See Robert L. Friedly, "Journalism," *Encyclopedia of the Stone-Campbell Movement,* 435.

57. Marshall Keeble, "Among the Colored Brethren," *Gospel Advocate* 96 (Jan. 7, 1954):20–21.

58. Marshall Keeble, "Among the Colored Brethren," *Gospel Advocate* 96 (Jan. 21, 1954):63.

59. Marshall Keeble, "Among the Colored Brethren," *Gospel Advocate* 96 (Jan. 28, 1954):78.

60. Marshall Keeble, "Among the Colored Brethren," *Gospel Advocate* 96 (Mar. 4, 1954):183.

61. Marshall Keeble, "Among the Colored Brethren," *Gospel Advocate* 96 (May 6, 1954):356–57.

62. Luke Miller (1904–1962), a native of Decatur, Alabama, converted to Churches of Christ after hearing Keeble preach in 1920. He later emerged as a noteworthy church planter and church stabilizer in the state of Texas. See Tuggle, *Our Ministers and Song Leaders,* 110.

63. John Oscar Williams and Oswell Lamar Aker (1884–1963) were both converts of Keeble. Williams, a native of Georgia, was baptized in 1930; Aker, also a native Georgian, converted from Methodism to Churches of Christ in Sheffield, Alabama, in 1926. See Tuggle, *Our Ministers and Song Leaders,* 8, 154; and "Obsequies of Brother O. L. Aker," *Christian Echo* 58 (Nov. 1963):4.

64. Jesse T. Burson was born in Fort Payne, Alabama, in 1905; he converted from the Baptist faith to Churches of Christ in 1932 under the preaching of Alonzo Jones. After entering the preaching ministry, Burson preached in St. Petersburg, Florida, before relocating to Texas. See Tuggle, *Our Ministers and Song Leaders,* 25.

65. Otha Dean Fikes, a native of Arnett, Texas, began preaching at the North Shepherd Church of Christ in Houston, Texas, in 1950. See Baxter and Young, *Preachers of Today* 1:114.

66. Marshall Keeble, "Among the Colored Brethren," *Gospel Advocate* 96 (July 8, 1954):541–42.

67. Robert Lewis Butler, born in Valdosta, Georgia, in 1923, became a member of Churches of Christ in 1933, began preaching the following year, and started preaching for the Franklin Street Church of Christ in Huntsville, Alabama, in 1950. See Carl E. Gaines and John C. Whitley, eds., *Black Preachers of Today: Churches of Christ* (n.p.: John C. Whitley and Carl E. Gaines, 1974), 10–11; and Baxter and Young, *Preachers of Today* 1:59.

68. Marshall Keeble, "Among the Colored Brethren," *Gospel Advocate* 96 (Nov. 4, 1954):878.
69. Ibid.
70. Athens Clay Pullias (1910–1985) was president of David Lipscomb College from 1946 to 1977 in addition to working as a staunch supporter of the Nashville Christian Institute. See Robert E. Hooper, "Lipscomb University," *Encyclopedia of the Stone-Campbell Movement*, 483.
71. Marshall Keeble, "Among the Colored Brethren," *Gospel Advocate* 97 (Feb. 10, 1955):119.
72. Marshall Keeble, "Among the Colored Brethren," *Gospel Advocate* 97 (Mar. 17, 1955):222–23.
73. Marshall Keeble, "Among the Colored Brethren," *Gospel Advocate* 97 (Mar. 31, 1955):262.
74. Marshall Keeble, "Among the Colored Brethren," *Gospel Advocate* 97 (May 5, 1955):357.
75. Marshall Keeble, "Among the Colored Brethren," *Gospel Advocate* 97 (Nov. 3, 1955):1002.
76. Marshall Keeble, "Among the Colored Brethren," *Gospel Advocate* 98 (May 3, 1956):429.
77. Marshall Keeble, "Among the Colored Brethren," *Gospel Advocate* 98 (Oct. 18, 1956):855.
78. Marshall Keeble, "Among the Colored Brethren," *Gospel Advocate* 100 (July 31, 1958):495.
79. A native of Cotton Plant, Arkansas, Berry B. Minor was baptized by T. H. York in 1932. After earning a degree from Tuskegee University in Alabama, Minor began serving churches in Arkansas, Mississippi, New Mexico, and California. See Gaines and Whitley, *Black Preachers*, 53.
80. Marshall Keeble, "Among the Colored Brethren," *Gospel Advocate* 101 (Oct. 22, 1959):687.
81. Marshall Keeble, "Among the Colored Brethren," *Gospel Advocate* 101 (Dec. 24, 1959):827.
82. J. Harold Thomas, a native of Glenrio, New Mexico, served as president for the Northeastern Institute for Christian Education in Villanova, Pennsylvania, from 1958 until 1962. Baxter and Young, *Preachers of Today* 4:315.
83. James Burton Coffman, a native of Taylor, Texas, served congregations in Texas and Washington, D.C., before relocating to Manhattan in New York City. Baxter and Young, *Preachers of Today* 3:79.
84. A member of Churches of Christ, Pat Boone rapidly rose to prominence as a popular singer and entertainer. In 1969, he announced that he had received the baptism of the Holy Ghost. See Byron C. Lambert, "Doctrine of the Holy Spirit," *Encyclopedia of the Stone-Campbell Movement*, 405.

Chapter 6
The Global Evangelist: Keeble in the 1960s

1. Franklin, *From Slavery to Freedom*, 505–61.
2. Marshall Keeble, *From Mule Back to Super Jet with the Gospel* (Nashville: Gospel Advocate, 1962). Used by permission.
3. This young man was Freeman T. Wyche. A native of Valdosta, Georgia, Wyche, after attending the Nashville Christian Institute in the 1940s, served the U.S. armed forces from 1949 to 1953 and from 1956 to 1965. See Gaines and Whitley, *Black Preachers*, 77.
4. In the 1960 Olympics in Rome, Wilma Rudolph (1940–1944), a native of Clarksville, Tennessee, won three gold medals in the 100-meter dash, 200-meter dash, and 4-x-100-meter relay for the United States.
5. Perhaps Adlai E. Stevenson II (1900–1965), who was governor of Illinois in 1948 and made two U.S. presidential bids in the 1950s.
6. Essien's diligent evangelistic efforts, which led to the establishment of sixty-five churches, earned him the title "the Alexander Campbell of Africa." See Stanley E. Granberg, "Missions in Africa," *Encyclopedia of the Stone-Campbell Movement*, 8. See also Choate, *Roll Jordan Roll*, 125–30.
7. Lucien Palmer was a close friend of Marshall Keeble, and he served as president of the Nashville Christian Institute.
8. Marshall Keeble, "Nashville Christian Institute to Close," *Gospel Advocate* 109 (Mar. 16, 1967):166. The desegregation of public schools led to a declining enrollment at the NCI. This fact, coupled with the death of A. M. Burton in 1966, NCI's chief benefactor, caused the school to close. When the defunct school's assets were transferred to David Lipscomb College, race relations in Churches of Christ were soured. See Hughes, *Reviving the Ancient Faith*, 292–95; and Holloway and York, *Unfinished Reconciliation*, 140–43.

Chapter 7
The Importance of Trained Ministers

1. This lecture is significant for three reasons. First, Keeble cancelled a preaching engagement in Los Angeles, California, to address the predominantly white lectureship audience at Abilene Christian College in Abilene, Texas. Second, Keeble's speech shifted the burden of black uplift on the shoulders of whites in Churches of Christ, and it focused on the need and importance of education for African American preachers. Third, Keeble challenged his predominantly white audience to view the black man his equal. Keeble expressed optimism over the prospect of the fledgling black school, the Southern Bible Institute (now Southwestern Christian College) in Terrell, Texas.
2. Don H. Morris (1902–1974) was president of Abilene Christian College from 1940 to 1969.

3. John G. Young, a medical doctor from Dallas, Texas, was appointed chairman of the Southern Bible Institute (now Southwestern Christian College).
4. The Southern Bible Institute was established in Fort Worth, Texas, in 1948 by G. P. Bowser (1874–1950), G. E. Steward (1906–1970), Levi Kennedy (1899–1970), R. N. Hogan (1902–1997), and J. S. Winston (1906–2002). This institution within a few years relocated to Terrell, Texas, and became Southwestern Christian College. See Edward J. Robinson, "Southwestern Christian College," *Encyclopedia of the Stone-Campbell Movement,* 695.
5. Athens Clay Pullias (1910–1985) was president of David Lipscomb College from 1946 to 1977.
6. Hugh Tiner was president of Pepperdine College from 1939 to 1957.
7. Nicholas B. Hardeman (1874–1965) was often called "the Prince of Preachers" in Churches of Christ. He often gave verbal, emotional, and material support to Marshall Keeble and other black evangelists.
8. Keeble never forgot this experience, which probably happened when he first preached in Jackson, Tennessee, where Lane College, a black Methodist school, trained aspiring ministers. Keeble mentioned the incident when lecturing at David Lipscomb College in 1948, at Abilene Christian College in 1950, and at Harding College in 1952. See Marshall Keeble, "Jesus, Misunderstood" (Nashville: Lipscomb Lectures, 1948), 123–24; and Marshall Keeble, "A Prepared Ministry" (Austin, Texas: Firm Foundation, 1952), 262 63.

    Keeble's disinterest in Koine Greek actually reflected his Booker T. Washington–like characteristics. Washington said that the African American who acquired knowledge of classical languages during the Reconstruction era felt like a "very superior human being, something bordering almost on the supernatural." Washington, however, insisted that black Americans should focus on acquiring practical skills. "One man may go into a community prepared to supply the people there with an analysis of Greek sentences. The community may not at that time be prepared for, or feel the need of, Greek analysis, but it may feel its need of bricks and houses and wagons. If the man can supply the need for those, then, it will lead eventually to a demand for the first product, and with the demand will come the ability to appreciate it and to profit by it." Booker T. Washington, *Up from Slavery* (New York: Oxford Univ. Press, 1995 [1901]), 47, 91. Like Washington, Keeble was a practical man, but he soon came to realize the necessity of quality trained black preachers.
9. Foy L. Kirkpatrick, an Abilene Christian College graduate in 1946, served as business manager for the newly established Southern Bible Institute (now Southwestern Christian College).
10. Edward W. McMillan (1889–1991), a native of New Baden, Texas, was a distinguished educator at Lubbock Christian College, Columbian Christian College in Portland, Oregon, and Southwestern Christian College in Terrell, Texas, respectively. See Shaun A. Casey, "Edward Washington McMillan," *Encyclopedia of the Stone-Campbell Movement,* 509–10.
11. A paraphrase of Acts 10:1–48.

12. J. W. Dunn was a noteworthy white evangelist for Churches of Christ in Texas.
13. James Wilson Brents (1884–1963) chaired the Bible Department at the Nashville Christian Institute (Tennessee) and trained approximately five hundred young men to preach.
14. Wife of Arthur Reeves Holton, president of the short-lived Throp Spring Christian School in Hood County, Texas.
15. Samuel Henry Hall (1877–1961) was an influential white minister and supporter of Keeble and other black evangelists.
16. Benton Cordell Goodpasture (1894–1977), a white benefactor of Keeble and an influential editor of the *Gospel Advocate* from 1939 to 1977.
17. Keeble, "A Prepared Ministry," in *Harding College Bible Lectures,* 261–63.
18. Even though Keeble's was limited to the seventh grade, he compensated for his lack of biblical knowledge and understanding by digesting materials that white leaders in Churches of Christ published. Keeble's theology was shaped by whites in Churches of Christ.
19. Here Keeble probably meant Jackson, Tennessee. See Marshall Keeble, "Report of Work," *Gospel Advocate* 70 (Sept. 13, 1928):886–87.
20. Marshall Keeble, "Humility," in *Lecture Outlines* (Henderson, Tenn.: Freed-Hardeman College, 1953), 36. Taking his cue from Jesus and Moses, Keeble understood humility to be submission to the will of God. Many whites in Churches of Christ, like the southern racist culture they lived and moved in, viewed "humility" and "meekness" as a black man willing to "stay in his place." Foy E. Wallace Jr. (1896–1970), a white leader in Churches of Christ and editor of the *Bible Banner,* praised Keeble as the "greatest colored preacher that has ever lived. Luke Miller was brought up under his teaching and has imbibed the same spirit of meekness and humility. These men know their work and do it. They know their place and stay in it, even when some white brethren try to take them out of it." See Foy E. Wallace, "From Marshall Keeble," *Bible Banner* 3 (Apr. 1941):5.
21. Marshall Keeble, "The Life of the Preacher," in *Lecture Outlines* (Henderson, Tenn.: Freed-Hardeman College, 1955), 22.

Selected Bibliography

Blair, Tracy L. "For a Better Tomorrow: Marshall Keeble and George Philip Bowser, African-American Ministers." Master's thesis, Middle Tennessee State Univ., 1996.
Bowers, Calvin H. *Realizing the California Dream: The Story of Churches of Christ in Los Angeles.* N.p.: Calvin H. Bowers, 2001.
Boyd, R. Vernon. *Undying Dedication: The Story of G. P. Bowser.* Nashville: Gospel Advocate, 1985.
Broking, Darrell. "Marshall Keeble and the Implementation of a Grand Strategy: Erasing the Color Line in the Church of Christ." Master's thesis, East Tennessee State Univ., 2003.
Casey, Michael. *Saddlebags, City Streets, and Cyberspace: A History of Preaching in the Churches of Christ.* Abilene, Texas: Abilene Christian Univ. Press, 1995.
Cato, Willie. *His Hand and His Heart: The Wit and Wisdom of Marshall Keeble.* Winona, Miss.: J. C. Choate, 1990.
Choate, J. E. *Roll Jordan Roll: A Biography of Marshall Keeble.* Nashville: Gospel Advocate, 1974.
Cummings, Gwendolyn D. "Revisiting Laura Keeble." *Christian Woman* 19 (Nov.–Dec. 2003):16–17.
Evans, Jack, Sr. "Marshall Keeble: Dreamer of Dreams for Blacks and Whites." *21st Century Christian Magazine* 56 (Nov. 1993):13–15.
Foster, Douglas A., Paul M. Blowers, Anthony L. Dunnavant, and D. Newell Williams, eds. *The Encyclopedia of the Stone-Campbell Movement.* Grand Rapids, Mich.: Eerdmans, 2004.
Goodpasture, B. C., ed. *Sermons and Biography of Marshall Keeble, Evangelist.* Nashville: Gospel Advocate, 1966.
Gray, Fred D. *Bus Ride to Justice: Changing the System by the System, the Life and Works of Fred D. Gray.* Montgomery, Ala.: Black Belt Press, 1995.
Harlan, Louis R. *Booker T. Washington: The Making of a Black Leader, 1856–1901.* New York: Oxford Univ. Press, 1972.

———. *Booker T. Washington: The Wizard of Tuskegee, 1901–1915.* New York: Oxford Univ. Press, 1983.
Harrell, David Edwin, Jr. . *Quest for a Christian America: The Disciples of Christ and American Society to 1866.* 1966. Reprint, Tuscaloosa: Univ. of Alabama Press, 2003.
———. *Sources of Division in the Disciples of Christ, 1865–1900: A Social History of the Disciples of Christ.* Vol. 2. 1973. Reprint, Tuscaloosa: Univ. of Alabama Press, 2003.
———. *White Sects and Black Men in the Recent South.* Nashville: Vanderbilt Univ. Press, 1971.
Haymes, Don. "Marshall Keeble." In Foster, Blowers, Dunnavant, and Williams, *Encyclopedia of the Stone-Campbell Movement.*
Holloway, Gary, and John H. York, eds. *Unfinished Reconciliation: Justice, Racism, and Churches of Christ.* Abilene, Texas: Abilene Christian Univ. Press, 2003.
Hooper, Robert E. *A Distinct People: A History of the Churches of Christ in the 20th Century.* West Monroe, La.: Howard Publishing, 1993.
Hughes, Richard T. *Reviving the Ancient Faith: The Story of Churches of Christ in America.* Grand Rapids, Mich.: Eerdmans, 1996.
Lincoln, C. Eric., and Lawrence H. Mamiya. *The Black Church in the African American Experience.* 1990. Reprint, Durham, N.C.: Duke Univ. Press, 1999.
Maxwell, James. "The Restoration Movement." *Gospel Advocate* 132 (Jan. 1990):15–16.
Miller, Luke. *Miller's Sermons.* Austin, Texas: Firm Foundation, 1940.
Overton, Basil. "She Reached Age 104, August 6, 2002! Recorded Interview with Mrs. Marshall Keeble Available!" *World Evangelist* 31 (Jan. 2003):18.
Phillips, C. Myer. "A Historical Study of the Attitude of the Churches of Christ toward Other Denominations." Ph.D. diss., Baylor Univ., 1983.
Phillips, Paul D. "The Interracial Impact of Marshall Keeble, Black Evangelist, 1878–1968." In *The Stone-Campbell Movement: An International Religious Tradition,* edited by Michael Casey and Douglas A. Foster. Knoxville: Univ. of Tennessee Press, 2002.
Pitts, Carroll, Jr. . "A Critical Study of Civil Rights Practices, Attitudes and Responsibilities in Churches of Christ." Master's thesis, Pepperdine Univ., 1969.
Rhoads, Forrest Neil. "A Study of the Sources of Marshall Keeble's Effectiveness as a Preacher." Ph.D. diss., Southern Illinois Univ., 1970.
Robinson, Edward J. "'Like Rats in a Trap': Samuel Robert Cassius and the 'Race Problem' in Churches of Christ." Ph.D. diss., Mississippi State Univ., 2003.
———. *"Show Us How You Do It": Marshall Keeble and the Rise of Black Churches of Christ in the United States, 1914–1968.* Tuscaloosa: Univ. of Alabama Press, 2008.
———. *To Save My Race from Abuse: The Life of Samuel Robert Cassius.* Tuscaloosa: Univ. of Alabama Press, 2007.
———. "'The Two Old Heroes': Samuel W. Womack, Alexander Campbell, and the Origins of Black Churches of Christ in the United States." *Discipliana* 65 (Spring 2005):3–20.
Sernett, Milton C. *Bound for the Promised Land: African American Religion and the Great Migration.* Durham, N.C.: Duke Univ. Press, 1997.
Smith, Arthur Lee, Jr. "A Rhetorical Analysis of the Speaking of Marshall Keeble." Master's thesis, Pepperdine Univ., 1965.

Smithson, John, III. "Restoration Leaders: Marshall Keeble." In *New Beginnings: God, Man and Redemption in Genesis, 65th Annual Freed-Hardeman University Lectureship.* Henderson, Tenn.: Freed-Hardeman Univ., 2001.

Tuggle, Annie C. *Another World Wonder.* N.p., n.d.

———. *Our Ministers and Song Leaders of the Church of Christ.* Detroit: Annie C. Tuggle, 1945.

Whitaker, Chris. "Restoration Women: Mrs. Marshall (Laura) Keeble." In *When We Hurt: Tragedy and Triumph in Job: Sixty-Seventh Annual Freed-Hardeman University Lectureship.* Henderson, Tenn.: Freed-Hardeman Univ., 2003.

Index

A
Abilene Christian College, xx, 104, 105, 136, 137
Adams, Henry, xvi
Aker, O. L., 72, 134
Allen, D. C., 20, 126, 127
Apostolic Times, 38

B
Bates, Ruby, xviii
Baxter, Batsell Barrett, 37
Bethune, Mary McLeod, 121
"Birth of a Nation, The," xvii
Boatright, O. H., 37, 41, 42, 130
Boone, Pat, 79, 135
Bowser, Fannie, 130
Bowser, George P., xxii, 4, 22, 36, 68, 104, 114, 122, 130
Brents, J. W., xi, xii, 41, 42, 46, 112, 138
Brown v. Board of Education, xix
Brown, L., 72
Burson, Jesse T., 72, 134
Burton, Andrew M., xv, xviii, xx, xxii, 3, 13, 15, 17, 18, 19, 21, 22, 24, 27, 35, 38, 101, 120, 122, 126
Burton-Keeble Scholarship Fund, 102
Busby, T. H., 9, 123
Butler, Robert, 72, 134
Bynum, D. J., 8, 123

C
Campbell, Alexander (black preacher), xiv, xvii, 2, 7, 10, 13, 20, 123
Campbell, Alexander (white preacher), xiv, 122
Campbell, Lambert, 37, 46
Caperton, C. L., 59
Carrey, Jim, 117
Carter, A. C., 126
Carter, W. M., 72
Cassius, Amos L., 34, 35, 68, 127, 130
Cassius, Samuel Robert, 13, 25, 104, 126, 129
Cathey, Frances, 123
Cathey, Nathan, 8, 123
Cato, Willie, xiv, 79
Central Tennessee College, xvi. *See also* Walden University
Choate, J. E., 129
Christian Echo, xxii
Christian Leader, xxii, 123
Christian Worker, xxii
Civil Rights Act of 1964, 87
Clansman, The, xvii
Claus, G. E., 26
Clay, Henry, 15, 20
Clipp, Wendell, 37
Coffman, James Burton, 135
Collins, Willard, 37
Columbian Christian College (Oregon), 137

Congress of Racial Equality (CORE), xix
Cook, Wilton H., 127
Crooms, Bose, 6

D

David Lipscomb College, xvii, 9, 30, 37, 41, 74, 102, 105, 135, 137
David Lipscomb High School, 42
Davis, O. Jennings, Jr., 133
Dixon, Thomas, Jr., xvii
Dowell, Calvin, 15, 20, 125
Duncan, Michael Clarke, 117
Dunn, J. W., 31, 111, 112, 137
Dye, M. A., 125

E

Elam, Edwin A., 9, 123
English, D., 30, 34, 129, 130, 134
Essien, C. A. O., 97, 98, 136
Evers, Medgar, 87
Exodusters, xvi

F

Fanning, Tolbert, 1, 123
Farley, Christopher John, xi, 117
Fikes, Otha D., 72, 134
Finley, I. N., 37
Firm Foundation, xxii, 38, 68
Fisk Jubilee Singers, xvi
Fisk University, xvi, 107, 130
Freed, A. G., 125
Freed-Hardeman College, 16, 125, 138
From Mule Back to Super Jet with the Gospel, xx, 88–101

G

Gibbs, G. F., 21
Gibbs, Shelton T. W., 128
Glenn, E. N., xii, xiv, xv
Goodman, Andrew, 87
Goodpasture, B. C., 25, 26, 38, 112, 138
Gospel Advocate, xiv, xv, xx, xxii, 10, 11, 14, 16, 25, 34, 38, 68, 76, 77, 124, 130
Gossett, Robert Carl, 133

Graves, W. C., 17, 18
Gray, Fred D., xxi
Gray, H. H., 36
Great Depression, xviii, 25
Green, J. M., 2

H

Hall, Samuel H., xv, 22, 37, 112, 127, 138
Hannon, J., 7, 9
Hardeman, Nicholas B., xv, xvii, xx, 1, 6, 105, 123, 137
Harding College, 137
Harris, Hal, 9
Harris, John, 133
Hogan, Richard N., 34, 36, 68, 104, 120, 130, 137
"Hold to God's Unchanging Hand," xxi
Holt, A. C., 30, 33, 68, 129
Holton, A. R., 41, 46, 112, 138
Holtzclaw, William H., 126
Hooks, Dan, 59
Horton, Floyd H., xii, xiii

I

Ickes, Harold L., 121

J

Jackson, Erma, 78
Jackson, Jimmie Lee, 87
Jeffcoats, H. D., 28
Johnson, James Weldon, xvii
Johnson, Laura (Keeble's second wife), xiv
Johnson, Sutton, 68
Jones, Alonzo, 20, 34, 134
Jones, C. P., 126
Jonesboro Orphan Home (Arkansas), 28
Jorgenson, E. L., 123

K

Keeble, Laura, 101, 102
Keeble, Marshall: as a "Magic Negro," xi–xxii; at Abilene Christian College (Texas), xx, 104–13; birth, xvi; children, 124; commits to full-time evan-

gelism, xvii; in Alabama, 17, 18, 23, 30, 31, 58, 59; in California, xii, 20, 34; in Florida, 23, 26, 28, 30, 34, 72, 79; in Georgia, 39; in Kentucky, 23, 29, 59, 107; in Michigan, 14, 67; in Mississippi, 19, 27; in Missouri, 29; in New York, 79, 80; in Oklahoma, xi, 31; in Ontario, Canada, 72; in Pennsylvania, 79; in South Carolina, 21; in Tennessee, 29, 30, 31, 34, 58, 59; in Texas, xiii, xv, 29, 32, 71, 72; travels abroad (Europe, Asia, and Africa), 88–101
Kennedy, John F., xx
Kennedy, Levi, 36, 137
Kennedy, Robert F., xx
King, Jr., Martin Luther, xx, xxi, 87
Kirkpatrick, Foy L., 106, 137
Ku Klux Klan, xvii, xix

L

Lane College (Tennessee), 22, 103, 129, 137
Lane Isaac, 22
Larimore, Emma Page, 127
Larimore, T. B., 11, 20, 124, 127
Lee, Fred, 118
Lee, William, 29, 30, 31, 32
Lewis, Vanderbilt, 55, 132
Lipscomb, A. B., 9, 11, 15, 16, 17, 26, 124
Lipscomb, David, xvii, 9, 10, 16, 18, 68, 123, 124
Liuzzo, Viola, 87
Little Rock Nine Episode, xix
Lubbock Christian College, 137

M

Martin, T. Q., 8
Mason, Charles H., 126
McMillan, E. W., 56, 107, 111, 113, 132, 137
McPherson, Joe, xv, xvii, 15, 18, 124, 126
McQuiddy, J. C., 9, 11, 16, 124
McQuiddy, Leon B., 38
Meharry Medical College (Tennessee), xvi
Millen, P. G., 26
Miller, Luke, 26, 27, 68, 72, 77, 138

Mingle, W. R., 3, 4, 9, 14
Minor, Berry, 78, 135
Montgomery Bus Boycott, xix
Morris, Don H., 104, 112, 113, 136
Myers, Jack, 79
Myers, M. B., 30

N

Nashville Christian Institute (NCI), xvi, xx, xxi, 33, 35, 36, 37, 40, 41, 42, 46, 53, 55, 56, 57, 59, 60, 62, 73, 74, 76, 77, 78, 79, 88, 101, 102, 103, 114, 115, 132
National Freedmen's Savings Bank (Tennessee), xvi

O

Owen, Felix, 20

P

Palmer, Lucien, 88, 91, 94, 98, 100, 101
Panic of 1873, xvi
Patton, Will, 117
Pepperdine College, 34, 55, 132, 137
Phillips, W. C., 26
Pittman, S. P., 15, 124
Plessy v. Ferguson, xvii
Price, Victoria, xviii
Pullias, A. C., 74, 105, 135, 137

R

Ramsey, John T., 132
"Red Summer," xvii
Richardson, "Pop," 125
Ricks, George, 133
Ricks, Percy, 58, 59, 78, 133
Roosevelt, Franklin D., xviii, xix
Rose, Alonzo, 37, 130
Rose, Floyd, 130
Rose, Jimmy, 130
Rose, Marshall Keeble, 130
Rose, Richard, 130
Rose, Sylvia, 130
Rucks, Thomas, 58, 132
Rudolph, Wilma, 136

Ruth, Babe, 112
Rutherford, H. N., 26

S
Schwerner, Michael, 87
Scott, Harvey, 29, 128
Scottsboro Incident, xviii
Sewell, Elisha G., xv, xvii, 10, 18, 124
Shanks, David, 56
Shearer, Tobin, 118
Show, David, 56
Showalter, G. H. P., 68, 134
Simmons, A. S., 132
Simmons, William J., xvii
Singleton, Benjamin "Pap," xvi
Smith, F. W., 15, 16, 124
Smith, G. Dallas, 3, 122
Smith, Lonnie, 125, 128
Smith v. Allwright, xix
Smith, Will, xi
Southern Bible Institute (Texas), 136, 137
Southern Christian Leadership Conference (SCLC), xix
Southwestern Christian College (Texas), xx, 56, 114, 130, 132, 136, 137
Srygley, F. B., xv, 15, 34, 124, 125, 130
Stevenson, Adlai E., 136
Steward, G. E., 36, 137
Stone, Barton W., xiv
Stovall, E. W., 59, 133
Stubblefield, James, 3
Swayze, Patrick, 117
Sweeney, R. L., 19

T
Taylor, Preston, 1, 25, 26
Thomas, A. A., 37
Thomas, C. B., 27, 28
Thomas, Harold, 79, 135

Thompson, F. L., 34, 68, 130
Thurmond, Strom, xix
Till, Emmett, xix
Tiner, Hugh, 105, 137
Trone, O. L., 67, 134
Tuggle, Annie C., 2, 4, 122
Turner, Rex, 30

V
Vaughn, J. Roy, 28
Vaughner, John R., 29, 31, 34, 68, 77, 129
Voting Rights Act of 1965, 87

W
Walden University, xvi. *See also* Central Tennessee College
Wallace, Foy E., Jr., 138
Washington, Booker T., xii, xvii, 103, 137
West, Earl I., 123
West Tennessee Christian College, 125
Whitaker, William, 30
White Citizens Council, xix
White, George L., xvi
Whittle, D. B., 28
Wilhelm, Jack, 59
William, John O., 72, 134
Winston, J. S., 36, 137
Womack, Minnie (Keeble's first wife), xiv, xvii, 2, 4, 10, 122
Womack, Sallie (Keeble's mother-in-law), xiv
Womack, Samuel, xiv, xv, xvii, 2, 4, 5, 7, 10, 13, 15, 17, 18, 68, 114, 123
World War II, xix
Worley, Joe, 3, 4
Wyche, Freeman T., 136

Y
Young, F. L., xii
Young, John G., 104, 106, 113, 137

www.ingramcontent.com/pod-product-compliance
Lightning Source LLC
Chambersburg PA
CBHW030325080526
44584CB00012B/712